P9-CRC-048

HOLIDAY & CELEBRATIONS

BRINGING LOVED ONES TOGETHER

Celebrations begin with the welcome opening of your front door. Whether you're a veteran cook, a first-time host, or simply have been asked to bring a dish to pass, this brand-new edition of *Taste of Home Holiday & Celebrations* is your go-to guide for creating a memorable event. You'll find 264 delicious recipes and innovative ideas for throwing the ultimate party for any occasion, formal holidays and everyday celebrations alike. This colorful cookbook is sure to become your most trusted source for meal prep, holiday fun, cozy get-togethers, party planning and creative ways to add a special touch to any gathering. Our hope is these inspiring recipes, secrets and tips will be warmly welcomed at your table, add to lively conversations and create memories that will last a lifetime.

Visit us at **tasteofhome.com** for other *Taste of Home* books and products.

International Standard Book Numbers:
D 978-1-61765-993-5
U 978-1-61765-994-2
International Standard Serial Number:
1535-2781
Component Numbers:
D 118000100H
U 118000102H

Executive Editor: Mark Hagen
Senior Art Director: Raeann Thompson
Editor: Amy Glander
Assistant Art Director: Courtney Lovetere
Designer: Jazmin Delgado
Copy Editor: Amy Rabideau Silvers
Senior Food Editor: Peggy Woodward, RDN

Cover Photography:
Photographer: Mark Derse
Set Stylist: Stephanie Marchese
Food Stylists: Josh Rink, Shannon Norris

Pictured on front cover:
Vanilla Ring Cake, p. 4; Easter Sugar Cookies, p. 141
Pictured on back cover:
Easter Sugar Cookies, p. 141

Printed in USA
1 3 5 7 9 10 8 6 4 2

TABLE OF CONTENTS

'TIS THE SEASON

GIVING THANKS

EASTER GATHERINGS

SPECIAL CELEBRATIONS

BEAUTIFUL BUNDTS

Bakers, dust off your apron and grab your favorite fluted tube pan. There's no better way to celebrate any occasion, big or small, than with cake. Bundt cakes combine old-fashioned charm with festive and modern appeal. See just how easy it is to stack two beautiful Bundts adorned with cutout cookies as the crowning touch. No matter how you decorate them, they make centerpiece-worthy desserts every time!

Get the recipe...

VANILLA RING CAKE

Yes, you're reading this recipe right—my tube cake calls for a whopping 2 tablespoons of vanilla! A friend who loved the taste of vanilla shared it with me years ago. I use high-quality Mexican vanilla when I make this to get that authentic flavor that makes it taste so good.
—Joan Hallford, North Richland Hills, TX

Prep: 15 min. • **Bake:** 55 min. + cooling
Makes: 1 cake (12 servings)

- **1 cup shortening**
- **2 cups sugar**
- **4 large eggs, room temperature**
- **2 Tbsp. vanilla extract**
- **3 cups all-purpose flour**
- **1 tsp. baking powder**
- **½ tsp. baking soda**
- **1 cup buttermilk**

DRIZZLE

- **1 cup confectioners' sugar**
- **½ tsp. vanilla extract**
- **1 to 2 Tbsp. 2% milk**

1. Preheat oven to 350°. Grease and flour a 10-in. fluted tube pan. In a large bowl, cream shortening and sugar until light and fluffy, about 5 minutes. Add eggs, 1 at a time, beating well after each addition. Beat in the vanilla. Combine the flour, baking powder and baking soda; add to the creamed mixture alternately with buttermilk, beating well after each addition.

2. Pour batter into prepared pan. Bake until a toothpick inserted in the center comes out clean, 55-65 minutes. Cool for 10 minutes before removing from pan to a wire rack to cool completely.

3. Combine the confectioners' sugar, vanilla extract and enough milk to achieve desired consistency; drizzle over cake.

1 slice: 466 cal., 18g fat (5g sat. fat), 71mg chol., 132mg sod., 68g carb. (44g sugars, 1g fiber), 6g pro.

These cakes were baked in the Brilliance Bundt Pan by Nordic Ware. Visit *nordicware.com* for details.

For the stacked look shown above, make two cakes and a double batch of icing. Add cookies and edible decorations as desired.

RECIPE FOR SUGAR COOKIES ON P. 141

One Cake, So Many Ways

Behold the world's most customizable cake! Tailor your creation to fit any holiday or event—such as Easter, Mardi Gras, Fourth of July, Halloween or a birthday party—by adding an array of decorative touches and embellishments. Think outside the cake box with cutout sugar cookies, candies, sprinkles, jimmies and other edible accents. Balloons and other food-safe party favors also make fun toppers—just be sure no one eats them!

You can even get a head start by baking the cakes in advance. After baking, remove the cakes to wire racks to cool. Once they cool, just wrap in plastic and freeze for up to 4 months. Be sure to wait to frost, glaze and decorate until the day you plan to serve the cakes.

'TIS THE SEASON

The merriest month of the year arrives bringing with it a host of holiday delights. We start the season off with eagerness and excitement, and before we know it, we're running full speed ahead decorating the tree, baking batches of our favorite cookies and wrapping all the presents. After weeks of preparation, it's finally time to enjoy the warmth and love of the Yuletide season with those we love most. Turn to these recipes, tips and ideas to help make your season sparkle.

HAPPY HOLIDAY APPETIZERS

Pass the happy! Here's to fun finger foods and other merry munchies that prove that good things come in small packages. Cheesy, flaky, stuffed and spicy—there is something for everyone in this lineup of miniature pop-in-your-mouth party pleasers!

Slow-Cooked Cranberry Hot Wings (p. 15) **Cheesy Snack Mix** (p. 12)

LEMON-HERB OLIVES
WITH GOAT CHEESE

LEMON-HERB OLIVES WITH GOAT CHEESE

Greek olives have a fruity flavor that comes into play when you mix them with lemon and fresh herbs. Spoon over goat cheese and slather on crackers.
—Jeanne Ambrose, Milwaukee, WI

Takes: 15 min. • **Makes:** 6 servings

- **3 Tbsp. olive oil**
- **2 tsp. grated lemon zest**
- **1 garlic clove, minced**
- **½ tsp. minced fresh oregano or rosemary**
- **¼ tsp. crushed red pepper flakes**
- **½ cup assorted pitted Greek olives**
- **1 pkg. (5.3 oz.) fresh goat cheese**
- **1 Tbsp. minced fresh basil**
- **Assorted crackers**

1. In a skillet, combine the first 5 ingredients; heat over medium heat just until fragrant, 2-3 minutes, stirring occasionally. Stir in the olives; heat through, allowing flavors to blend. Cool completely.
2. To serve, place cheese on a serving plate. Stir minced basil into olive mixture; spoon over cheese. Serve with crackers.

1 serving: 135 cal., 13g fat (3g sat. fat), 17mg chol., 285mg sod., 2g carb. (0 sugars, 0 fiber), 3g pro.

BROCCOLI & CHIVE STUFFED MINI PEPPERS

Crunchy peppers perfectly balance the creamy filling in these party appetizers. Fresh chives help them stand out.
—Jean McKenzie, Vancouver, WA

Takes: 30 min. • **Makes:** 2 dozen

- **12 miniature sweet peppers**
- **1 pkg. (8 oz.) cream cheese, softened**
- **⅓ cup minced fresh chives**
- **⅛ tsp. salt**
- **⅛ tsp. pepper**
- **⅔ cup finely chopped fresh broccoli**
- **⅔ cup shredded cheddar cheese**

1. Preheat oven to 400°. Cut the peppers lengthwise in half; remove seeds. In a bowl, mix cream cheese, chives, salt and pepper; stir in broccoli. Spoon into pepper halves.
2. Place on a foil-lined baking sheet; bake until heated through, 9-11 minutes. Sprinkle with cheddar cheese. Bake until cheese is melted, 3-4 minutes longer. Cool slightly before serving.

1 stuffed pepper half: 48 cal., 4g fat (2g sat. fat), 14mg chol., 68mg sod., 1g carb. (1g sugars, 0 fiber), 1g pro.

HAM & BRIE PASTRIES

HAM & BRIE PASTRIES

Growing up, I loved pocket pastries. Now with a busy family, I need quick bites, and my spin on the classic ham and cheese delivers at snack or supper time.
—Jenn Tidwell, Fair Oaks, CA

Takes: 30 min. • **Makes:** 16 pastries

- **1 sheet frozen puff pastry, thawed**
- **⅓ cup apricot preserves**
- **4 slices deli ham, quartered**
- **8 oz. Brie cheese, cut into 16 pieces**

Preheat oven to 400°. On a lightly floured surface, unfold puff pastry. Roll pastry to a 12-in. square; cut into sixteen 3-in. squares. Place 1 tsp. preserves in center of each square; top with ham, folding as necessary, and cheese. Overlap 2 opposite corners of pastry over filling; pinch tightly to seal. Place on a parchment-lined baking sheet. Bake 15-20 minutes or until golden brown. Cool on pan 5 minutes before serving.

Freeze option: Freeze cooled pastries in a freezer container, separating layers with waxed paper. To use, reheat pastries on a baking sheet in a preheated 400° oven until heated through.

1 appetizer: 144 cal., 8g fat (3g sat. fat), 17mg chol., 192mg sod., 13g carb. (3g sugars, 1g fiber), 5g pro.

With a buttery texture and an edible, slightly salty rind, Brie cheese is ideal for pairing with fruit, nuts and sweet preserves. The interior has a soft spreadable consistency when served at room temperature.

CHEESY SNACK MIX

Our penchant for Mexican food inspired me to add taco seasoning to a basic party mix. The flavor is zesty but mild, so even kids love it.
—Elizabeth Wynne, Aztec, NM

Prep: 10 min. • **Cook:** 5 min. + cooling
Makes: 12 servings (2½ qt.)

- 3 **cups Corn Chex**
- 3 **cups Rice Chex**
- 3 **cups cheddar miniature pretzels**
- ¼ **cup butter, melted**
- 1 **envelope cheesy taco seasoning**
- 2 **cups white cheddar popcorn**

1. In a large microwave-safe bowl, combine cereal and pretzels. In a small bowl, mix the melted butter and taco seasoning; drizzle over cereal mixture and toss to coat.
2. Microwave, uncovered, on high until heated through, 3-3½ minutes, stirring once every minute. Stir in popcorn. Transfer to a baking sheet to cool completely. Store snack mix in an airtight container.
¾ cup: 151 cal., 5g fat (3g sat. fat), 11mg chol., 362mg sod., 23g carb. (2g sugars, 1g fiber), 3g pro. **Diabetic exchanges:** 1½ starch, 1 fat.

TOMATO-BACON DIP WITH FOCACCIA

BLT lovers, meet your new favorite dip! Enjoy it with crunchy veggies or crackers, or spread it on bread for a zesty flavor booster.
—Marsha Postar, Lubbock, TX

Prep: 20 min. + chilling
Makes: 12 servings

- 1 **cup mayonnaise**
- 1 **cup sour cream**
- ½ **lb. bacon strips, cooked and crumbled**
- 1 **large tomato, seeded and finely chopped**
- ½ **small onion, finely chopped**
- **Crumbled cooked bacon and minced fresh parsley, optional**
- **Focaccia bread, sliced and lightly toasted**

1. In a small bowl, mix mayonnaise and sour cream. Stir in the bacon, tomato and onion. Refrigerate until cold, about 1 hour.
2. If desired, sprinkle with bacon and parsley; serve with focaccia.
¼ cup dip: 211 cal., 21g fat (5g sat. fat), 27mg chol., 228mg sod., 2g carb. (1g sugars, 0 fiber), 3g pro.

MARINATED CHEESE

This special appetizer always makes it to our neighborhood parties and is the first to disappear at the buffet table. It's attractive, delicious and so easy!
—Laurie Casper, Coraopolis, PA

Prep: 30 min. + marinating
Makes: 32 servings (about 2 lbs.)

- 2 **blocks (8 oz. each) white cheddar cheese**
- 2 **pkg. (8 oz. each) cream cheese**
- ¾ **cup chopped roasted sweet red peppers**
- ½ **cup olive oil**
- ¼ **cup white wine vinegar**
- ¼ **cup balsamic vinegar**
- 3 **Tbsp. chopped green onions**
- 3 **Tbsp. minced fresh parsley**
- 2 **Tbsp. minced fresh basil**
- 1 **Tbsp. sugar**
- 3 **garlic cloves, minced**
- ½ **tsp. salt**
- ½ **tsp. pepper**
- **Assorted crackers or toasted sliced French bread**

1. Slice each block of cheddar cheese into twenty ¼-in. slices. Cut each block of cream cheese into 18 slices. Create four 6-in.-long blocks of stacked cheeses, sandwiching 9 cream cheese slices between 10 cheddar slices for each stack. Place in a 13x9-in. dish.
2. In a small bowl, combine the roasted peppers, olive oil, vinegars, onions, herbs, sugar, garlic, salt and pepper; pour over cheese stacks.
3. Cover and refrigerate overnight, turning cheese blocks once. Drain excess marinade. Serve cheese with crackers or toasted bread.
1 oz. cheese: 121 cal., 11g fat (6g sat. fat), 30mg chol., 153mg sod., 1g carb. (0 sugars, 0 fiber), 5g pro.

BUFFALO CHICKEN POCKETS

Here's my idea of pub food made easy: biscuits flavored with Buffalo wing sauce and blue cheese. They're my Friday night favorite!
—Maria Regakis, Saugus, MA

Takes: 30 min. • **Makes:** 8 servings

- ¾ **lb. ground chicken**
- ⅓ **cup Buffalo wing sauce**
- 1 **tube (16.3 oz.) large refrigerated buttermilk biscuits**
- ½ **cup shredded cheddar cheese**
- **Blue cheese salad dressing, optional**

1. Preheat oven to 375°. In a skillet, cook chicken over medium heat until no longer pink, breaking into crumbles, 5-7 minutes; drain. Remove from heat; stir in wing sauce.
2. On a lightly floured surface, roll each biscuit into a 6-in. circle; top each with ¼ cup chicken mixture and 2 Tbsp. cheese. Fold dough over filling; pinch edge to seal.
3. Transfer to an ungreased baking sheet. Bake until golden brown, 12-14 minutes. If desired, serve with blue cheese dressing.
Freeze option: Freeze cooled pockets in a freezer container. To use, reheat pockets on an ungreased baking sheet in a preheated 375° oven until heated through.
1 pocket: 258 cal., 12g fat (5g sat. fat), 35mg chol., 987mg sod., 25g carb. (3g sugars, 1g fiber), 12g pro.

BUFFALO CHICKEN POCKETS

HOLIDAY APPETIZER MEATBALLS

These beefy meatballs are a perennial favorite at our holiday parties. You won't believe how easy these are to make.
—Pat Waymire, Yellow Springs, OH

Prep: 15 min. • **Bake:** 50 min.
Makes: 18 servings

- **1 large egg, lightly beaten**
- **½ cup soft bread crumbs**
- **¼ cup 2% milk**
- **⅓ cup finely chopped onion**
- **1 tsp. salt**
- **½ tsp. Worcestershire sauce**
- **1 lb. ground beef**

SAUCE

- **½ cup ketchup**
- **½ cup chopped onion**
- **⅓ cup sugar**
- **⅓ cup vinegar**
- **1 Tbsp. Worcestershire sauce**
- **⅛ tsp. pepper**

1. In a bowl, combine the first 6 ingredients. Crumble ground beef over mixture and mix well. Shape into 1-in. balls.
2. In a large skillet over medium heat, brown meatballs; drain. Place in a 2½-qt. baking dish. Combine the sauce ingredients. Pour over meatballs. Bake, uncovered, at 350° for 50-60 minutes or until meatballs are no longer pink.
2 meatballs: 84 cal., 4g fat (1g sat. fat), 29mg chol., 245mg sod., 7g carb. (5g sugars, 0 fiber), 6g pro.

TEST KITCHEN TIP

If you're making several batches of meatballs to serve a crowd, consider preparing in bulk to save on time. Make meatballs, bake, cool and then freeze until needed. When ready to use, partially thaw in the refrigerator overnight. Reheat on a greased baking pan in a 350° oven until heated through.

SLOW-COOKED CRANBERRY HOT WINGS

SLOW-COOKED CRANBERRY HOT WINGS

Cranberry wings bring back fond memories of all the fun celebrations and parties we've had through the years, where they always made an appearance. Now my daughter and her friends can't get enough of them.

—Noreen McCormick Danek, Cromwell, CT

Prep: 45 min. • **Cook:** 3 hours
Makes: 4 dozen

- **1 can (14 oz.) jellied cranberry sauce**
- **½ cup orange juice**
- **¼ cup Louisiana-style hot sauce**
- **2 Tbsp. soy sauce**
- **2 Tbsp. honey**
- **1 Tbsp. packed brown sugar**
- **1 Tbsp. Dijon mustard**
- **2 tsp. garlic powder**
- **1 tsp. dried minced onion**
- **1 garlic clove, minced**
- **5 lbs. chicken wings (about 24 wings)**
- **1 tsp. salt**
- **4 tsp. cornstarch**
- **2 Tbsp. cold water**

1. Whisk together first 10 ingredients. For chicken, use a sharp knife to cut through 2 wing joints; discard wing tips. Place wings in a 6-qt. slow cooker; sprinkle with salt. Pour cranberry mixture over top. Cook, covered, on low until tender, 3-4 hours.

2. To serve, remove wings to a 15x10x1-in. pan; arrange in a single layer. Preheat broiler.

3. Transfer cooking juices to a skillet; skim fat. Bring juices to a boil; cook until the mixture is reduced by half, 15-20 minutes, stirring occasionally. Mix cornstarch and water until smooth; stir into juices. Return mixture to a boil, stirring constantly; cook and stir until thickened, 1-2 minutes.

4. Meanwhile, broil wings 3-4 in. from heat until lightly browned, 2-3 minutes. Brush with glaze before serving. Serve with the remaining glaze.

1 piece: 71 cal., 4g fat (1g sat. fat), 15mg chol., 122mg sod., 5g carb. (3g sugars, 0g fiber), 5g pro.

REUBEN WAFFLE POTATO APPETIZERS

I love Reubens, so I turned the classic sammie into a bite-sized appetizer with corned beef and sauerkraut on waffle fries.

—Gloria Bradley, Naperville, IL

Prep: 30 min. • **Bake:** 10 min./batch
Makes: about 4 dozen

- **1 pkg. (22 oz.) frozen waffle-cut fries**
- **4 oz. cream cheese, softened**
- **2 cups shredded fontina cheese, divided**
- **⅓ cup Thousand Island salad dressing**
- **3 Tbsp. chopped sweet onion**
- **1½ tsp. prepared horseradish**
- **12 oz. sliced deli corned beef, coarsely chopped**
- **1 cup sauerkraut, rinsed, well drained and chopped**
- **2 Tbsp. minced fresh chives**

1. Prepare waffle fries according to package directions for baking. Meanwhile, in a small bowl, beat the cream cheese, 1 cup fontina cheese, salad dressing, onion and horseradish until blended.

2. Remove fries from oven; reduce oven setting to 400°. Top each waffle fry with about ¼ oz. corned beef and 1 tsp. each cream cheese mixture, sauerkraut and remaining fontina cheese. Bake until cheese is melted, 8-10 minutes. Sprinkle with chives.

1 appetizer: 62 cal., 4g fat (2g sat. fat), 12mg chol., 168mg sod., 4g carb. (0 sugars, 0 fiber), 3g pro.

A REGAL CHRISTMAS DINNER

On Christmas Day, gather loved ones around the table for an unforgettable feast. It's easier than you think to host a dinner with a formal ambiance when you turn to these impressive dishes. Use the timeline on p. 18 as your road map for a stunning, yet stress-free, holiday meal.

Peppercorn-Dijon Beef Roast (p. 22) **Swiss Cheese Potatoes** (p. 22)
Herbed Accordion Dinner Rolls (p. 21)

Christmas Day Countdown

It's the most wonderful day of the year! Many of the dishes in this menu can be prepared in advance, while others are best to make the day of. Use this timeline as your guide to get a jump on all the festivities.

A FEW WEEKS BEFORE

☐ Prepare two grocery lists—one for nonperishable items to buy now and one for perishable items to buy a few days before Christmas.

☐ Mix together the ingredients for the Cranberry Bourbon. Store in a cool, dry place for 2-4 weeks.

TWO DAYS BEFORE

☐ Buy remaining grocery items.

☐ Bake the Peppermint Cream Pound Cake, but do not glaze. Store the cake in an airtight container.

☐ Bake the Lacy Brandy Snaps, but do not fill with cream mixture. Store the cookies in an airtight container.

☐ Start the Easy Smoked Salmon recipe. Cover and refrigerate salmon for 4-8 hours.

☐ Wash china, stemware and linens.

THE DAY BEFORE

☐ Bake the Herbed Accordion Dinner Rolls. Let rolls cool and store in an airtight container.

☐ Mix together the Creamy Horseradish Sauce. Refrigerate until serving.

☐ Remove Easy Smoked Salmon from the refrigerator. Bake and cool to room temperature. Cover and refrigerate overnight.

☐ Prepare the Pickled Mushrooms with Garlic. Refrigerate overnight.

☐ Blanch snow peas for Snow Pea Holiday Wreath. Pat dry; store in an airtight container in the refrigerator.

CHRISTMAS DAY

☐ About 2-3 hours before dinner, prepare the Peppercorn-Dijon Beef Roast and let stand for 15 minutes before slicing. Keep warm until serving.

☐ About 2 hours before dinner, remove the cream cheese for the Snow Pea Holiday Wreath and set on the counter to soften.

☐ About 1 hour before dinner, mix together the glaze for the pound cake. Add glaze to cake. Keep covered until serving.

☐ About 40 minutes before dinner, prepare the Swiss Cheese Potatoes. Keep warm until serving.

RIGHT BEFORE DINNER

☐ Just before guests arrive, arrange snow peas in a wreath and mix the dip for Snow Pea Holiday Wreath.

☐ Just before guests arrive, remove the Easy Smoked Salmon and the Pickled Mushrooms with Garlic from the refrigerator. Transfer to platters or hors d'oeuvres trays and serve as appetizers.

☐ As guests arrive, bring out the Cranberry Bourbon. Strain and discard cranberries, cinnamon and orange zest. Transfer to a glass container and add to cocktails.

☐ Warm dinner rolls in the oven just before serving.

☐ Remove Creamy Horseradish Sauce from the refrigerator. Serve with beef roast.

☐ Following dinner, mix together the filling for the Lacy Brandy Snaps. Pipe cream mixture into cookies and sprinkle ends with chocolate if desired. Cut and serve pound cake.

CRANBERRY BOURBON

The subtle tang of cranberry and warm winter spices make this bourbon just right for holiday toasts—neat, on the rocks or in a cocktail.
—James Schend, Pleasant Prairie, WI

Prep: 10 min. + standing
Makes: 20 servings

- 3 **cups bourbon**
- 1 **cup dried cranberries**
- 1 **cinnamon stick (3 in.)**
- 4 **orange zest strips (3 in.)**

ADDITIONAL INGREDIENTS FOR CRANBERRY MANHATTAN (FOR EACH SERVING)

- **Ice cubes**
- ¾ **oz. sweet vermouth**
- **Dash bitters**

ADDITIONAL INGREDIENTS FOR CRANBERRY OLD-FASHIONED (FOR EACH SERVING)

- 1 **orange slice**
- 4 **dried cranberries**
- 2 **dashes bitters**
- **Ice cubes**
- 3 **oz. lemon-lime soda**
- 1 **tsp. orange juice**

In an airtight glass container, combine the bourbon, cranberries, cinnamon stick and orange zest. Store in a cool, dry place for 2-4 weeks. Strain, discarding cranberries, cinnamon and orange zest. Return bourbon to glass container. Store in a cool, dry place.
1 oz. bourbon: 64 cal., 0 fat (0 sat. fat), 0 chol., 0 sod., 0 carb. (0 sugars, 0 fiber), 0 pro.
To prepare a cranberry Manhattan: Fill a shaker three-fourths full with ice. Add 2 oz. Cranberry Bourbon, sweet vermouth and bitters; cover and shake until cold. Strain into a cocktail glass.
To prepare a cranberry old-fashioned: In a rocks glass, muddle orange slice, cranberries and bitters. Add ice cubes. Pour in 1½ oz. of Cranberry Bourbon, soda and juice.

TEST KITCHEN TIP

A well-stocked bar includes the tools to tackle all kinds of cocktails. Common items include an ice bucket, bar spoon, muddler, wine and beer bottle openers, a jigger (for measuring shots), a cocktail shaker and strainer. If you'll be making a variety of cocktails, it's nice to have a combination of short, tall and stemmed glasses. And don't forget fun extras like stir sticks, cute beverage napkins, embossed coasters and frilled toothpicks.

SNOW PEA HOLIDAY WREATH

SNOW PEA HOLIDAY WREATH

Santa himself might stop to sample this pretty-as-a-picture finger food! Crunchy green pea pods and juicy red tomatoes add a natural fresh, festive holiday note to my buffet table.
—Carol Schneck, Lodi, CA

Takes: 25 min. • **Makes:** 20 servings

- ½ **lb. fresh snow peas, strings removed**
- 3 **oz. cream cheese, softened**
- ¼ **tsp. garlic powder**
- ¼ **tsp. seasoned salt**
- 2 **cups grape tomatoes**

1. In a large saucepan, bring 6 cups water to a boil. Add snow peas; cook, uncovered, just until crisp-tender and they turn bright green, 1-2 minutes. Drain and immediately drop into ice water. Drain and pat dry.
2. In a small bowl, combine the cream cheese, garlic powder and seasoned salt. Place bowl in the center of a serving platter. Arrange snow peas and tomatoes around the bowl.
1 serving: 23 cal., 2g fat (1g sat. fat), 5mg chol., 33mg sod., 2g carb. (1g sugars, 0 fiber), 1g pro.

PICKLED MUSHROOMS WITH GARLIC

I'm always asked to bring these tempting tidbits to holiday gatherings. Easy to make ahead and transport, they're something to celebrate on a festive relish tray.
—Joyce Anderson, Chico, CA

Prep: 10 min. + marinating • **Makes:** 4½ cups

- ⅔ **cup white wine vinegar**
- ½ **cup vegetable oil**
- 2 **Tbsp. water**
- 1 **tsp. salt**
- **Dash pepper**
- **Dash hot pepper sauce**
- 1 **lb. small whole fresh mushrooms**
- 1 **medium onion, thinly sliced**
- 2 **to 4 garlic cloves, thinly sliced**

In a large glass jar with a tight-fitting lid, combine the first 6 ingredients. Add the mushrooms, onion and garlic. Cover and shake gently to coat. Refrigerate for 8 hours or overnight. Drain before serving.
¼ cup: 25 cal., 2g fat (0 sat. fat), 0 chol., 132mg sod., 2g carb. (0 sugars, 0 fiber), 1g pro.

HERBED ACCORDION DINNER ROLLS

HERBED ACCORDION DINNER ROLLS

To dress up everyday dinner rolls, brush herbed butter over the dough, then form accordion rolls. The aroma while baking is incredible!
—Taste of Home *Test Kitchen*

Prep: 40 min. + rising • **Bake:** 20 min.
Makes: 2 dozen

- **2 pkg. (¼ oz. each) active dry yeast**
- **½ cup warm water (110° to 115°)**
- **1 tsp. plus ⅓ cup sugar, divided**
- **1¼ cups warm 2% milk (110° to 115°)**
- **½ cup butter, melted**
- **2 large eggs, room temperature**
- **1½ tsp. salt**
- **6 to 6½ cups all-purpose flour**
- **3 Tbsp. butter, softened**
- **1 tsp. Italian seasoning**
- **1 large egg white, beaten**

1. In a large bowl, dissolve yeast in warm water with 1 tsp. sugar. Add the milk, melted butter, eggs, salt, 3 cups flour and remaining sugar; beat until smooth. Stir in enough remaining flour to form a soft dough.
2. Turn onto a floured surface; knead until smooth and elastic, 6-8 minutes. Place in a greased bowl, turning once to grease the top. Cover and let rise in a warm place until doubled, about 1 hour.
3. Punch dough down; place on a lightly floured surface. Divide into 4 portions. Roll each portion into a 14x6-in. rectangle. Combine the softened butter and Italian seasoning; spread over dough.
4. Score each rectangle widthwise at 2-in. intervals. Using marks as a guide, fold dough accordion-style back and forth along score lines. Cut folded dough into six 1-in. pieces. Place pieces cut side down in greased muffin cups. Cover and let rise until doubled, about 30 minutes.
5. Preheat oven to 375°. Uncover and let stand another 10 minutes before baking. Brush with egg white. Bake until golden brown, 18-22 minutes. Remove from pans to wire racks.
1 roll: 186 cal., 6g fat (4g sat. fat), 32mg chol., 200mg sod., 28g carb. (4g sugars, 1g fiber), 5g pro.
Basil & oregano dinner rolls: Substitute ½ tsp. each dried oregano and basil for Italian seasoning.
Fresh herb dinner rolls: Substitute 1½ tsp. minced fresh parsley and ½ tsp. minced fresh thyme for Italian seasoning.

EASY SMOKED SALMON

EASY SMOKED SALMON

I found this in a magazine years ago, and it became my favorite way to prepare salmon. It's such an elegant appetizer!
—Norma Fell, Boyne City, MI

Prep: 10 min. + marinating
Bake: 35 min. + chilling
Makes: 16 servings

- **1 salmon fillet (about 2 lbs.)**
- **2 Tbsp. brown sugar**
- **2 tsp. salt**
- **½ tsp. pepper**
- **1 to 2 Tbsp. liquid smoke**

1. Place salmon, skin side down, in an 11x7-in. baking pan coated with cooking spray. Sprinkle with brown sugar, salt and pepper. Drizzle with liquid smoke. Cover and refrigerate for 4-8 hours.
2. Drain salmon, discarding liquid. Bake, uncovered, at 350° until fish flakes easily with a fork, 35-45 minutes. Cool to room temperature. Cover and refrigerate for 8 hours or overnight.
1½ oz. cooked salmon: 95 cal., 5g fat (1g sat. fat), 28mg chol., 324mg sod., 2g carb. (2g sugars, 0 fiber), 10g pro.

PEPPERCORN-DIJON BEEF ROAST

Dinner guests will be surprised to hear this festive entree only calls for five ingredients. It's the perfect choice for serving a large group.
—Mary Ann Griffin, Bowling Green, KY

Prep: 15 min. • **Bake:** 2 hours + standing
Makes: 16 servings

- 2 **Tbsp. Dijon mustard**
- 1 **Tbsp. coarsely ground pepper**
- 1 **Tbsp. minced fresh mint or 1 tsp. dried mint**
- 1 **Tbsp. minced fresh rosemary or 1 tsp. dried rosemary, crushed**
- 1 **beef sirloin tip roast (4 lbs.)**

1. Preheat the oven to 350°. Mix the first 4 ingredients.
2. Place roast on a rack in a roasting pan; spread with mustard mixture. Roast until desired doneness (a thermometer should read 135° for medium-rare, 140° for medium and 145° for medium-well), about 2 hours.
3. Remove from oven; tent with foil. Let stand 15 minutes before slicing.
3 oz. cooked beef: 146 cal., 5g fat (2g sat. fat), 72mg chol., 78mg sod., 1g carb. (0 sugars, 0 fiber), 23g pro. **Diabetic exchanges:** 3 lean meat.

CREAMY HORSERADISH SAUCE

This sauce complements a variety of foods, but my favorite way to use it is on cold roast beef sandwiches.
—Florence Palmer, Marshall, IL

Takes: 15 min. • **Makes:** 3½ cups

- 1 **cup heavy whipping cream**
- 1 **cup mayonnaise**
- ⅛ **tsp. salt**
- ¼ **cup prepared horseradish**

In a bowl, whip cream until soft peaks form. Add mayonnaise and salt; blend thoroughly. Fold in horseradish. Chill until serving. Use as a condiment with roast beef, corned beef, pork or sandwiches.
2 Tbsp.: 87 cal., 9g fat (3g sat. fat), 15mg chol., 63mg sod., 0 carb. (0 sugars, 0 fiber), 0 pro.

SWISS CHEESE POTATOES

You'll find a dish like this in German-Swiss restaurants, but it's super simple to pull together at home.
—Wolfgang Hanau, West Palm Beach, FL

Prep: 30 min. • **Broil:** 5 min.
Makes: 12 servings

- 8 **large potatoes, peeled and cubed (about 4 lbs.)**
- 1½ **tsp. salt, divided**
- 2 **cups chopped celery**
- ¾ **cup chopped onion**
- 1½ **cups shredded Swiss cheese, divided**
- ⅔ **cup 2% milk**
- 3 **Tbsp. butter**
- ¼ **tsp. pepper**

1. Place potatoes and 1 tsp. salt in a Dutch oven; add water to cover. Bring to a boil. Reduce the heat; cook, uncovered, for 10 minutes. Add celery and onion; cook until vegetables are tender, 10-15 minutes. Drain; transfer to a large bowl.
2. Mash potato mixture, gradually adding ¾ cup cheese, milk, butter, pepper and remaining salt. Transfer to a greased 8-in. square baking pan; sprinkle with remaining cheese. Broil 3-4 in. from the heat until cheese is lightly browned, 5-8 minutes.
¾ cup: 235 cal., 8g fat (5g sat. fat), 21mg chol., 368mg sod., 36g carb. (4g sugars, 3g fiber), 7g pro.

PEPPERCORN-DIJON BEEF ROAST

LACY BRANDY SNAPS

These cream-filled crisps are the perfect sweet treat. Include them on a holiday cookie platter or serve at the end of the meal with coffee or tea.

—Natalie Bremson, Plantation, FL

Prep: 30 min. • **Bake:** 10 min./batch + cooling
Makes: 4 dozen

- **6 Tbsp. unsalted butter, cubed**
- **⅓ cup sugar**
- **3 Tbsp. light corn syrup**
- **⅔ cup all-purpose flour**
- **2 tsp. brandy**
- **1 tsp. ground ginger**

FILLING

- **4 cups heavy whipping cream**
- **1¾ cups confectioners' sugar**
- **½ cup brandy**
- **Grated chocolate, optional**

1. In a small saucepan, combine the butter, sugar and corn syrup. Cook and stir over medium heat until butter is melted. Remove from the heat. Stir in flour, brandy and ginger.
2. Drop by teaspoonfuls, 3 at a time, 3 in. apart onto a parchment-lined baking sheet. Bake at 350° until golden brown, 7-8 minutes.
3. Cool for 30-45 seconds. Working quickly, loosen each cookie and curl around a thick wooden spoon handle. (If cookies become too cool to shape, return to oven for 1 minute to soften.) Remove to a wire rack to cool completely.
4. For filling, in a large bowl, beat cream until it begins to thicken. Add confectioners' sugar and brandy; beat until stiff peaks form. Just before serving, pipe the cream mixture into cookies. Sprinkle ends with grated chocolate if desired.
1 cookie: 119 cal., 9g fat (5g sat. fat), 31mg chol., 9mg sod., 9g carb. (6g sugars, 0 fiber), 1g pro.

PEPPERMINT CREAM POUND CAKE

PEPPERMINT CREAM POUND CAKE

I came up with this recipe when I was looking for a twist on traditional pound cake. I love the look and flavor of peppermint, especially at Christmas, so it seemed like a natural pairing. Everyone at work loved the results, and my family did, too.

—Carolyn Webster, Winston-Salem, NC

Prep: 35 min. • **Bake:** 1 hour + cooling
Makes: 12 servings

- **1 cup unsalted butter, softened**
- **½ cup butter-flavored shortening**
- **2 cups sugar**
- **6 large eggs, room temperature**
- **1 tsp. vanilla extract**
- **½ tsp. peppermint extract**
- **3 cups all-purpose flour**
- **1 tsp. baking powder**
- **1 cup heavy whipping cream**
- **½ cup finely crushed peppermint candies**

GLAZE

- **1½ cups confectioners' sugar**
- **1 tsp. unsalted butter, melted**
- **¼ tsp. vanilla extract**
- **⅛ tsp. salt**
- **4 to 5 Tbsp. heavy whipping cream**
- **Additional crushed peppermint candies**

1. Preheat oven to 325°. In a large bowl, cream the butter, shortening and sugar until light and fluffy. Add 1 egg at a time, beating well after each addition. Beat in extracts. Combine flour and baking powder; add to creamed mixture alternately with whipping cream. Fold in candies.

2. Transfer to a well-greased and floured 10-in. fluted tube pan. Bake until a toothpick inserted in the center of the cake comes out clean, 1-1¼ hours. Cool for 10 minutes before removing from pan to a wire rack to cool completely.

3. In a small bowl, combine the confectioners' sugar, butter, vanilla and salt. Stir in enough cream to achieve a drizzling consistency. Drizzle over cake. Sprinkle with additional candies. Refrigerate leftovers.

1 slice: 649 cal., 35g fat (18g sat. fat), 181mg chol., 107mg sod., 77g carb. (50g sugars, 1g fiber), 7g pro.

Family Traditions

While some holiday traditions remain the same year after year, it's never too late to start a new one. Try a fresh tradition that you and your family will look forward to in years to come—and make some new memories. Take a peek at some of these reader stories for inspiration.

HOLIDAY POETRY SLAM

The in-law side of my family has a tradition of reciting poems over homemade appetizers. We work on the poems the week leading up to Christmas and, before opening presents, we take turns sharing.

—Ginger Scott, Glendale, AZ

GENEROUS SPIRITS

We keep all the charity solicitations that arrive in the mail in a basket all year. On the eighth night of Hanukkah, instead of getting gifts, we all sit around and discuss the different organizations and give each family member money to contribute to the organizations they deem most worthy.

—Jessica Tolmach, Greenwich, CT

A VERY PINTEREST NEW YEAR

On New Year's Day, we invite a group of friends and family to each pick a Pinterest recipe and then we spend the day making the dishes.

—Cheryl Blanco, Austin, TX

PAJAMA PARTY

Each year I make my kids a Christmas Eve box. It includes a new pair of jammies, microwave popcorn, their favorite movie snacks, hot cocoa mix and a Christmas movie. We all watch the Christmas movie before bed, with a roaring fire. We started it 17 years ago with our oldest and have never missed a year!

—Erin Wright, Wallace, KS

WHEN FRIENDS ARE FAMILY

We celebrate Tamale Day (or so we have named it) with our friends just before the holidays. As the name suggests, everyone brings their favorite tamales; each couple usually leaves with five dozen.

—Krysti Roush, Phoenix, AZ

HOLIDAY BAKING

Bakers, start your ovens! Here is your time to shine. Show off your baking prowess with a stand-out baked beauty. From velvety cheesecake to a whimsical gingerbread chalet, these recipes show how to bring the "wow" to your next holiday party or potluck.

Cocoa Frosting Yule Log (p. 30)

Baking Pantry Staples

Keep these ingredients handy for when the baking bug strikes—or when an unexpected potluck invite comes your way! These are the building blocks for homemade cakes, breads, cheesecakes and more.

THE ESSENTIALS

- Baking chocolate bars (bittersweet)
- Baking powder and soda
- Chocolate chips (semisweet)
- Cinnamon
- Cocoa powder
- Extracts (almond and vanilla)
- Flour
- Oil (canola or vegetable)
- Old-fashioned oats
- Salt
- Shredded coconut
- Sugar (confectioners', granulated and light brown)
- Sprinkles

NICE TO HAVE

- Applesauce
- Cream of tartar
- Raisins
- Peanut butter
- Shortening
- Pudding mix

CREAM-FILLED CINNAMON COFFEE CAKE

CREAM-FILLED CINNAMON COFFEE CAKE

When guests stay overnight, they often request this cinnamon coffee cake for breakfast. You can prepare it in advance to make the morning easy.
—Arlene Wengerd, Millersburg, OH

Prep: 25 min. • **Bake:** 20 min. + cooling
Makes: 12 servings

- ½ cup butter, softened
- 1 cup sugar
- 2 large eggs, room temperature
- 1 tsp. vanilla extract
- 1½ cups all-purpose flour
- ½ tsp. baking soda
- ½ tsp. salt
- 1 cup sour cream

TOPPING

- ½ cup sugar
- ½ cup chopped pecans
- 2 tsp. ground cinnamon

FILLING

- 1 Tbsp. cornstarch
- ¾ cup 2% milk
- ¼ cup butter, softened
- ¼ cup shortening
- ½ cup sugar
- ½ tsp. vanilla extract
- Caramel ice cream topping, optional

1. In a large bowl, cream butter and sugar until light and fluffy. Add eggs, 1 at a time, beating well after each addition. Beat in the vanilla. Combine flour, baking soda and salt; add to creamed mixture alternately with sour cream, beating just until combined.
2. Pour the batter into 2 greased and waxed paper-lined 9-in. round baking pans. Combine topping ingredients; sprinkle over the batter. Lightly cut through with a knife to swirl.
3. Bake at 350° until a toothpick inserted in the center comes out clean, 20-25 minutes. Cool for 10 minutes; remove from pans to wire racks to cool completely.
4. In a small saucepan, combine cornstarch and milk until smooth. Bring to a boil; cook and stir for 1-2 minutes or until thickened. Cover and refrigerate until chilled. In a small bowl, cream the butter, shortening and sugar until light and fluffy. Add vanilla and chilled milk mixture; beat on medium speed until smooth and creamy, about 10 minutes.
5. Place 1 cake on a serving plate; spread with filling. Top with remaining cake. Store in the refrigerator. If desired, serve with caramel topping.
1 slice: 419 cal., 24g fat (11g sat. fat), 67mg chol., 268mg sod., 49g carb. (35g sugars, 1g fiber), 4g pro.

GERMAN STOLLEN

My family and friends agree that the holidays just wouldn't be the same without this traditional German bread.
—Valeria Mauk, Elkhart Lake, WI

Prep: 1½ hours + rising
Bake: 25 min. + cooling
Makes: 2 loaves (14 slices each)

- ¾ cup raisins
- ½ cup chopped mixed candied fruit
- ¼ cup dried currants
- ¾ cup apple juice
- 4½ to 5 cups all-purpose flour
- 2 pkg. (¼ oz. each) active dry yeast
- ¼ cup sugar
- 1 tsp. salt
- 1 cup 2% milk
- ½ cup butter, cubed
- 2 large eggs, room temperature
- 2 Tbsp. grated orange zest
- 1 Tbsp. grated lemon zest
- ½ tsp. almond extract
- ½ cup chopped almonds
- Confectioners' sugar, optional

GLAZE

- 1 cup confectioners' sugar
- 3 to 4 Tbsp. milk

1. In a large bowl, soak the raisins, fruit and currants in apple juice for 1 hour; drain and set aside.
2. In a large bowl, combine 1½ cups flour, yeast, sugar and salt. In a small saucepan, heat milk and butter to 120°-130°. Add to the dry ingredients; beat just until moistened. Add the eggs, zest and extract; beat until smooth. Stir in the almond, fruit mixture and enough of the remaining flour to form a soft dough.
3. Turn onto a floured surface; knead until smooth and elastic, 6-8 minutes. Place dough in a greased bowl, turning once to grease the top. Cover and let rise in a warm place until doubled, about 1 hour.
4. Punch dough down; divide in half. Cover dough and let rest for 10 minutes. On a lightly floured surface, roll each half into a 12x8-in. oval. Fold 1 long side over to within 1 in. of the opposite side; press edges lightly to seal. Place on greased baking sheets. Cover and let rise until almost doubled, about 30 minutes.
5. Bake at 350° for 25-30 minutes or until golden brown. Cool on wire racks. Dust with confectioners' sugar or combine glaze ingredients and drizzle over loaves.
1 slice: 214 cal., 6g fat (3g sat. fat), 30mg chol., 155mg sod., 36g carb. (16g sugars, 2g fiber), 4g pro.

COCOA FROSTING YULE LOG

Here is a berry-trimmed version of the traditional yule log that is sure to cause murmurs of appreciation. It is one of my most requested Christmas recipes.
—*Jane Birch, Edison, NJ*

Prep: 45 min.
Bake: 20 min.
Makes: 14 servings

- **1⅓ cups finely ground walnuts**
- **¾ cup all-purpose flour**
- **½ cup baking cocoa**
- **10 large eggs, separated, room temperature**
- **1⅓ cups sugar, divided**
- **1 tsp. vanilla extract**
- **1 tsp. salt**
- **½ tsp. cream of tartar**
- **Additional baking cocoa**

FILLING

- **2 cups heavy whipping cream**
- **½ cup confectioners' sugar**
- **1 tsp. vanilla extract**

COCOA FROSTING

- **3¾ cups confectioners' sugar**
- **⅓ cup baking cocoa**
- **1 cup butter, softened**
- **1 tsp. vanilla extract**
- **3 to 5 Tbsp. 2% milk**
- **Optional: Confectioners' sugar and fresh raspberries**

1. Line 2 greased 15x10x1-in. baking pans with parchment. Grease parchment and set aside. In a bowl, combine the walnuts, flour and cocoa; set aside.
2. In a large bowl, beat egg yolks on high until light and fluffy. Gradually add ⅔ cup sugar, beating until mixture is thick and light yellow, about 10 minutes. Beat in vanilla. Add cocoa mixture; stir until combined.
3. In another large bowl, beat the egg whites, salt and cream of tartar on medium speed until soft peaks form. Gradually beat in the remaining sugar, 1 Tbsp. at a time, on high until stiff glossy peaks form and the sugar is dissolved. Gently fold ⅓ of the meringue into cocoa mixture until thoroughly incorporated; fold in remaining meringue in 2 additions.
4. Spread batter into prepared pans. Bake at 350° for 18-20 minutes or until cake springs back when lightly touched. Cool cakes in pans for 5 minutes. Turn each onto a kitchen towel dusted with additional cocoa. Gently peel off parchment. Working quickly, roll up each cake in a towel, starting with the short side. Cool completely on a wire rack.
5. For filling, in a large bowl, beat the cream until it begins to thicken. Gradually add the confectioners' sugar and vanilla; beat until stiff peaks form. Unroll cakes and spread evenly with cream mixture to within ½ in. of edges. Roll up each cake again.
6. Place 1 cake roll seam side down on a serving plate. Use the second cake roll for the branches. To make branches, measure 3 in. from top right corner of the second cake roll; cut at an angle from that point to the bottom right corner. Measure 3 in. from the top left corner; cut at an angle from that point to the bottom left corner. Save the end pieces for another use. Measure 3 in. from the top right and 3 in. from bottom right; cut between the marks. Place cut cake sections along sides of cake for branches.
7. For frosting, sift confectioners' sugar and cocoa together into a large bowl. In a another large bowl, beat the butter and vanilla until blended. Beat in confectioners' sugar mixture alternately with enough milk to reach desired consistency. Frost top and sides of cake with cocoa frosting. Using an offset spatula, make short strokes in the frosting to create bark pattern. If desired, dust with confectioners' sugar and garnish with fresh raspberries.
1 piece: 594 cal., 35g fat (18g sat. fat), 207mg chol., 336mg sod., 66g carb. (56g sugars, 2g fiber), 9g pro.

GOLDEN SANTA BREAD

A friend of mine shared this fun idea. She made it with store-bought frozen dough, but I wanted to try it with homemade. The finished Santa looks complicated, but he's actually simple to create.
—*Vicki Melies, Elkhorn, NE*

Prep: 30 min. + rising
Bake: 25 min. + cooling
Makes: 1 loaf (18 servings)

- **4 to 4½ cups bread flour**
- **½ cup sugar**
- **2 pkg. (¼ oz. each) active dry yeast**
- **1½ tsp. salt**
- **½ cup 2% milk**
- **¼ cup water**
- **¼ cup butter, cubed**
- **2 large eggs, room temperature**
- **2 raisins**
- **2 large egg yolks**
- **2 to 3 drops red food coloring**

1. In a large bowl, combine 2 cups flour, sugar, yeast and salt. In a small saucepan, heat milk, water and butter to 120°-130°. Add to the dry ingredients; beat just until moistened. Beat in eggs until smooth. Stir in enough remaining flour to form a stiff dough.
2. Turn onto a floured surface; knead until smooth and elastic, 6-8 minutes. Place in a greased bowl, turning once to grease top. Cover dough and let rise in a warm place until doubled, about 1 hour.
3. Preheat oven to 350°. Punch dough down. Turn onto a lightly floured surface; divide into 2 portions, 1 slightly larger than the other.
4. Shape the larger portion into an elongated triangle with rounded corners for Santa's head and hat.
5. Divide the smaller portion in half. Shape and flatten 1 half into a beard. Place beard over face; using a sharp knife, cut deep slits to resemble hair.
6. Use remaining dough for the mustache, nose, eyebrows, hat pompom and brim. Shape a portion of dough into a mustache; flatten and place on face over beard. Using sharp knife, cut slits to resemble hair. Place a small ball above mustache for nose. With scissors, cut 2 slits for eyes; insert raisins into slits. Form another small portion of dough into eyebrows; flatten and place above eyes. Roll out a narrow piece of dough to create a hat brim; position below hat. Fold tip of hat over and add dough ball for pompom. If desired, using scissors or sharp knife, cut small lines along edges of brim and pompom to resemble fur.
7. In separate small bowls, beat egg each yolk. Add red food coloring to 1 yolk; carefully brush over hat. Brush plain yolk over the remaining dough.
8. Cover loosely with foil. Bake 15 minutes. Uncover and bake until golden brown, 10-12 minutes longer. Cool on a wire rack.
1 piece: 175 cal., 4g fat (2g sat. fat), 49mg chol., 230mg sod., 29g carb. (6g sugars, 1g fiber), 5g pro.

GOLDEN
SANTA BREAD

ALMOND PASTRY PUFFS

This tender, nutty coffee cake is one of my favorite brunch treats. It looks and tastes so special, people won't believe you made it yourself. It's good that the recipe makes two!
—*Betty Claycomb, Alverton, PA*

Prep: 40 min. • **Bake:** 20 min. + cooling
Makes: 2 pastries (11 servings each)

- **2 cups all-purpose flour, divided**
- **¼ tsp. salt**
- **1 cup cold butter, divided**
- **2 Tbsp. plus 1 cup cold water, divided**
- **¼ tsp. almond extract**
- **3 large eggs**

FROSTING

- **1½ cups confectioners' sugar**
- **2 Tbsp. butter, softened**
- **4 tsp. water**
- **¼ tsp. almond extract**
- **⅔ cup chopped almonds, toasted**

1. In a large bowl, combine 1 cup flour and salt; cut in ½ cup butter until mixture resembles coarse crumbs. Add 2 Tbsp. cold water; stir with a fork until blended. Shape dough into a ball; divide in half. Place dough 3 in. apart on an ungreased baking sheet; pat each into a 12x3-in. rectangle.
2. In a large saucepan, bring remaining butter and water to a boil. Remove from the heat; stir in the extract and remaining flour until a smooth ball forms. Remove from heat; let stand for 5 minutes. Add eggs, 1 at a time, beating well after each addition. Continue beating until mixture is smooth and shiny.
3. Spread over rectangles. Bake at 400° until the topping is lightly browned, 18-20 minutes. Cool for 5 minutes before removing from pan to wire racks.
4. For frosting, in a small bowl, combine the confectioners' sugar, butter, water and almond extract; beat until smooth. Spread over the pastries; sprinkle with almonds.
1 piece: 189 cal., 12g fat (6g sat. fat), 54mg chol., 130mg sod., 18g carb. (8g sugars, 1g fiber), 3g pro.

FESTIVE HOLIDAY CHEESECAKE

Make Christmas dinner dazzle with this show-stopping cheesecake. The top is adorned with pretty garnishes.
—Taste of Home *Test Kitchen*

Prep: 30 min. • **Bake:** 1½ hours + chilling
Makes: 16 servings

- **1½ cups graham cracker crumbs**
- **½ cup pecans, toasted and finely chopped**
- **2 Tbsp. light brown sugar**
- **6 Tbsp. butter, melted**

FILLING

- **4 pkg. (8 oz. each) cream cheese, softened**
- **1 cup sugar**
- **3 tsp. vanilla extract**
- **4 large eggs, room temperature, lightly beaten**
- **1 cup miniature semisweet chocolate chips**

TOPPING

- **2 cups sour cream**
- **¼ cup sugar**
- **Optional: Chocolate and vanilla star meringues, chocolate shavings, chocolate curls, candied orange peel, chopped pistachios**

1. Place an ungreased 9-in. springform pan on a double thickness of heavy-duty foil (about 18 in. square). Securely wrap foil around pan.
2. In a small bowl, combine cracker crumbs, pecans and brown sugar; stir in melted butter. Press onto bottom and 1½ in. up the sides of prepared pan. Place on a baking sheet. Bake at 350° for 5 minutes. Cool on a wire rack.
3. In a large bowl, beat the cream cheese, sugar and vanilla until smooth. Add eggs; beat on low speed just until combined. Fold in chocolate chips. Pour into crust. Place in a larger baking pan; add 1 in. of hot water to larger pan.
4. Bake at 325° for 1½ hours or until center is just set and top appears dull. In a small bowl, combine sour cream and sugar until smooth; spoon over hot cheesecake and spread to cover. Bake for 5 minutes longer or until the topping is just set.
5. Remove springform pan from water bath. Cool on a wire rack for 10 minutes. Carefully run a knife around edge of pan to loosen; cool 1 hour longer. Refrigerate overnight. Remove the sides of pan. If desired, top with optional garnishes.
1 slice: 499 cal., 38g fat (20g sat. fat), 122mg chol., 285mg sod., 36g carb. (29g sugars, 1g fiber), 7g pro.

FESTIVE HOLIDAY CHEESECAKE

HOLIDAY FRUITCAKE

After some experimenting in the kitchen, I finally came up with my ideal fruitcake. I think it has just the right mix of nuts and fruit.
—Allene Spence, Delbarton, WV

Prep: 20 min. • **Bake:** 2 hours + cooling
Makes: 16 servings

- **1½ cups whole red candied cherries**
- **1½ cups whole green candied cherries**
- **3 cups diced candied pineapple**
- **1 lb. walnut halves**
- **10 oz. golden raisins**
- **1 cup shortening**
- **1 cup sugar**
- **5 large eggs, room temperature**
- **4 Tbsp. vanilla extract**
- **3 cups all-purpose flour**
- **3 tsp. baking powder**
- **1 tsp. salt**

1. Preheat oven to 300°. Combine fruit and nuts. In another bowl, cream shortening and sugar until light and fluffy. Beat in eggs and vanilla. Combine flour, baking powder and salt; add to creamed mixture and mix well. Pour over fruit and nuts; stir to coat.
2. Transfer to a greased and floured 10-in. tube pan. Bake until a toothpick inserted in center comes out clean, about 2 hours. Cool 10 minutes; remove from pan to a wire rack to cool completely. Wrap tightly and store in a cool place. Bring to room temperature before serving; slice with a serrated knife.
1 slice: 686 cal., 32g fat (5g sat. fat), 58mg chol., 342mg sod., 92g carb. (61g sugars, 4g fiber), 10g pro.

Be patient as the cake cools after baking. Fruitcake needs to cool completely before being removed from the pan.

GINGERBREAD CHALET

GINGERBREAD CHALET

The A-frame design on this pretty winter chalet is easy enough for even first-timers builders to construct. Make it for a decoration. Enjoy it for dessert!

—Peggy Anderson, Haughton, LA

Prep: 25 min. • **Bake:** 15 min. + assembly
Makes: 1 chalet (32 servings)

DOUGH

- **1 cup butter, softened**
- **1½ cups packed dark brown sugar**
- **1 large egg, room temperature**
- **2 Tbsp. molasses**
- **1 Tbsp. dark corn syrup**
- **4 cups all-purpose flour**
- **4 tsp. ground cinnamon**
- **1 Tbsp. ground cloves**
- **2 tsp. ground nutmeg**
- **2 Tbsp. hot brewed coffee**
- **2 tsp. baking soda**

ICING AND ASSEMBLY

- **2 large pasteurized egg whites, room temperature**
- **3¾ cups confectioners' sugar**
- **Warm water**

1. In a large bowl, cream butter and brown sugar until light and fluffy, 5-7 minutes. Beat in egg, molasses and corn syrup. Combine flour, cinnamon, cloves and nutmeg; gradually beat into the creamed mixture. In a small bowl, combine coffee and baking soda; gradually beat into the dough. Divide dough in half. Shape each into a disk; wrap and refrigerate 1 hour or until firm enough to roll.

2. Visit the web address (in sidebar at right) to download and print patterns for chalet (see Fig. 2 at right). Trace the patterns onto waxed paper and cut out.

3. Preheat the oven to 350°. Lightly grease 2 baking sheets. Divide dough in half. Using a lightly floured rolling pin, roll out the dough directly onto baking sheets to ⅛-in. thickness.

4. Position patterns on dough. Using a sharp knife, cut out according to quantities noted on each pattern piece. Remove patterns. Remove dough scraps; cover and refrigerate dough scraps to re-roll if desired.

5. Bake until set, 10-12 minutes. Cool on pans for 5 minutes before removing to wire racks to cool completely.

6. For the icing, in the bowl of a stand mixer fitted with paddle attachment, beat the egg whites until foamy. Gradually add sugar until completely incorporated. Increase speed and continue to beat until stiff, glossy peaks form and sugar is dissolved, 8-12 minutes, adding a few drops of warm water as needed. Spoon half the icing into another bowl. To 1 portion, stir in additional warm water, a few drops at a time, until the icing reaches a thin flood consistency. If necessary, stir in additional confectioners' sugar to the remaining portion of icing to form a stiff icing. Place a damp cloth over bowls and cover tightly between uses.

7. To decorate, insert a #3 round tip into 2 pastry bags. Fill 1 with flood consistency icing and the other with stiff consistency icing. Working with 1 piece at a time, pipe a border using stiff icing. Fill the area inside border with flood icing; pop any air bubbles with a toothpick. When all pieces have been iced, set aside and allow to dry for several hours or overnight. Icing must be completely dry and hard to the touch prior to stenciling. Working with 1 piece at a time, place food-safe stencil on surface of dried icing; using an offset spatula, spread a very thin layer of stiff icing over stencil. Carefully remove stencil; wipe off stencil between uses. When all pieces have been decorated with stencil set aside to dry for several hours or overnight.

8. Before assembling the chalet, test cookie pieces to make sure they fit together snugly. If necessary, file edges carefully with a serrated knife to make them fit.

9. Insert #5 round tips into pastry bag; fill bag two-thirds full with stiff icing. Beginning with the chimney, pipe a wide strip of icing along the longest edge of chimney piece A. Angle and press the longest edge of chimney piece B against it; set aside.

10. Ice along the 2 longer edges of chimney piece C. Press 1 edge against the shortest edge of chimney piece A and 1 edge against the shortest edge of chimney piece B to form a triangle. Gently press all 3 chimney pieces together (see Fig. 1 at right). Set aside to dry completely, 3-4 hours.

11. Meanwhile, pipe icing along the 2 longest edges of both front and back chalet pieces. With longest sides pointing up, position 1 A-frame roof piece, then the other, at about a 45° angle between the front and back house pieces. Press pieces gently together. Prop with canned goods and set chalet aside to dry, 3-4 hours.

12. Referring to the photo at left, center the chimney on 1 side of chalet. Ice the bottom edge of chimney piece C and press onto peak of chalet so that the chimney rises above it.

13. Ice the back of the door and center it on front of chalet, as indicated on pattern. Press into place. If desired, use reserved dough scraps and icing to create tree and deer cutout cookies.

1 serving: 189 cal., 5g fat (3g sat. fat), 19mg chol., 120mg sod., 34g carb. (22g sugars, 1g fiber), 2g pro.

Gingerbread Chalet Patterns

For full-scale patterns to build your own chalet, visit: *www.tasteofhome.com/recipes/gingerbread-chalet*. Look for the Download Patterns link at the bottom of the page.

FIG. 1
Forming the roof and chimney

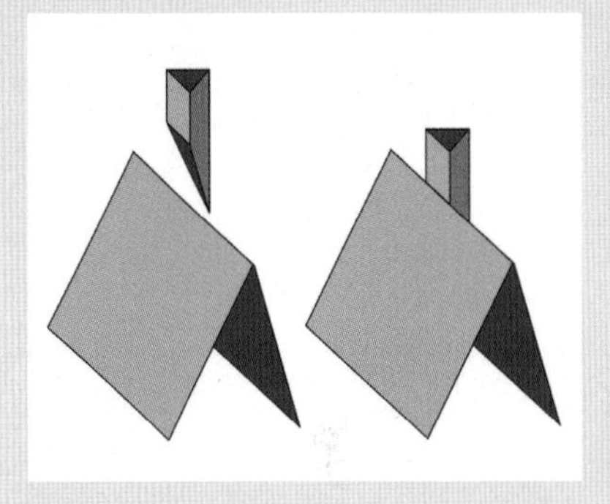

FIG. 2
Individual cutouts

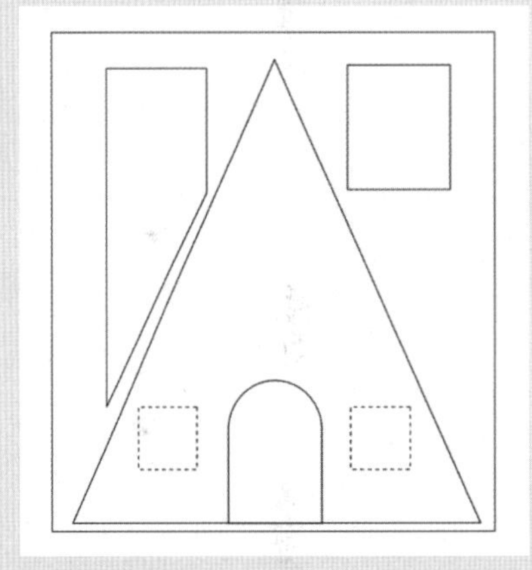

STENCIL LIKE A PRO
After you have applied a thin layer of stiff icing over the stencil, use a frosting scraper to gently wipe away any excess.

CHRISTMAS MOVIE MARATHON

Recreate your favorite Christmas movies with recipes inspired by famous holiday flicks. These foods are perfect for a jolly potluck with friends, or enjoy them with family while wrapping presents and decorating the tree. From the Grinch's roast "beast" to Clark Griswold's eggnog, we've got you covered!

Gingerbread Fruitcake Cookies (p. 39)
Old-Fashioned Eggnog (p. 41) **Homemade Pizza** (p. 43)

TRIM WEAVE TIE STRIP SHRED STAMP FOLD CURL STRAP EMBELLISH BIND
NATIONAL LAMPOON'S
Made in the USA

ROAST BEEF WITH PEPPERS

ROAST BEEF WITH PEPPERS

INSPIRED BY ROAST BEAST FROM *HOW THE GRINCH STOLE CHRISTMAS*

This moist, flavorful entree gets a bit of Italian flair from oregano and garlic. The sauteed peppers are a fresh-tasting accompaniment to the meat and they look beautiful arranged around the sliced roast on a platter.

—Jeanne Murray, Scottsbluff, NE

Prep: 35 min. • **Bake:** 3 hours + standing
Makes: 10 servings

- **1 beef rump roast or bottom round roast (3 lbs.)**
- **3 Tbsp. vegetable oil**
- **3 cups hot water**
- **4 tsp. beef bouillon granules**
- **1 Tbsp. dried oregano**
- **1 to 2 garlic cloves, minced**
- **½ tsp. salt**
- **½ tsp. pepper**
- **3 medium bell peppers, julienned**
- **3 Tbsp. butter**
- **Fresh oregano sprigs, optional**

1. In a Dutch oven, brown roast on all sides in oil over medium-high heat; drain. Combine the water, bouillon, oregano, garlic, salt and pepper; pour over roast.
2. Cover and bake at 350° for 3 hours or until meat is tender. Remove roast to a warm serving platter and let stand for 10 minutes before slicing.
3. Meanwhile, in a large skillet, saute peppers in butter until tender. Serve peppers and pan juices with the roast. If desired, garnish with fresh oregano sprigs.

1 serving: 253 cal., 14g fat (5g sat. fat), 91mg chol., 512mg sod., 3g carb. (1g sugars, 1g fiber), 27g pro.

DID YOU KNOW?

Bell peppers add crunch, sweetness, color and vitamin C to recipes. Green bell peppers are actually unripened versions of the sweeter-tasting red and orange peppers. Green peppers are less expensive than sweet peppers because they're faster to market. Select firm peppers with little give when squeezed. The surface should be bright in color and shiny. If it's dull, wrinkled, spotted or discolored, the pepper is too old. You can also check your store's salad bar for ready-chopped peppers.

GINGERBREAD FRUITCAKE COOKIES

GINGERBREAD FRUITCAKE COOKIES

INSPIRED BY GINGERBREAD COOKIES FROM *JINGLE ALL THE WAY*

Here's a recipe that combines two classics—gingerbread and fruitcake—into one yummy treat. I add a simple glaze of confectioners' sugar tinged with tangy orange juice.

—Jamie Jones, Madison, GA

Prep: 20 min. • **Bake:** 10 min./batch + cooling
Makes: 3 dozen

- **1 pkg. (14½ oz.) gingerbread cake/cookie mix**
- **¼ cup butter, melted**
- **¼ cup water**
- **1 container (8 oz.) chopped mixed candied fruit**
- **½ cup chopped pecans**
- **½ cup raisins**
- **1¼ cups confectioners' sugar**
- **1 to 2 Tbsp. orange juice**

1. Preheat oven to 350°. In a large bowl, mix cookie mix, melted butter and water to form a soft dough. Stir in candied fruit, pecans and raisins. Drop dough by tablespoonfuls 2 in. apart onto ungreased baking sheets.
2. Bake 8-10 minutes or until set. Cool on pans 1 minute. Remove from pans to wire racks to cool completely.
3. In a small bowl, mix confectioners' sugar and enough orange juice to reach desired consistency. Spread or drizzle over cookies. Let stand until set.

1 cookie: 111 cal., 4g fat (1g sat. fat), 3mg chol., 91mg sod., 19g carb. (15g sugars, 1g fiber), 1g pro.

CREAMY MACARONI & CHEESE

INSPIRED BY MACARONI AND CHEESE FROM *HOME ALONE*

Looking for the ultimate mac and cheese? Look no further. My version is creamy, thick and rich, with a wonderful cheddar flavor. Once you taste it, you'll be hooked.
—Cindy Hartley, Chesapeake, VA

Prep: 20 min. • **Bake:** 35 min.
Makes: 6 servings

- **2 cups uncooked elbow macaroni**
- **½ cup butter, cubed**
- **½ cup all-purpose flour**
- **1½ to 2 cups 2% milk**
- **1 cup sour cream**
- **8 oz. cubed Velveeta**
- **¼ cup grated Parmesan cheese**
- **½ tsp. salt**
- **½ tsp. ground mustard**
- **½ tsp. pepper**
- **2 cups shredded cheddar cheese**

1. Cook macaroni according to package directions.
2. Meanwhile, preheat oven to 350°. In a large saucepan, melt the butter. Stir in flour until smooth. Gradually add 1½ cups milk. Bring to a boil; cook and stir for 2 minutes or until thickened. Reduce the heat; stir in the sour cream, process cheese, Parmesan cheese, salt, mustard and pepper until smooth and cheese is melted, adding additional milk to reach desired consistency.
3. Drain macaroni; toss with cheddar cheese. Transfer to a greased 3-qt. baking dish. Stir in cream sauce.
4. Bake, uncovered, 35-40 minutes or until golden brown and bubbly.
1 cup: 653 cal., 46g fat (30g sat. fat), 143mg chol., 1141mg sod., 35g carb. (8g sugars, 1g fiber), 25g pro.

SPAGHETTI WITH ITALIAN MEATBALLS

INSPIRED BY BUDDY'S SPAGHETTI WITH MAPLE SYRUP FROM *ELF*

This hearty spaghetti is a family favorite. The versatile red sauce can be served over almost any type of pasta.
—Sharon Crider, Junction City, KS

Prep: 20 min. • **Cook:** 1¼ hours
Makes: 10 servings

- **¾ cup chopped onion**
- **1 Tbsp. olive oil**
- **1 garlic clove, minced**
- **1 can (28 oz.) Italian crushed tomatoes, undrained**
- **1 can (6 oz.) tomato paste**
- **1 cup water**
- **1½ tsp. dried oregano**
- **½ tsp. salt**
- **½ tsp. pepper**

MEATBALLS

- **4 slices white bread, torn**
- **½ cup water**
- **2 large eggs, lightly beaten**
- **½ cup grated Parmesan cheese**
- **1 garlic clove, minced**
- **1 tsp. dried basil**
- **1 tsp. dried parsley flakes**
- **½ tsp. salt**
- **1 lb. lean ground beef (90% lean)**
- **2 Tbsp. olive oil, divided**
- **1 pkg. (16 oz.) spaghetti**

1. In a large saucepan, cook onion in oil until tender. Add garlic; cook 1 minute longer. Stir in the tomatoes, tomato paste, water, oregano, salt and pepper. Bring to a boil. Reduce heat; cover and simmer for 30 minutes.
2. Meanwhile, in a small bowl, soak bread in water for 5 minutes. Squeeze out excess liquid. In a large bowl, combine the eggs, cheese, garlic, basil, parsley, salt and bread. Crumble beef over mixture and mix well. Shape into 1-in. balls.
3. In a large skillet, heat 1 Tbsp. oil over medium heat. In batches, brown meatballs, adding more oil as needed. Remove to paper towels to drain.
4. Add meatballs to sauce; return to a boil. Reduce the heat; simmer, uncovered, for 30 minutes or until the meatballs are no longer pink.
5. Cook spaghetti according to package directions; drain. Serve with the meatballs and sauce.
½ cup sauce with 3 meatballs and ⅔ cup cooked spaghetti: 385 cal., 11g fat (3g sat. fat), 69mg chol., 612mg sod., 49g carb. (7g sugars, 4g fiber), 21g pro.

OLD-FASHIONED EGGNOG

INSPIRED BY CLARK'S EGGNOG FROM *NATIONAL LAMPOON'S CHRISTMAS VACATION*

Celebrating the holidays with eggnog is an American tradition dating back to Colonial days. We toast the season with this smooth and creamy concoction that keeps family and friends coming back from more.
—*Pat Waymire, Yellow Springs, OH*

Prep: 40 min. + chilling
Makes: 16 servings (about 3 qt.)

- **12 large eggs**
- **1½ cups sugar**
- **½ tsp. salt**
- **2 qt. whole milk, divided**
- **2 Tbsp. vanilla extract**
- **1 tsp. ground nutmeg**
- **2 cups heavy whipping cream**
- **Whipped cream, additional nutmeg and cinnamon sticks, optional**

1. In a heavy saucepan, whisk together the eggs, sugar and salt. Gradually add 1 qt. milk. Cook and stir over low heat until a thermometer reads 160°, about 25 minutes. Pour into a large bowl; stir in vanilla, nutmeg and remaining milk. Place bowl in an ice-water bath; stir frequently until cool. If mixture separates, process in a blender until smooth. Cover and refrigerate at least 3 hours.
2. When ready to serve, beat cream in a bowl on high until soft peaks form; whisk gently into cooled mixture. Pour into a chilled 5-qt. punch bowl. If desired, top servings with dollops of whipped cream, sprinkle with nutmeg and serve with cinnamon sticks.
¾ cup: 308 cal., 18g fat (10g sat. fat), 186mg chol., 188mg sod., 26g carb. (26g sugars, 0 fiber), 9g pro.

Eggnog may be stored, covered, in the refrigerator for several days. Whisk it before serving.

If you're entertaining the 21-and-over crowd, spike this easy eggnog recipe with bourbon or dark rum.

HOMEMADE PIZZA

HOMEMADE PIZZA

INSPIRED BY CHEESE PIZZA FROM
HOME ALONE 2: LOST IN NEW YORK

This recipe is a hearty, zesty main dish with a crisp, golden crust. Feel free to use whatever toppings your family enjoys.
—Marianne Edwards, Lake Stevens, WA

Prep: 25 min. + rising • **Bake:** 25 min.
Makes: 2 pizzas (3 servings each)

- 1 **pkg. (¼ oz.) active dry yeast**
- 1 **tsp. sugar**
- 1¼ **cups warm water (110° to 115°)**
- ¼ **cup canola oil**
- 1 **tsp. salt**
- 3½ **to 4 cups all-purpose flour**
- ½ **lb. ground beef**
- 1 **small onion, chopped**
- 1 **can (15 oz.) tomato sauce**
- 3 **tsp. dried oregano**
- 1 **tsp. dried basil**
- 1 **medium green pepper, diced**
- 2 **cups shredded part-skim mozzarella cheese**

1. In large bowl, dissolve yeast and sugar in water; let stand for 5 minutes. Add oil and salt. Stir in flour, 1 cup at a time, until a soft dough forms.
2. Turn onto floured surface; knead until smooth and elastic, 2-3 minutes. Place in a greased bowl, turning once to grease the top. Cover and let rise in a warm place until doubled, about 45 minutes. Meanwhile, cook the beef and onion over medium heat until no longer pink; drain.
3. Punch down dough; divide in half. Press each into a greased 12-in. pizza pan. Combine the tomato sauce, oregano and basil; spread over each crust. Top with beef mixture, green pepper and cheese.
4. Bake at 400° for 25-30 minutes or until crust is lightly browned.
2 slices: 537 cal., 19g fat (7g sat. fat), 40mg chol., 922mg sod., 64g carb. (5g sugars, 4g fiber), 25g pro.

PECAN FUDGE PIE

INSPIRED BY MA BAILEY'S PIES FROM
IT'S A WONDERFUL LIFE

This fudgy pie with a chocolaty twist is the perfect showcase for crunchy pecans. Top it with whipped cream, and you won't wait long for compliments!
—Jacquelyn Smith, Soperton, GA

Prep: 10 min. • **Bake:** 55 min. + cooling
Makes: 8 servings

- 1¼ **cups light corn syrup**
- ½ **cup sugar**
- ⅓ **cup baking cocoa**
- ⅓ **cup all-purpose flour**
- ¼ **tsp. salt**
- 3 **large eggs**
- 3 **Tbsp. butter, softened**
- 1½ **tsp. vanilla extract**
- 1 **cup chopped pecans**
- 1 **unbaked pastry shell (9 in.)**
- **Whipped cream, optional**

In a large bowl, beat the first 8 ingredients until smooth. Stir in nuts; pour into pie crust. Bake at 350° for 55-60 minutes or until set. Cool completely. Garnish with whipped cream if desired.
1 slice: 512 cal., 24g fat (7g sat. fat), 96mg chol., 303mg sod., 73g carb. (40g sugars, 2g fiber), 6g pro.

HOME-STYLE GLAZED MEAT LOAF

INSPIRED BY MEAT LOAF FROM
A CHRISTMAS STORY

Grated carrots and cheese add a hint of color to this down-home classic. We look forward to meat loaf sandwiches the next day!
—Sandra Etelamaki, Ishpeming, MI

Prep: 15 min. • **Bake:** 1 hour + standing
Makes: 12 servings

- 2 **large eggs, beaten**
- ⅔ **cup 2% milk**
- 1½ **cups shredded cheddar cheese**
- 1 **cup crushed saltines (about 30 crackers)**
- 1 **cup finely shredded carrots**
- ½ **cup finely chopped onion**
- ½ **tsp. salt**
- ¼ **tsp. garlic powder**
- ¼ **tsp. pepper**
- 2 **lbs. lean ground beef**
- ½ **cup packed brown sugar**
- ½ **cup ketchup**
- 2 **Tbsp. Dijon mustard**

1. In a large bowl, combine the eggs, milk, cheese, saltines, carrots, onion, salt, garlic powder and pepper. Crumble ground beef over mixture and mix well. Shape into a loaf. Place in a greased 13x9-in. baking dish. Bake, uncovered, at 350° for 50 minutes.
2. For glaze, in a small saucepan, bring the brown sugar, ketchup and mustard to a boil. Reduce heat; simmer, uncovered, until heated through, 3-5 minutes. Spoon over meat loaf.
3. Bake 10-15 minutes longer or until the meat is no longer pink and a thermometer reads 160°. Drain; let meat loaf stand for 10 minutes before slicing.
1 slice: 266 cal., 12g fat (6g sat. fat), 100mg chol., 494mg sod., 18g carb. (12g sugars, 1g fiber), 20g pro.

PEANUT BUTTER SNOWBALLS

INSPIRED BY EDIBLE SNOWBALLS FROM
THE NIGHTMARE BEFORE CHRISTMAS

These creamy treats incorporate white chocolate, which is a nice change from the typical milk chocolate and peanut butter combination. This recipe is easy, and kids love to get in on the fun of making them. I prepared a big batch of these for a bake sale at my granddaughter's school and to share with neighbors at Christmas.
—Wanda Regula, Birmingham, MI

Prep: 15 min. + chilling • **Makes:** 2½ dozen

- 1 **cup confectioners' sugar**
- ½ **cup creamy peanut butter**
- 3 **Tbsp. butter, softened**
- 1 **lb. white candy coating, coarsely chopped**
- **Chopped peanuts, optional**

1. In a bowl, combine the sugar, peanut butter and butter. Chill in freezer for 30 minutes or until easy to handle. Shape into 1-in. balls and place on a waxed paper-lined baking sheet. Freeze for 30 minutes or until firm.
2. Meanwhile, melt the candy coating in a microwave-safe bowl. Dip balls and place on waxed paper to harden. If desired, sprinkle with chopped peanuts.
1 piece: 132 cal., 8g fat (5g sat. fat), 3mg chol., 27mg sod., 16g carb. (15g sugars, 0 fiber), 1g pro.

GRANDMA’S BEST CHRISTMAS

She knows the secrets to making Christmas feel effortlessly special. From the dishes you look forward to all year to the traditions that become lasting memories, here’s how Grandma creates holiday magic time and again.

Grandma’s Yeast Rolls (p. 48) **Cran-Raspberry Gelatin Salad** (p. 50)
Party Cheese Balls (p. 47)

PARTY
CHEESE BALLS

PARTY CHEESE BALLS

As a grandmother who loves to cook, I send many food gifts to my grandkids at college. They can hardly wait to come home for the holidays to enjoy these tangy cheese balls. The ingredients create a colorful presentation and a savory combination of flavors. Try them at your next gathering!
—Shirley Hoerman, Nekoosa, WI

Prep: 20 min. + chilling
Makes: 2 cheese balls (1¾ cups each)

- **1 pkg. (8 oz.) cream cheese, softened**
- **2 cups shredded cheddar cheese**
- **1 jar (5 oz.) sharp American cheese spread**
- **1 jar (5 oz.) pimiento cheese spread**
- **3 Tbsp. finely chopped onion**
- **1 Tbsp. lemon juice**
- **1 tsp. Worcestershire sauce**
- **Dash garlic salt**
- **½ cup chopped pecans, toasted**
- **½ cup minced fresh parsley**
- **Assorted crackers**

1. In a large bowl, beat the first 8 ingredients until blended. Cover and refrigerate until easy to handle, about 45 minutes.
2. Shape mixture into 2 balls; roll in parsley and pecans. Cover and refrigerate. Remove from the refrigerator 15 minutes before serving. Serve with crackers.

2 Tbsp.: 99 cal., 9g fat (5g sat. fat), 25mg chol., 188mg sod., 2g carb. (1g sugars, 0 fiber), 4g pro.

PICKLED PEPPERONCINI DEVILED EGGS

It's hard to resist these tasty deviled eggs on our buffet table. The avocado filling has pepperoncini and cilantro for extra zip.
—Carmell Childs, Clawson, UT

Takes: 30 min. • **Makes:** 1 dozen

- **6 hard-boiled large eggs**
- **1 jar (16 oz.) garlic and dill pepperoncini**
- **1 medium ripe avocado, peeled and pitted**
- **1 Tbsp. minced fresh cilantro, divided**
- **¼ tsp. salt**
- **⅛ tsp. pepper**
- **1 Tbsp. minced sweet red pepper**
- **¼ tsp. chili powder**

1. Cut eggs lengthwise in half. Remove yolks, reserving whites. Mash yolks. Stir in 1 tsp. minced garlic from the pepperoncini jar and 2 tsp. pepperoncini juice. Add 3 Tbsp. minced pepperoncini and the whole avocado; mash with a fork until smooth. Stir in 2 tsp. cilantro, salt and pepper.
2. Transfer the avocado mixture to a pastry bag fitted with a medium star tip. Pipe mixture into egg whites, swirling upward to resemble Christmas trees if desired. Sprinkle filled eggs with minced red pepper, chili powder and the remaining cilantro.
3. Cut open and seed 1 large pepperoncini; slice into 12 small diamond shapes to top the eggs. Refrigerate, covered, until serving. Save remaining pepperoncini for another use.

1 stuffed egg half: 59 cal., 4g fat (1g sat. fat), 93mg chol., 125mg sod., 1g carb. (0 sugars, 1g fiber), 3g pro.

CRANBERRY BRIE PECAN PINWHEELS

These pinwheels are a fun twist on baked Brie. They are delicious and make the kitchen smell amazing. The recipe is one of my family's top requests for special occasions.
—Jacquie Franklin, Hot Springs, MT

Prep: 20 min. • **Bake:** 15 min.
Makes: about 2 dozen

- **1 lb. Brie cheese, rind removed**
- **1 pkg. (17.3 oz.) frozen puff pastry, thawed**
- **⅔ cup whole-berry cranberry sauce**
- **1 large egg**
- **1 Tbsp. water**
- **½ cup chopped pecans**

1. Preheat oven to 400°. Beat trimmed Brie on medium until smooth and creamy, about 5 minutes.
2. On a lightly floured surface, unfold 1 sheet puff pastry; spread half the Brie to within ½ in. of edges. Spread half the cranberry sauce over Brie. Starting with a short side, roll up jelly-roll style. Cut crosswise into 12 slices. Place pastries on parchment-lined baking sheets. Whisk egg with water; brush over slices. Sprinkle with chopped pecans. Repeat with remaining puff pastry. Bake until golden brown, 15-20 minutes.

1 pastry: 193 cal., 13g fat (5g sat. fat), 27mg chol., 193mg sod., 15g carb. (2g sugars, 2g fiber), 6g pro.

GREENS WITH HOT BACON DRESSING

Growing up in a German community, I ate this salad often. It's a beloved dish that goes back generations—I recall my grandmother talking about her mother making this recipe. As a variation, the old-timers in my family cut up some boiled potatoes on dinner plates, then serve the warm salad mixture on top.
—Robert Enigk, Canastota, NY

Takes: 20 min. • **Makes:** 8 servings

- **4 cups torn fresh spinach**
- **4 cups torn iceberg lettuce**
- **3 celery ribs, sliced**
- **½ cup chopped red onion**
- **4 bacon strips, diced**
- **1 large egg**
- **⅔ cup water**
- **⅓ cup cider vinegar**
- **2 tsp. sugar**
- **2 tsp. cornstarch**
- **½ tsp. salt**
- **¼ tsp. pepper**

In a salad bowl, toss spinach, lettuce, celery and onion; set aside. In a large skillet, cook the bacon until crisp; remove bacon with a slotted spoon to paper towels to drain. Discard all but 2 Tbsp. drippings. In a small bowl, beat egg; add water and mix well. Add to the drippings. Combine vinegar, sugar, cornstarch, salt and pepper; add to skillet. Bring to a boil; stirring constantly. Remove from the heat; pour over salad. Add bacon. Toss and serve immediately.

1 serving: 93 cal., 7g fat (3g sat. fat), 34mg chol., 266mg sod., 5g carb. (3g sugars, 1g fiber), 3g pro.

MASHED POTATOES WITH HORSERADISH

MASHED POTATOES WITH HORSERADISH

Say *adios* to plain mashed potatoes and try this unique recipe that incorporates prepared horseradish. My family requests it on holidays. It's also a great pairing with classic roast beef.
—Cynthia Gobeli, Norton, OH

Takes: 25 min. • **Makes:** 8 servings

- **6 medium potatoes, peeled and cubed**
- **¼ cup butter, melted**
- **¾ tsp. salt**
- **⅛ tsp. pepper**
- **½ cup sour cream**
- **2 Tbsp. prepared horseradish**

Place potatoes in a large saucepan and cover with water. Bring to a boil. Reduce heat and cook for 10 minutes or until tender; drain. Add butter, salt and pepper. Mash potatoes. Beat in the sour cream and horseradish.
1 cup: 175 cal., 8g fat (5g sat. fat), 25mg chol., 301mg sod., 23g carb. (2g sugars, 2g fiber), 3g pro.

GRANDMA'S YEAST ROLLS

(ALSO PICTURED ON PAGE 45)

My grandmother used to make these tender rolls for family get-togethers. The applesauce may be an unexpected ingredient, but it adds so much flavor.
—Nancy Spoth, Festus, MO

Prep: 20 min. + rising • **Bake:** 15 min.
Makes: 2 dozen

- **1 pkg. (¼ oz.) active dry yeast**
- **1 cup 2% milk (110° to 115°)**
- **¼ cup sugar**
- **¼ cup unsweetened applesauce**
- **2 large egg whites, room temperature, beaten**
- **1 tsp. salt**
- **3½ to 4 cups all-purpose flour**

1. In a large bowl, dissolve yeast in warm milk. Add the sugar, applesauce, egg whites, salt and 2 cups flour; beat until smooth. Stir in enough remaining flour to form a soft dough.
2. Turn onto a lightly floured surface; knead until smooth and elastic, 6-8 minutes (dough will be slightly sticky). Place in a bowl coated with cooking spray, turning once to coat top. Cover and let rise in a warm place until doubled, about 1 hour.
3. Turn dough onto a lightly floured surface; divide into 24 pieces. Shape each portion into an 8-in. rope; tie into a knot. Place on 2 baking sheets coated with cooking spray.
4. Cover and let rise until doubled, about 30 minutes. Bake at 375° until golden brown, 12-16 minutes. Remove from pans to wire racks to cool.
1 serving: 83 cal., 1g fat (1g sat. fat), 1mg chol., 109mg sod., 17g carb. (0 sugars, 1g fiber), 3g pro.
Diabetic exchanges: 1 starch.

HERBED RIB ROAST

The aromatic mixture of herbs and garlic turns this tender roast into a star attraction. My kids and grandkids look forward to it for Christmas and other special family occasions.
—Carol Jackson, South Berwick, ME

Prep: 10 min. • **Bake:** 2 hours
Makes: 10 servings

- **1 beef ribeye roast (4 to 5 lbs.)**
- **2 to 3 garlic cloves, thinly sliced**
- **1 tsp. salt**
- **½ tsp. pepper**
- **½ tsp. dried basil**
- **½ tsp. dried parsley flakes**
- **½ tsp. dried marjoram**

Cut 15-20 slits in the ribeye roast; insert garlic. Combine the salt, pepper, basil, parsley and marjoram; rub over roast. Place fat side up on a rack in a roasting pan. Bake, uncovered at 325° until meat reaches the desired doneness (for medium-rare, a thermometer should read 135°; medium, 140°; medium-well, 145°), 2-2½ hours.
4 oz. cooked beef: 397 cal., 29g fat (12g sat. fat), 107mg chol., 319mg sod., 0 carb. (0 sugars, 0 fiber), 32g pro.

DID YOU KNOW?

A rub is a blend of dry seasonings, such as fresh or dried herbs and spices, that coats the surface of uncooked meat to add flavor. Rubs add a lot of flavor, but they do not tenderize meats.

HERBED
RIB ROAST

CRAN-RASPBERRY GELATIN SALAD

GINGERBREAD

CRAN-RASPBERRY GELATIN SALAD

Just like my mom's version, this pretty gelatin salad has full berry flavor without being too tart. It's perfect for any holiday dinner.
—Rosemary Burch, Phoenix, AZ

Prep: 15 min. + chilling • **Makes:** 10 servings

- **2 pkg. (3 oz. each) raspberry gelatin**
- **1 cup boiling water**
- **1 can (14 oz.) whole-berry cranberry sauce**
- **1 can (8 oz.) crushed pineapple, undrained**
- **1 cup orange juice**
- **Sugared cranberries, optional**

1. In a large bowl, dissolve gelatin in boiling water. Stir in the cranberry sauce, pineapple and orange juice. Pour into a 6-cup ring mold coated with cooking spray.
2. Cover and refrigerate until set, about 4 hours. Unmold onto a serving platter. If desired, garnish with sugared cranberries.
1 serving: 155 cal., 0 fat (0 sat. fat), 0 chol., 49mg sod., 39g carb. (32g sugars, 1g fiber), 2g pro.

GINGERBREAD

My grandmother first made this spiced cake over 100 years ago. As a child, I remember her kitchen smelled like heaven whenever she made it. The only thing better was when she took the cake out of the oven and served it with a topping of fresh whipped cream.
—Ellouise Halstead, Union Grove, WI

Prep: 15 min. • **Bake:** 20 min.
Makes: 9 servings

- **1 large egg, room temperature, beaten**
- **½ cup sugar**
- **½ cup molasses**
- **5 Tbsp. butter, melted**
- **⅔ cup cold water**
- **1½ cups all-purpose flour**
- **1 tsp. baking soda**
- **1 tsp. ground ginger**
- **½ tsp. salt**
- **Whipped cream**

Combine the egg, sugar, molasses, butter and water; mix well. In a large bowl, stir together the flour, baking soda, ginger and salt; add the molasses mixture. Beat until well mixed. Pour into a greased 8-in. square baking pan. Bake at 350° until cake tests done, 20-25 minutes. Cut into squares; serve warm with whipped cream.
1 piece: 232 cal., 7g fat (4g sat. fat), 41mg chol., 350mg sod., 40g carb. (22g sugars, 1g fiber), 3g pro.

Gram's Plan

It didn't matter if 30 people showed up for Christmas dinner, Grandma knew how to get everything on the table right on time and delicious as ever. How did she do it all? A few *Taste of Home* Field Editors share Grandma's simple secrets for a memory-making holiday.

"My grandmother used to keep her gravy in two large Thermos containers. That way it stayed hot but didn't take up extra stove space. She'd pour it into her gravy boat to serve."
—Susan Seymour, Valatie, NY

"If you're making roast, cook, cool and slice it the day before (it's much easier to slice when cold), and arrange it in an oven-safe serving dish, drizzled with pan juices. The host can visit with guests while the roast warms at 325° in the oven."
—Helen Nelander, Boulder Creek, CA

"She would write out and post the menu for holiday meals on the refrigerator, always noting prep time needed, baking time and temperature. The menu list was written in order of time to start prep so everyone knew in what order things needed done."
—Julie Peterson, Crofton, MD

"My grandmother made cookie decorating an event. She had every Christmasy color of frosting imaginable, along with pretty sprinkles and sparkles—you couldn't help but be in the Christmas spirit!"
—Gina Dolieslager, Conway Springs, KS

"One of her secrets was borne out of necessity, as kitchen real estate was at a premium: She stored all the desserts in the mudroom/laundry room just off the kitchen to free up space on the kitchen table and counter. We had cookies, pies, cakes and more on top of the washer, dryer and deep freezer! A bonus: It kept everything a little cooler."
—Allison Ochoa, Hays, KS

"My grandma's secret was to let the kids open up gifts right away. That way the kids played away while she was able to finish cooking our meal."
—Anna Miller, Churdan, IA

COOKIES & COCKTAILS

What’s Christmas without the cookies? This year skip the plain glass of milk and host a grown-up affair complete with your favorite libations. Enjoy a night of fun, laughter, jazzy cocktails and homemade cookies.

DOUBLE CHOCOLATE MARTINI

DOUBLE CHOCOLATE MARTINI

Is it a beverage or a dessert? No matter how you define it, you're sure to love it. But don't let its chocolaty appearance fool you—this martini is potent!
—Deborah Williams, Peoria, AZ

Takes: 5 min. • **Makes:** 1 serving

- **Grated chocolate**
- **1 maraschino cherry**
- **Chocolate syrup, optional**
- **Ice cubes**
- **2½ oz. half-and-half cream**
- **1½ oz. vodka**
- **1½ oz. chocolate liqueur**
- **1½ oz. creme de cacao**

1. Sprinkle grated chocolate on a plate. Moisten the rim of a martini glass with water; hold the glass upside down and dip rim into chocolate. Place cherry in glass. If desired, garnish glass with chocolate syrup.
2. Fill a mixing glass or tumbler three-fourths full with ice. Add the cream, vodka, chocolate liqueur and creme de cacao; stir mixture until condensation forms on the outside of glass. Strain into martini glass; serve immediately.
1 serving: 717 cal., 8g fat (5g sat. fat), 38mg chol., 49mg sod., 60g carb. (26g sugars, 0 fiber), 3g pro.

RASPBERRY MERRY

Looking for a lighter cocktail with a fruity flair? You'll love this one that boasts a festive look and flavor.
—Taste of Home *Test Kitchen*

Takes: 5 min. • **Makes:** 1 serving

- **5 fresh raspberries**
- **¼ cup crushed ice**
- **1 navel orange wedge**
- **1 oz. pomegranate-flavored vodka**
- **1½ oz. Prosecco**

GARNISH

- **Pomegranate seeds**

1. In a shaker, muddle raspberries. Add ice. Squeeze the juice from the orange wedge into the shaker; add orange wedge and vodka. Cover and shake for 10-15 seconds or until condensation forms on outside of shaker.
2. Strain into a chilled cocktail glass. Stir in Prosecco. Garnish with pomegranate seeds.
1 serving: 112 cal., 0 fat (0 sat. fat), 0 chol., 0 sod., 5g carb. (3g sugars, 1g fiber), 0 pro.

ANISE PIZZELLE

ANISE PIZZELLE

These lovely, golden brown pizzelle cookies have a crisp texture and delicate anise flavor. I create them using an electric pizzelle iron.
—Barbara Colucci, Rockledge, FL

Prep: 15 min. • **Cook:** 5 min./batch
Makes: about 2 dozen

- **3 large eggs, room temperature**
- **¾ cup sugar**
- **½ cup butter, melted**
- **1¾ cups all-purpose flour**
- **2 tsp. baking powder**
- **1 tsp. aniseed**
- **½ tsp. vanilla extract**
- **½ tsp. anise extract**

1. In a large bowl, beat the eggs, sugar and butter until smooth. Combine the flour and baking powder; gradually to egg mixture and mix well. Stir in aniseed and extracts.
2. Bake in a preheated pizzelle iron according to manufacturer's directions until golden brown. Remove to wire racks to cool. Store in an airtight container.
1 cookie: 76 cal., 3g fat (2g sat. fat), 27mg chol., 52mg sod., 10g carb. (5g sugars, 0 fiber), 1g pro.

Add a light drizzle of melted chocolate to add a little extra flair to these pizzelles.

HOLIDAY MOCHA SPRITZ

I had fun learning to use my spritz cookie press this past Christmas. I play around with a new dough and disk every time I make them. This is my favorite flavor combination.
—Shelly Bevington, Hermiston, OR

Prep: 35 min. • **Bake:** 10 min./batch
Makes: about 10 dozen

- **1½ cups unsalted butter, softened**
- **1 cup sugar**
- **1 large egg, room temperature**
- **1 Tbsp. instant coffee granules**
- **1 tsp. vanilla extract**
- **3½ cups all-purpose flour**
- **⅓ cup dark baking cocoa or baking cocoa**
- **2 tsp. instant espresso powder**
- **1 tsp. baking powder**
- **½ tsp. salt**
- **½ tsp. ground nutmeg**
- **⅓ cup orange juice**
- **Colored sugar, optional**

1. Preheat oven to 375°. In a large bowl, beat the butter and sugar until light and fluffy. Combine egg, instant coffee and vanilla; beat into creamed mixture. In another bowl, whisk the flour, cocoa, espresso powder, baking powder, salt and nutmeg; add to creamed mixture alternately with orange juice, beating well after each addition.

2. Using a cookie press fitted with a disk of your choice, press dough 1 in. apart onto ungreased baking sheets. If desired, sprinkle cookies with colored sugar. Bake until set, 8-10 minutes (do not brown). Remove from pans to wire racks to cool.

1 cookie: 42 cal., 2g fat (1g sat. fat), 8mg chol., 15mg sod., 5g carb. (2g sugars, 0 fiber), 1g pro.

TEST KITCHEN TIP

If the dough is sticky, chill it in the freezer for 10-15 minutes before loading it into the press. If your find your dough works fine at room temperature, chill the cookie sheets before pressing. This will prevent the dough from spreading too fast.

HOLIDAY MOCHA SPRITZ

LEMON-SPICE SWIRLS

My grandma used to send us spiced cookies every Christmas. This is my lemony twist on her recipe. I like making slice-and-bake cookies because the dough is easy to do in advance and you can bake them when you need them. Just wrap the log of dough in freezer paper and freeze in an airtight container.
—Elisabeth Larsen, Pleasant Grove, UT

Prep: 30 min. + chilling • **Bake:** 15 min./batch
Makes: 2 dozen

- **1 cup butter, softened**
- **1 cup sugar**
- **2 large eggs, room temperature**
- **1½ tsp. vanilla extract**
- **3 cups all-purpose flour**
- **½ tsp. salt**
- **1 tsp. ground ginger**
- **1 tsp. ground cinnamon**
- **½ tsp. ground nutmeg**
- **¼ tsp. ground cardamom**
- **¼ tsp. ground cloves**
- **2 tsp. grated lemon zest**
- **½ tsp. lemon extract**
- **Yellow food coloring, optional**

1. In a large bowl, cream the butter and sugar until light and fluffy. Beat in eggs and vanilla. In another bowl, whisk flour and salt; gradually beat into creamed mixture. Divide dough in half. Mix ginger, cinnamon, nutmeg, cardamom and cloves into 1 half; mix lemon zest, lemon extract and if desired, yellow food coloring into remaining half. Cover and refrigerate until firm enough to roll, 1-2 hours.
2. On baking sheets, roll each dough portion between 2 sheets of waxed paper to ¼-in. thickness, forming 8x12-in. rectangles. Refrigerate for 30 minutes. Remove waxed paper. Place spice rectangle on top of lemon rectangle. Starting with a long side, roll up tightly jelly-roll style. Wrap and refrigerate until firm, about 6 hours or overnight.
3. Preheat oven to 350°. Unwrap and cut dough crosswise into ½-in. slices. Place 2½ in. apart on parchment-lined baking sheets. Bake until set, 15-17 minutes. Remove from pans to wire racks to cool.
1 cookie: 165 cal., 8g fat (5g sat. fat), 36mg chol., 116mg sod., 21g carb. (8g sugars, 1g fiber), 2g pro.

APRICOT-WALNUT CRESCENT COOKIES

Crescent-shaped cookies are classics on a holiday dessert platter. If you'd like a larger filled cookie, place half the cutouts on a baking sheet and place 1 teaspoon filling in the center of each. Top each with another cutout and press the edges to seal. Bake a minute or two longer than recipe directs.
—Angela Lott, Neshanic Station, NJ

Prep: 45 min. • **Bake:** 15 min./batch + cooling
Makes: 40 cookies

- **1 pkg. (6 oz.) dried apricots**
- **½ cup walnut halves**
- **½ cup sugar**
- **2 Tbsp. water**
- **3 sheets refrigerated pie pastry**
- **3 Tbsp. 2% milk**
- **2 Tbsp. coarse sugar**

ICING

- **1½ cups confectioners' sugar**
- **3 to 5 Tbsp. apricot brandy**
- **½ cup finely chopped walnuts**

1. Place apricots and walnut halves in a food processor; cover and process until finely chopped.
2. In a small saucepan, combine the sugar, water and apricot mixture. Cook over medium heat for 4-5 minutes or until heated through, stirring occasionally. Cool mixture to room temperature.
3. Meanwhile, on a lightly floured surface, unroll 1 crust. Roll out to ⅛-in. thickness. Cut with a 2½-in. round cookie cutter. Spoon about 1 tsp. apricot filling on half of each circle. Fold crust over; seal edges. Place 2 in. apart on ungreased baking sheets. Repeat with the remaining crusts and filling. Brush cookies with milk; sprinkle with coarse sugar.
4. Bake at 375° for 12-15 minutes or until golden brown. Cool for 2 minutes before removing from pans to wire racks to cool completely.
5. For icing, in a small bowl, combine confectioners' sugar and enough brandy to achieve desired consistency. Place chopped walnuts in another small bowl. Dip rounded edges of cookies in icing and then in walnuts. Drizzle any remaining icing over cookies if desired. Let stand until set.
1 cookie: 133 cal., 6g fat (2g sat. fat), 3mg chol., 61mg sod., 18g carb. (10g sugars, 1g fiber), 1g pro.

CARAMEL
WHISKEY COOKIES

CARAMEL WHISKEY COOKIES

A bit of yogurt replaces part of the butter in this cookie, but the secret is yours because no one will ever be able to tell. I get so many requests for these bites that I never make a cookie tray without them.
—Priscilla Yee, Concord, CA

Prep: 30 min. • **Bake:** 10 min./batch
Makes: 4 dozen

- **½ cup butter, softened**
- **½ cup sugar**
- **½ cup packed brown sugar**
- **¼ cup plain Greek yogurt**
- **2 Tbsp. canola oil**
- **1 tsp. vanilla extract**
- **2½ cups all-purpose flour**
- **2 tsp. baking powder**
- **1 tsp. baking soda**
- **¼ tsp. salt**

TOPPING

- **24 caramels**
- **1 Tbsp. whiskey**
- **3 oz. semisweet chocolate, melted**
- **½ tsp. kosher salt, optional**

1. Preheat oven to 350°. In a large bowl, beat butter and sugars until crumbly. Beat in yogurt, oil and vanilla. In another bowl, whisk flour, baking powder, baking soda and salt; gradually beat into sugar mixture.
2. Shape into 1-in. balls; place 2 in. apart on ungreased baking sheets. Flatten with the bottom of a glass dipped in flour. Bake until edges are light brown, 7-9 minutes. Cool on pans 2 minutes. Remove to wire racks to cool completely.
3. In a microwave, melt caramels with whiskey; stir until smooth. Spread over cookies. Drizzle with melted chocolate; sprinkle with salt if desired. Let stand until set. Store in an airtight container.
1 cookie: 93 cal., 4g fat (2g sat. fat), 6mg chol., 83mg sod., 14g carb. (9g sugars, 0 fiber), 1g pro.

LIMONCELLO SPRITZER

A perfect hint of lemon highlights this smooth and sweet spritzer. Guests will say *grazie* and ask for more.
—Taste of Home *Test Kitchen*

Takes: 5 min. • **Makes:** 1 serving

- **¾ to 1 cup crushed ice**
- **1 lemon wedge**
- **½ cup club soda, chilled**
- **1 oz. vodka**
- **1 oz. limoncello**

Place ice in a wine glass. Squeeze lemon wedge over ice; drop lemon into the glass. Pour the club soda, vodka and limoncello into the glass; stir.
1 serving: 170 cal., 0 fat (0 sat. fat), 0 chol., 25mg sod., 12g carb. (11g sugars, 0 fiber), 0 pro.

CHAI SPICED CRANBERRY COOKIES

This recipe brings the warming flavors of chai into a cookie. It saves time with a box mix and always gets rave reviews.
—Jess Apfe, Berkeley, CA

Prep: 30 min. • **Bake:** 10 min./batch
Makes: 4 dozen

- **½ cup sugar**
- **2 tsp. ground cinnamon**

COOKIE DOUGH

- **1 pkg. yellow cake mix (regular size)**
- **½ cup canola oil**
- **2 large eggs, room temperature**
- **1½ tsp. ground cinnamon**
- **1 tsp. ground cardamom**
- **1 tsp. ground ginger**
- **¼ tsp. ground allspice**
- **¼ tsp. ground cloves**
- **½ cup dried cranberries**

1. In a small bowl, combine the sugar and cinnamon; set aside.
2. In a large bowl, combine the cake mix, oil, eggs and spices; mix well. Stir in cranberries. Shape into 1-in. balls. Roll in sugar mixture and place 2 in. apart on greased baking sheets.
3. Bake at 375° until the edges are lightly browned, 8-10 minutes. Cool for 2 minutes before removing from pans to wire racks to cool completely. Store in an airtight container.
1 cookie: 78 cal., 3g fat (0 sat. fat), 8mg chol., 81mg sod., 13g carb. (8g sugars, 0 fiber), 1g pro.

Playing Dress-Up

Give ho-hum beverages a makeover with these easy garnishes.

KEEP IT COOL
Frost a glass by placing it in the freezer 15-30 minutes before using. Fill with ice and cold beverages.

SWEET OR SASSY?
Coat the rim of a glass with sugar or salt. Invert the glass, dip the rim in water, then dip it into a plate of salt, sugar or colored sugar.

ADD A POP OF COLOR.
Attach fresh fruit—pineapple wedges, citrus slices or whole strawberries—to the rim of the glass. Cut a slit partway through the fruit so it will rest on the rim without falling.

CURLS ARE IN.
For colorful citrus curls, use a citrus stripper to remove a long continuous strip of zest. Tightly wind the strip around a straw and secure the end with waterproof tape. Let stand at least 20 minutes. Remove the tape and slide the curl off the straw for a garnish.

MAKE A STAR STATEMENT.
Skewer a slice of star fruit and place it vertically into a clear drink. Or use a small cookie cutter to cut stars or other decorative shapes from slices of melon. Thread a few pieces onto skewers for cocktail stirrers.

TRY A WEAVE.
Weave a long, wide strip of citrus zest onto a skewer accordion-style. If desired, add a piece of fruit or mint to the top for extra color.

SAY IT WITH CHOCOLATE.
Pipe melted dark chocolate into interesting designs on waxed paper; let them stand until set. Be careful, though—if the design is too thin, it is more likely to break. Use to top iced coffee, shakes and other cold beverages.

ROSEMARY SHORTBREAD CHRISTMAS TREE COOKIES

These treats are a tradition on our Christmas cookie platter. Because the scent of rosemary and the shape of its leaves remind me of pine needles, I cut these using a Christmas-tree cookie cutter. Feel free to use any shapes. These are fragile, so handle the dough and baked cookies carefully.
—Amy Bartlett, Depew, NY

Prep: 25 min. + chilling • **Bake:** 20 min./batch
Makes: 15 cookies

- **1 cup unsalted butter, softened**
- **½ cup sugar**
- **2 cups all-purpose flour**
- **2 Tbsp. minced fresh rosemary**
- **⅛ tsp. sea salt**
- **Colored sugar, optional**

1. In a large bowl, cream butter and sugar until light and fluffy. In another bowl, whisk flour, rosemary and sea salt; gradually beat into creamed mixture.
2. Divide dough in half. Shape each into a disk. Cover and refrigerate for 1 hour or until firm enough to roll.
3. Preheat oven to 350°. On a lightly floured surface, roll each portion of dough to ¼-in. thickness. Cut with a floured 4½x2½-in. tree-shaped cookie cutter. Place 1 in. apart on parchment-lined baking sheets. If desired, decorate with colored sugar.
4. Bake until cookie edges begin to brown, 14-16 minutes. Let cool for 5 minutes before removing from pans to wire racks. Store in an airtight container.
1 cookie: 196 cal., 12g fat (8g sat. fat), 33mg chol., 18mg sod., 20g carb. (7g sugars, 0 fiber), 2g pro.

PEPPERMINT STICK COOKIES

With cool mint flavor and a festive look, these whimsical creations will make you feel like you are at the North Pole. The chilled dough is easy to shape, too.
—Nancy Knapke, Fort Recovery, OH

Prep: 1 hour + chilling
Bake: 10 min./batch + cooling
Makes: 4 dozen

- **1 cup unsalted butter, softened**
- **1 cup sugar**
- **1 large egg, room temperature**
- **2 tsp. mint extract**
- **½ tsp. vanilla extract**
- **2¾ cups all-purpose flour**
- **½ tsp. salt**
- **12 drops red food coloring**
- **12 drops green food coloring**
- **1½ cups white baking chips**
- **Crushed mint candies**

1. In a large bowl, cream the butter and sugar until light and fluffy. Beat in egg and extracts. Combine flour and salt; gradually add to the creamed mixture and mix well.
2. Set aside half the dough. Divide remaining dough in half; add the green food coloring to 1 portion and red food coloring to the other. Cover dough separately. Refrigerate 1-2 hours or until easy to handle.
3. Preheat oven to 350°. Divide green and red dough into 24 portions each. Divide the plain dough into 48 portions. Roll each into a 4-in. rope. Place each green rope next to a white rope; press together gently and twist. Repeat with red ropes and remaining white ropes. Place 2 in. apart on ungreased baking sheets.
4. Bake 10-12 minutes or until set. Cool for 2 minutes before carefully removing from pans to wire racks to cool completely.
5. In a microwave, melt white chips; stir until smooth. Dip cookie ends into melted chips; allow excess to drip off. Sprinkle with crushed candies and place on waxed paper. Let stand until set. Store in an airtight container.
1 serving: 107 cal., 6g fat (3g sat. fat), 15mg chol., 31mg sod., 13g carb. (7g sugars, 0 fiber), 1g pro. **Diabetic exchanges:** 1 starch, ½ fat.

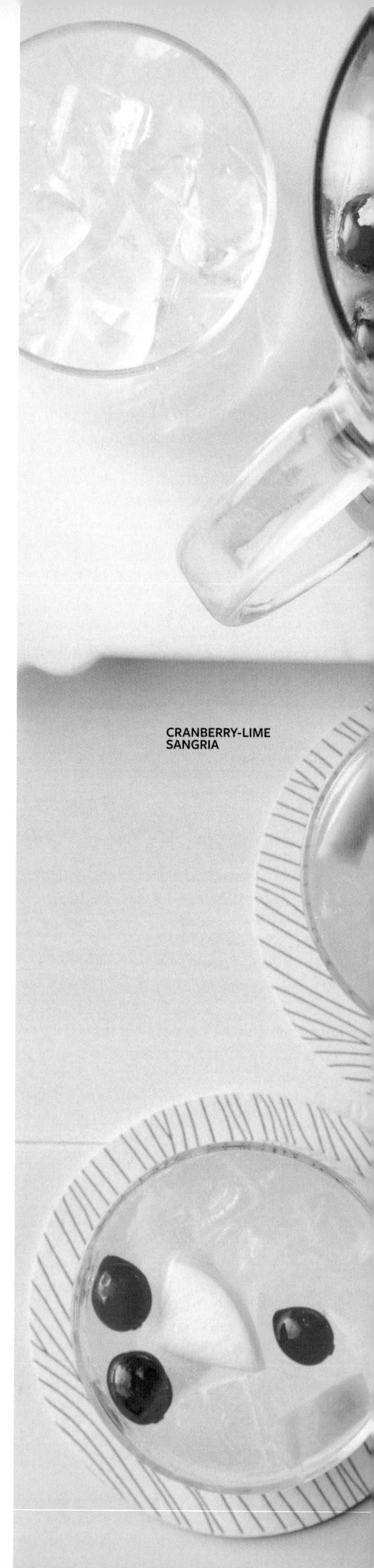
CRANBERRY-LIME SANGRIA

CRANBERRY-LIME SANGRIA

Don't wait for warm weather to enjoy this sangria. Tart, light, fruity and bursting with color, this party-worthy beverage is great for winter celebrations, too.
—Katy Joosten, Little Chute, WI

Takes: 20 min.
Makes: 13 servings (about 2½ qt.)

- **2 cups water**
- **1 cup fresh or frozen cranberries, thawed**
- **1 bottle (750 ml) white wine, chilled**
- **¾ cup frozen limeade concentrate, thawed**
- **1 each medium orange, lime and apple, peeled and diced**
- **1 bottle (1 liter) citrus soda, chilled**

1. In a small saucepan, combine water and cranberries. Cook over medium heat until berries pop, about 5 minutes. Drain and discard liquid; set cranberries aside.
2. In a pitcher, combine the wine and limeade concentrate. Stir in diced fruit and reserved cranberries; add the soda. Serve over ice.
¾ cup: 134 cal., 0 fat (0 sat. fat), 0 chol., 12mg sod., 24g carb. (21g sugars, 1g fiber), 0 pro.

IRISH CREAM NIGHTCAP

This simple yet delicious drink is perfect for cozy nights at home or cuddling near the fireplace. I make it every Christmas Eve.
—Brenda Peck, Bakersfield, CA

Takes: 15 min. • **Makes:** 10 servings

- **1 can (14 oz.) sweetened condensed milk**
- **1 cup heavy whipping cream**
- **1 cup brandy**
- **2 Tbsp. chocolate syrup**
- **3 tsp. instant coffee granules**
- **1 tsp. vanilla extract**
- **¼ tsp. almond extract**
- **10 Pirouette cookies**

In a saucepan, combine the first 5 ingredients; cook and stir over medium heat until heated through, 6-8 minutes or. Remove from heat; stir in extracts. Serve with cookies.
⅓ cup with 1 cookie: 338 cal., 15g fat (10g sat. fat), 46mg chol., 89mg sod., 34g carb. (30g sugars, 1g fiber), 4g pro.

WINTER’S JEWEL: POMEGRANATE

Brighten a cold, bleak day by whipping up a dish that calls for one of winter’s treasures. Vibrant, juicy pomegranates are the stars in this collection of recipes. And the pretty jewel-toned seeds add an elegant touch when used as garnish. *Pom appetit!*

Spiced Pomegranate-Pear Cake (p. 68)

POMEGRANATE BAKED OATMEAL

This baked oatmeal recipe is a new spin on a classic family favorite. A splash of citrus and the ruby red color make this the perfect breakfast for Christmas morning.
—Jennifer Bistline, Shippensburg, PA

Prep: 20 min. • **Bake:** 30 min.
Makes: 8 servings

- **1 medium orange**
- **3½ cups old-fashioned oats**
- **2 tsp. baking powder**
- **¼ tsp. ground cinnamon**
- **Dash salt**
- **3 large eggs, room temperature**
- **1½ cups 2% milk**
- **½ cup packed brown sugar**
- **¼ cup canola oil**
- **½ cup pomegranate seeds**
- **¼ cup chopped walnuts**

1. Preheat oven to 350°. Finely grate zest from orange to measure 4 tsp.; set aside. Cut orange crosswise in half and squeeze juice.
2. In a large bowl, mix oats, baking powder, cinnamon and salt. In another bowl, whisk eggs, milk, brown sugar, oil, orange juice and zest until blended; stir into oat mixture. Stir in pomegranate seeds and walnuts.
3. Transfer to a greased 2-qt. baking dish. Bake, uncovered, until set and edges are lightly browned, 30-35 minutes.
1 serving: 330 cal., 15g fat (2g sat. fat), 73mg chol., 191mg sod., 43g carb. (19g sugars, 4g fiber), 9g pro.

DID YOU KNOW?

Here are some fun facts about pomegranates.

FLAVOR: Wondering what exotic-looking pomegranate tastes like? Pomegranate arils taste a lot like cranberries—fairly tart with a bit of sweetness underneath.

STORAGE: Pomegranate arils can keep in the refrigerator for about three days. You can also keep them in the freezer for six months.

SUPERFRUIT STATUS: Pomegranates are some of the healthiest fruits on the planet, helping to lower blood pressure, risk of heart disease and cholesterol levels. They also offer anti-inflammatory benefits and may help fight some forms of cancer and arthritis.

POMEGRANATE, CHICKEN & FARRO SALAD

POMEGRANATE, CHICKEN & FARRO SALAD

This salad recipe is special—simple yet sophisticated—and never fails to win raves. I use quick-cooking farro, which takes only 10 minutes on the stovetop. Many stores now carry packaged pomegranate seeds in the refrigerated produce section year-round.
—David Dahlman, Chatsworth, CA

Prep: 15 min. • **Cook:** 25 min. + cooling
Makes: 8 servings

- **1½ cups uncooked farro, rinsed or wheat berries**
- **2 medium ripe avocados, peeled, pitted and chopped**
- **3 cups shredded rotisserie chicken**
- **¾ cup chopped dried apricots**
- **½ cup thinly sliced green onions**
- **½ cup chopped walnuts, toasted**
- **1 Tbsp. chopped seeded jalapeno pepper, optional**
- **¾ cup pomegranate seeds**
- **⅓ cup olive oil**
- **¼ cup orange juice**
- **3 Tbsp. white wine vinegar**
- **1 Tbsp. Dijon mustard**
- **½ tsp. salt**
- **½ tsp. pepper**

1. Place farro in large saucepan; add water to cover. Bring to a boil. Reduce heat; cook, covered, until tender, 25-30 minutes. Drain and cool.
2. Arrange farro, avocados, chicken, apricots, green onions, walnuts and, if desired, jalapeno on a platter. Sprinkle with the pomegranate seeds. In a small bowl, whisk the remaining ingredients until blended. Serve dressing with the salad.
1 serving: 482 cal., 24g fat (3g sat. fat), 47mg chol., 251mg sod., 44g carb. (9g sugars, 9g fiber), 23g pro.

CITRUS POMEGRANATE SPIRALS WITH CANDIED GINGER

Are you a fan of cinnamon rolls? Then you'll love these soft, tender rolls that boast a fruity twist. The flavor punch makes these citrusy-ginger-pomegranate bites disappear in no time. Add a citrus glaze if you like.
—Melissa Hansen, Ellison Bay, WI

Prep: 45 min. + rising • **Bake:** 25 min.
Makes: 2 dozen

- **1 pkg. (¼ oz.) active dry yeast**
- **¾ cup warm 2% milk (110° to 115°)**
- **1 medium lime**
- **½ cup warm orange juice (110° to 115°)**
- **¼ cup honey**
- **1 large egg, room temperature**
- **1 Tbsp. butter, melted**
- **1 tsp. salt**
- **1 cup white whole wheat flour**
- **3 to 3½ cups all-purpose flour**
- **1 cup orange marmalade**
- **1 cup pomegranate seeds**
- **¼ to ⅓ cup crystallized ginger, finely chopped**

1. In a small bowl, dissolve yeast in warm milk. Finely grate enough zest from lime to measure 1½ tsp. Cut lime crosswise in half; squeeze juice from lime. Transfer zest and juice to a large bowl. Add orange juice, honey, egg, butter, salt, yeast mixture, white whole wheat flour and 1½ cups all-purpose flour; beat on medium speed until smooth. Stir in enough remaining flour to form a soft dough (dough will be sticky).
2. Turn dough onto a floured surface; knead until smooth and elastic, 6-8 minutes. Place in a greased bowl, turning once to grease the top. Cover and let rise in a warm place until doubled, about 1 hour.
3. Punch down dough; divide in half. Turn 1 portion of dough onto a lightly floured surface; roll into an 12x9-in. rectangle. Brush with half the marmalade to within ¼ in. of edges; sprinkle with half the pomegranate seeds and crystallized ginger. Roll up jelly-roll style, starting with a long side; pinch seam to seal. Cut into 12 slices. Repeat with remaining dough and filling ingredients.
4. Place all slices in greased muffin cups, cut side down. Cover with kitchen towels; let rise in a warm place until almost doubled, about 45 minutes.
5. Preheat oven to 350°. Bake until golden brown, 25-30 minutes. Cool for 5 minutes before removing from muffin pans to wire racks. Serve warm.
1 roll: 151 cal., 1g fat (1g sat. fat), 10mg chol., 118mg sod., 32g carb. (14g sugars, 2g fiber), 4g pro. **Diabetic exchanges:** 2 starch.

How to Seed a Pomegranate

Here's the simplest way to get to those tart little gems inside a pomegranate. Enjoy them as a snack or as an addition to salads, roasts, drinks and more.

Cut the pomegranate in half along its middle. Hold it cut side down over a bowl of water, then, using a large spoon, give it a hearty smack on the skin. Keep smacking until all the seed pods—called arils—fall from the white membrane into the bowl. Discard the skin and membrane. Drain the water, reserving the arils. You can eat them whole, seeds and all.

POMEGRANATE SALSA WITH HOMEMADE CHIPS

Here's a fresh twist on homemade salsa. The ingredients blend beautifully to create a nice balance between sweet and tart.
—Taste of Home *Test Kitchen*

Prep: 25 min. + chilling • **Cook:** 5 min./batch
Makes: 3 servings

- **1½ cups pomegranate seeds**
- **½ cup finely chopped peeled ripe pear**
- **¼ cup finely chopped red onion**
- **1 Tbsp. chopped seeded jalapeno pepper**
- **1 garlic clove, minced**
- **1 Tbsp. minced fresh cilantro**
- **1 Tbsp. lime juice**
- **2 tsp. canola oil**
- **2 tsp. honey**
- **1 tsp. minced fresh basil**
- **¼ tsp. salt**
- **⅛ tsp. ground ginger**
- **Oil for deep-fat frying**
- **6 corn tortillas (6 in.), cut into 6 wedges**
- **1 tsp. kosher salt**
- **⅓ cup cubed avocado**

1. For salsa, in a serving bowl, combine the pomegranate seeds, pear, onion, jalapeno and garlic. In a small bowl, combine cilantro, lime juice, oil, honey, basil, salt and ginger. Drizzle over pomegranate mixture; toss to coat. Cover and refrigerate for 1 hour.
2. Line a 15x10x1-in. baking pan with a double thickness of paper towel; place a wire rack in pan. In an electric skillet or deep-fat fryer, heat oil to 375°. Fry tortilla wedges, a few at a time, for 1-1½ minutes on each side or until golden brown. Place the chips on wire rack; sprinkle with kosher salt.
3. Just before serving, gently stir avocado into salsa. Serve with chips.
½ cup salsa with 12 chips: 303 cal., 12g fat (1g sat. fat), 0 chol., 913mg sod., 48g carb. (20g sugars, 5g fiber), 4g pro.

ROASTED GREEN BEANS WITH POMEGRANATE SEEDS

Here's a simple side dish that requires only five ingredients. These green beans add a classy touch to any spread.
—Dalya Rubin, Boca Raton, FL

Takes: 30 min. • **Makes:** 8 servings

- **2 lbs. fresh green beans, trimmed**
- **2 Tbsp. olive oil**
- **¾ tsp. kosher salt**
- **4 garlic cloves, minced**
- **¼ cup pomegranate seeds**

1. Preheat oven to 425°. Place beans in a greased 15x10x1-in. baking pan. Drizzle with oil; sprinkle with salt. Toss to coat. Roast for 10 minutes, stirring once.
2. Add garlic to pan. Roast until green beans are crisp-tender, 5-7 minutes longer. Sprinkle with pomegranate seeds.
1 serving: 70 cal., 4g fat (1g sat. fat), 0 chol., 187mg sod., 9g carb. (4g sugars, 4g fiber), 2g pro. **Diabetic exchanges:** 1 vegetable, 1 fat.

CRANBERRY POMEGRANATE RELISH

This tart relish combines cranberry and pomegranate for a powerhouse of nutrients. It also captures the flavors of the holiday season and adds beautiful crimson color to any meal.
—Arlene Rakoczy, Gilbert, AZ

Prep: 25 min. + chilling • **Makes:** 1½ cups

- **2 cups fresh or frozen cranberries**
- **½ cup sugar**
- **½ cup water**
- **1 cup pomegranate seeds**
- **¼ tsp. ground cinnamon**
- **⅛ tsp. pumpkin pie spice**

1. In a small saucepan, combine the cranberries, sugar and water. Cook over medium heat until the berries pop, about 15 minutes.
2. Remove from the heat; stir in remaining ingredients. Transfer to a small bowl. Refrigerate until chilled.
¼ cup: 94 cal., 0 fat (0 sat. fat), 0 chol., 1mg sod., 24g carb. (22g sugars, 2g fiber), 0 pro.

POMEGRANATE FLUFF SALAD

My sister-in-law brought this salad to a family gathering one year and we all loved it. It's a fun way to introduce folks to pomegranate.
—Jennie Richards, Riverton, UT

Takes: 40 min. • **Makes:** 26 servings

- **5 cups pomegranate seeds (about 3 large pomegranates)**
- **3 cans (11 oz. each) mandarin oranges, drained**
- **1 pkg. (10½ oz.) pastel miniature marshmallows**
- **3 medium apples, chopped**
- **2 medium bananas, sliced**
- **½ cup sweetened shredded coconut**
- **½ cup chopped walnuts**
- **2 cups heavy whipping cream**
- **⅓ cup confectioners' sugar**
- **1 tsp. vanilla extract**

1. In a large bowl, combine first 7 ingredients. In another bowl, beat cream until it begins to thicken. Add confectioners' sugar and vanilla; beat until stiff peaks form.
2. Gently fold into fruit mixture. Serve salad immediately.
¾ cup: 178 cal., 9g fat (5g sat. fat), 25mg chol., 20mg sod., 25g carb. (19g sugars, 1g fiber), 2g pro.

MINT-PESTO LAMB CHOPS

The simple mint-cilantro pesto marries well with the lamb flavor in this recipe, while the pomegranate-balsamic reduction adds the perfect balance to finish off the dish. The entree is easy to prepare and sure to impress.
—Melanie Stevenson, Reading, PA

Prep: 40 min. • **Cook:** 20 min.
Makes: 8 servings

- **2 cups pomegranate juice**
- **1 cup balsamic vinegar**

PESTO

- **¼ cup fresh mint leaves**
- **¼ cup fresh cilantro leaves**
- **8 garlic cloves, peeled**
- **1 tsp. salt**
- **1 tsp. pepper**
- **¼ cup olive oil**

LAMB

- **8 double-cut lamb rib chops (2 in. thick and 4 oz. each)**
- **1 Tbsp. olive oil**
- **Optional: Pomegranate seeds and torn fresh mint leaves**

1. In a large saucepan, bring pomegranate juice and vinegar to a boil over medium heat; cook until reduced to ½ cup.
2. Meanwhile, for pesto, place the mint, cilantro, garlic cloves, salt and pepper in a small food processor; cover and pulse until chopped. While processing, gradually add olive oil in a steady stream.
3. Coat lamb chops with the pesto. In a large ovenproof skillet, brown lamb in oil on all sides.
4. In a 450° oven, bake chops,uncovered, for 15-20 minutes or until meat reaches the desired doneness (for medium-rare, a thermometer should read 135°; medium, 140°; medium-well, 145°). Drizzle with pomegranate sauce and, if desired, sprinkle with pomegranate seeds and mint leaves.
2 lamb chops with 1 Tbsp. sauce: 238 cal., 13g fat (3g sat. fat), 45mg chol., 352mg sod., 15g carb. (13g sugars, 0 fiber), 15g pro.
Diabetic exchanges: 2 lean meat, 1½ fat, 1 starch.

POMEGRANATE GINGER SPRITZER

A pitcher of this nonalcoholic beverage can conveniently be made hours before holiday guests arrive. Add the chilled club soda just before serving.

—Taste of Home *Test Kitchen*

Prep: 10 min. + chilling • **Makes:** 7 servings

- **½ cup sliced fresh gingerroot**
- **1 medium lime, sliced**
- **3 cups pomegranate juice**
- **¾ cup orange juice**
- **3 cups chilled club soda**
- **Optional: Lime wedges, pomegranate seeds and ice**

1. Place ginger and lime slices in a pitcher; stir in pomegranate and orange juices. Refrigerate overnight.

2. Just before serving, strain and discard ginger and lime. Stir club soda into the juice mixture.

1 cup: 80 cal., 0 fat (0 sat. fat), 0 chol., 35mg sod., 20g carb. (17g sugars, 0 fiber), 1g pro.

SPICED POMEGRANATE-PEAR CAKE

Featuring the tart flavor and rich color of pomegranate juice, this three-layer cake is a delicious combination of tender buttery cake, tangy fruit and sweet buttercream. It will be the star attraction of your meal and stays moist for days.

—*Kelly Koutahi, Moore, OK*

Prep: 1 hour + chilling
Bake: 20 min. + cooling
Makes: 16 servings

- **1½ cups pomegranate juice**
- **3 Tbsp. brown sugar**
- **1 tsp. ground ginger**
- **1 tsp. vanilla extract**
- **1 can (29 oz.) pear halves in juice, drained and cut into ⅛-in. slices**

CAKE

- **¾ cup 2% milk**
- **1 tsp. white vinegar**
- **10 Tbsp. butter, softened**
- **1¼ cups sugar**
- **4 large eggs, room temperature**
- **2 tsp. vanilla extract**
- **2 cups cake flour**
- **2 tsp. baking powder**
- **¼ tsp. salt**

BUTTERCREAM FROSTING

- **1½ cups butter, softened**
- **2 tsp. vanilla extract**
- **2 to 3 drops red food coloring, optional**
- **7½ cups confectioners' sugar**
- **4 to 5 Tbsp. 2% milk**
- **Pomegranate seeds**

1. In a small saucepan, combine juice, brown sugar and ginger. Cook and stir over medium heat until sugar is dissolved; remove from the heat. Stir in vanilla. Place pears in a bowl or shallow dish; pour juice mixture over pears and turn to coat. Cover and refrigerate at least 4 hours.

2. Meanwhile, preheat oven to 350°. Line bottoms of 3 greased 8-in. round baking pans with parchment; grease paper. In a small bowl, combine the milk and vinegar; let stand for 5 minutes until curdled. In a large bowl, cream the butter and sugar until light and fluffy. Add the eggs, 1 at a time, beating well after each addition. Beat in the vanilla. In another bowl, whisk flour, baking powder and salt; add to the creamed mixture alternately with milk mixture, beating well after each addition.

3. Transfer to prepared pans. Bake until a toothpick inserted in center comes out clean, 18-20 minutes. Cool in pans for 10 minutes before removing to wire racks; remove paper. Cool completely.

4. Drain pears, reserving marinade; pat dry. For frosting, in a large bowl, beat butter, 2 Tbsp. reserved marinade, vanilla and if desired, food coloring until blended. Beat in confectioners' sugar alternately with enough milk to reach spreading consistency.

5. To assemble cake, using a long serrated knife, cut each cake horizontally in half. Place 1 cake layer on a serving plate; brush with ¼ cup reserved marinade. Top with ⅔ cup pears. Top with another cake layer; spread with ½ cup frosting. Repeat layers, ending with remaining cake layer. Frost top and sides of cake with 2 cups frosting. Pipe remaining frosting around top and bottom edges. Sprinkle pomegranate seeds over top of cake. Refrigerate at least 2 hours before serving.

1 slice: 614 cal., 26g fat (16g sat. fat), 113mg chol., 321mg sod., 93g carb. (75g sugars, 1g fiber), 4g pro.

Frosting needs to be just the right consistency for spreading. If it's too thin, add a little confectioners' sugar. If it's too thick, add a little milk.

SPICED POMEGRANATE-PEAR CAKE

GIVING THANKS

What comes to mind when you think of the harvest season? For many, it's crisp air, crackling fires, football and the world awash in vibrant red and gold. With cooler temperatures, our thoughts turn to cozy meals—a big juicy turkey, apple cider, squash and warm pie. When it's finally Thanksgiving, we gather with loved ones to count blessings, celebrate traditions and enjoy good food. From turkey to stuffing to dessert and even breakfast, you'll find everything you need for a memorable feast. Soak in each moment of these near-perfect days.

THANKSGIVING DAY PARADE BRUNCH

Aside from the delicious dishes, the Macy's Thanksgiving Day Parade just might be the most beloved part of the holiday. Treat the family to a warm, comforting brunch as you all cozy up on the couch to watch the one of the world's most famous parades. Or look to these recipes as inspiration for an eye-opening breakfast any day of the year.

Ham & Feta Omelet (p. 81)

SLOW-COOKED
BIG BREAKFAST

SLOW-COOKED BIG BREAKFAST

We make this during holidays or on mornings when we know we're going to have a busy day. The hearty combination of fresh vegetables, eggs, meats, potatoes and cheese keeps us full and satisfied.

—Delisha Paris, Elizabeth City, NC

Prep: 30 min. • **Cook:** 3 hours + standing
Makes: 12 servings

- **1 lb. bulk pork sausage**
- **2 lbs. potatoes (about 4 medium), peeled and cut into ½-in. cubes**
- **¼ cup water**
- **1 large onion, finely chopped**
- **1 medium sweet red pepper, chopped**
- **2 cups fresh spinach**
- **1 cup chopped fresh mushrooms**
- **1 lb. cubed deli ham**
- **1 cup shredded cheddar cheese**
- **12 large eggs**
- **½ cup 2% milk**
- **1 tsp. garlic powder**
- **1 tsp. pepper**
- **½ tsp. salt**

1. In a large skillet, cook and crumble pork sausage over medium heat until no longer pink, 5-7 minutes; drain.
2. Meanwhile, place potatoes and water in a large microwave-safe dish. Microwave, covered, on high until potatoes are tender, about 6 minutes, stirring halfway. Drain and add to sausage.
3. Stir in onion, sweet red pepper, spinach, mushrooms, ham and cheese. Transfer to a greased 6-qt. slow cooker.
4. Whisk together remaining ingredients until blended; pour over sausage mixture. Cook, covered, on low until the eggs are set, 3-4 hours. Let stand, uncovered, 10 minutes before serving.
1 cup: 303 cal., 18g fat (6g sat. fat), 236mg chol., 873mg sod., 14g carb. (3g sugars, 1g fiber), 21g pro.

Resist the urge to remove the lid and peek at the food. Opening the slow cooker lets heat and moisture escape, and it slows the cooking process. Most slow cookers come with a glass lid so cooks can see the food as it cooks.

At-Home Coffee Bar

No need to make an impromptu coffee run on Thanksgiving morning. Recreate the experience of visiting your favorite coffee shop by setting up your own coffee bar stocked with all of the essentials. Now you and your guests can leisurely enjoy a hot cup o' joe while you watch the parade.

TURKEY SWISS QUICHE

If you're looking to use up leftover turkey, here's your answer. My family looks forward to having this the day after Thanksgiving.

—Lois Forehand, Little River-Academy, TX

Prep: 25 min. • **Bake:** 30 min. + standing
Makes: 6 servings

- **1 pastry shell (9 in.), unbaked**
- **1½ cups finely chopped cooked turkey**
- **4 large eggs**
- **¾ cup half-and-half cream**
- **2 cups shredded Swiss cheese**
- **4 green onions, finely chopped**
- **2 Tbsp. diced pimientos**
- **1 tsp. dried oregano**
- **1 tsp. dried parsley flakes**
- **Dash salt and pepper**
- **3 slices (¾ oz. each) Swiss cheese, cut into thin strips**

1. Preheat oven to 450°. Line unpricked crust with a double thickness of heavy-duty foil. Bake 8 minutes. Remove foil; bake until golden brown, 5-7 minutes longer. Reduce heat to 375°.
2. Sprinkle chopped turkey into crust. In a large bowl, whisk the eggs and cream. Stir in the shredded Swiss cheese, onions, pimientos, oregano, parsley, salt and pepper. Pour into crust.
3. Bake 20 minutes. Arrange Swiss cheese strips in a lattice pattern over quiche. Bake until a knife inserted in the center comes out clean, 10-15 minutes longer. Let stand 10 minutes before cutting.
1 piece: 489 cal., 31g fat (16g sat. fat), 234mg chol., 334mg sod., 21g carb. (4g sugars, 0 fiber), 30g pro.

10 Facts About the Macy's Thanksgiving Day Parade

Since 1924, millions of viewers have been delighted by Macy's department store's annual parade. That first year, it was called the Macy's Christmas Parade, held as a promotional event to officially kick off the holiday shopping season. The parade was an instant hit, and in 1927, the name was changed to reflect the fact that it always falls on Thanksgiving Day.

From featuring live musical productions to the world's biggest pop stars taking the stage, the parade's come a long way. But even if you have watched it every year, there's probably a lot you never knew about its history or behind-the-scenes workings. These fun facts might surprise you!

1. From 1924 to 1926, the parade included zoo animals.

2. Character balloons have been around since 1927.

3. From 1927 to 1932, handlers let the balloons fly away after the parade ended.

4. After the parade, there was a race to capture the free-floating balloons.

5. Macy's is the second largest consumer of helium in the world.

6. It takes 90 minutes to inflate the mega balloons...and only 15 minutes to deflate them.

7. The parade was canceled from 1942 to 1944 during World War II.

8. The person in charge of each balloon is called a balloon pilot.

9. The long ropes affixed to the bottom and sides of the balloons are called "bones."

10. The balloons are purposely designed to fit through the Lincoln Tunnel.

BACON & EGGS PIZZA

BACON & EGGS PIZZA

I tried a breakfast pizza at a resort in Florida and wanted to adapt it for home. I'm pleased with the results! It's a fun alternative to typical egg bakes.

—Noelle Myers, Grand Forks, ND

Takes: 30 min. • **Makes:** 6 slices

- **8 thick-sliced bacon strips, chopped**
- **¼ cup finely chopped onion**
- **4 large eggs**
- **¼ cup grated Parmesan cheese**
- **1 tsp. Italian seasoning**
- **¼ tsp. salt**
- **¼ tsp. pepper**
- **1 Tbsp. butter**
- **1 prebaked 12-in. pizza crust**
- **½ cup Alfredo sauce**
- **½ cup chopped roasted sweet red peppers**
- **⅔ cup shredded cheddar cheese**
- **½ cup crumbled queso fresco or shredded part-skim mozzarella cheese**

1. Preheat oven to 425°. In a large skillet, cook bacon over medium heat until crisp, stirring occasionally. Remove with a slotted spoon; drain on paper towels. Discard drippings, reserving 1 Tbsp. in pan.

2. Add onion to drippings; cook and stir over medium-high heat until tender. Remove from pan. Wipe skillet clean if necessary.

3. In a small bowl, whisk the eggs, Parmesan cheese and seasonings until blended. In same pan, heat butter over medium-high heat. Pour in egg mixture; cook and stir until eggs are almost set.

4. Place pizza crust on an ungreased baking sheet. Spread with Alfredo sauce. Top with red peppers, bacon, onion and scrambled eggs. Sprinkle with cheeses. Bake 6-8 minutes or until cheese is melted and eggs are set.

1 slice: 465 cal., 26g fat (12g sat. fat), 190mg chol., 1152mg sod., 34g carb. (3g sugars, 2g fiber), 24g pro.

DID YOU KNOW?

As long as you are cooking bacon for breakfast, you might as well cook the entire package at the same time. Leftover bacon can be used in many different ways, including in salad and as garnish for soups.

SAUSAGE & SWEET POTATO HASH

Meat and potatoes make up traditional hash. Our version uses sausage, sweet potatoes and a little salsa. Sometimes we enjoy this for dinner, too.

—Christy Scott Campbell, Blooming Grove, TX

Takes: 30 min. • **Makes:** 4 servings

- **½ lb. maple pork sausage**
- **1 large sweet potato, peeled and cut into ½-in. pieces**
- **1 medium red onion, chopped**
- **2 tsp. chili powder**
- **¼ tsp. plus ⅛ tsp. salt, divided**
- **¼ tsp. plus ⅛ tsp. pepper, divided**
- **½ cup shredded cheddar cheese**
- **1 Tbsp. butter**
- **4 large eggs**
- **Salsa, optional**

1. In a large nonstick skillet, cook sausage over medium heat 4-6 minutes or until no longer pink, breaking into crumbles; drain. Stir in sweet potato, onion, chili powder and ¼ tsp. each salt and pepper. Cook, uncovered, until potatoes are tender, stirring occasionally, 15-20 minutes. Remove from heat. Sprinkle with cheese; cover and let stand until cheese is melted.

2. Meanwhile, in another nonstick skillet, heat butter over medium-high heat. Break eggs, 1 at a time, into pan; immediately reduce heat to low. Cook, covered, 5-6 minutes or until whites are completely set and yolks just begin to thicken. If desired, carefully turn eggs and cook second side to preferred doneness. Sprinkle with the remaining salt and pepper. Serve hash with eggs and, if desired, salsa.

¾ cup hash with 1 egg: 440 cal., 29g fat (12g sat. fat), 249mg chol., 922mg sod., 26g carb. (11g sugars, 4g fiber), 20g pro.

PUMPKIN PANCAKES WITH CINNAMON-APPLE TOPPING

PUMPKIN PANCAKES WITH CINNAMON-APPLE TOPPING

People flock to the kitchen when these pumpkin pancakes are on the griddle. Grab a spoon and dollop each stack with buttery, cinnamon-spiced apples.
—Kami Button, Cheektowaga, NY

Takes: 30 min.
Makes: 8 pancakes (1 cup topping)

- **1 Tbsp. butter**
- **1 large tart apple, peeled and thinly sliced**
- **2 Tbsp. brown sugar**
- **2 Tbsp. maple syrup**
- **½ tsp. ground cinnamon**

PANCAKES

- **1 cup all-purpose flour**
- **1 Tbsp. sugar**
- **1½ tsp. baking powder**
- **1½ tsp. pumpkin pie spice**
- **½ tsp. salt**
- **2 large eggs, room temperature**
- **1 cup 2% milk**
- **⅓ cup canned pumpkin**
- **2 Tbsp. canola oil**
- **½ cup chopped walnuts, toasted**

1. In a skillet, heat butter over medium-high heat. Add apple; cook and stir until tender, 3-4 minutes. Stir in brown sugar, maple syrup and cinnamon; cook and stir 1 minute longer. Remove from heat; keep warm.
2. For pancakes, in a large bowl, whisk flour, sugar, baking powder, pie spice and salt. In another bowl, whisk eggs, milk, pumpkin and oil until blended. Add to flour mixture; stir just until moistened. Stir in walnuts.
3. Lightly grease a griddle; heat over medium heat. Pour batter by scant ⅓ cupfuls onto griddle. Cook until bubbles on top begin to pop and bottoms are golden brown. Turn; cook until second side is golden brown. Serve with apple topping.

Freeze option: Prepare pancakes only. Freeze cooled pancakes between layers of waxed paper in an airtight freezer container. To use, place pancakes on an ungreased baking sheet, cover with foil and reheat in a preheated 375° oven, 5-10 minutes. Meanwhile, prepare apple topping as directed; serve with pancakes.
2 pancakes with ¼ cup topping: 459 cal., 24g fat (5g sat. fat), 106mg chol., 537mg sod., 54g carb. (25g sugars, 3g fiber), 11g pro.

ARTICHOKE EGG CASSEROLE

This is a fabulous recipe for a brunch as well as breakfast. I serve it with fresh stir-fried asparagus, a fruit salad and croissants.
—Marilyn Moores, Indianapolis, IN

Prep: 15 min. • **Bake:** 35 min.
Makes: 9 servings

- **4 jars (6½ oz. each) marinated artichoke hearts**
- **½ cup chopped green onions**
- **1 Tbsp. canola oil**
- **2 to 3 garlic cloves, minced**
- **8 large eggs, lightly beaten**
- **1 jar (4½ oz.) sliced mushrooms, drained**
- **3 cups shredded sharp cheddar cheese**
- **1 cup butter-flavored cracker crumbs (about 25 crackers)**

1. Drain artichoke hearts, reserving ½ cup marinade. Set aside. Cut artichokes into slices; set aside. In a small skillet, saute green onions in oil until tender. Add garlic; cook 1 minute longer. Remove from the heat.
2. In a large bowl, combine eggs, artichokes, mushrooms, cheese, cracker crumbs, onion mixture and reserved marinade.
3. Transfer to a greased 13x9-in. baking dish. Bake, uncovered, at 350° until a knife inserted in the center comes out clean, 35-40 minutes. Let stand for 5 minutes before cutting.
1 serving: 304 cal., 22g fat (11g sat. fat), 229mg chol., 497mg sod., 11g carb. (2g sugars, 1g fiber), 15g pro.

ARTICHOKE
EGG CASSEROLE

CRANBERRY CREAM CHEESE
FRENCH TOAST

CRANBERRY CREAM CHEESE FRENCH TOAST

A friend made this French toast with blueberries for brunch. I make mine with cranberry sauce, but either way, it's divine.
—Sandie Heindel, Liberty, MO

Prep: 25 min. + chilling
Bake: 50 min. + standing
Makes: 12 servings

- **12 cups cubed French bread (about 12 oz.)**
- **2 pkg. (8 oz. each) cream cheese, cubed**
- **1 can (14 oz.) whole-berry cranberry sauce**
- **12 large eggs, lightly beaten**
- **2 cups 2% milk**
- **⅓ cup maple syrup**
- **2 tsp. ground cinnamon**
- **Dash ground nutmeg**
- **Additional maple syrup, optional**

1. Arrange half the bread in a single layer in a greased 13x9-in. baking dish; top with cream cheese and spoonfuls of cranberry sauce. Top with remaining bread.
2. In a large bowl, whisk eggs, milk, ⅓ cup syrup, cinnamon and nutmeg until blended. Pour over casserole. Refrigerate, covered, overnight.
3. Remove the casserole from refrigerator 30 minutes before baking. Preheat oven to 350°. Bake, uncovered, until a knife inserted in center comes out clean, 50-60 minutes. Let stand 10 minutes before serving. If desired, serve with additional maple syrup.
1 serving: 375 cal., 19g fat (10g sat. fat), 231mg chol., 382mg sod., 38g carb. (18g sugars, 1g fiber), 13g pro.

PEAR-OATMEAL BREAKFAST PUDDING

No on will be able to refuse this sweet and tasty variation of oatmeal. Have plenty prepared...they may ask for seconds!
—Joyce Robbins, Old Hickory, TN

Prep: 15 min. • **Bake:** 30 min.
Makes: 6 servings

- **1 can (29 oz.) pear halves**
- **2 cups whole milk**
- **2 Tbsp. brown sugar, divided**
- **1 Tbsp. butter**
- **¼ tsp. salt**
- **¼ tsp. ground cinnamon**
- **1½ cups old-fashioned oats**
- **¼ cup raisins**
- **Half-and-half cream or additional milk**

1. Preheat oven to 350°. Drain pears and reserve 1 cup syrup in a saucepan. Set pears aside. To the syrup, add the milk, 1 Tbsp. brown sugar, butter, salt and cinnamon; heat until simmering. Chop all but 2 pear halves; stir into syrup mixture. Add oats and raisins. Heat until bubbly. Pour into a greased 1½-qt. baking dish.
2. Bake for 20 minutes; stir. Slice remaining pear halves; arrange over top. Sprinkle with remaining 1 Tbsp. brown sugar. Bake another 10-15 minutes. Serve hot with cream or milk.
1 cup: 278 cal., 6g fat (3g sat. fat), 16mg chol., 167mg sod., 53g carb. (33g sugars, 4g fiber), 6g pro.

PEANUT BUTTER & BANANA WAFFLES

These are a refreshing change from your everyday waffles. I make big batches, so I can freeze the leftovers and reheat them later for a quick breakfast.
—Christina Addison, Blanchester, OH

Prep: 10 min. • **Cook:** 5 min./batch
Makes: 16 waffles

- **1¾ cups all-purpose flour**
- **2 Tbsp. sugar**
- **3 tsp. baking powder**
- **¼ tsp. salt**
- **¾ cup creamy peanut butter**
- **½ cup canola oil**
- **2 large eggs, room temperature**
- **1¾ cups 2% milk**
- **1 cup mashed ripe bananas (about 2 medium)**
- **Maple syrup, optional**

In a large bowl, whisk the flour, sugar, baking powder and salt. Place the peanut butter in another bowl; gradually whisk in oil. Whisk in eggs and milk. Add to dry ingredients; stir just until moistened. Stir in the bananas. Bake in a preheated waffle maker according to the manufacturer's directions until golden brown.
Freeze option: Cool waffles on wire racks. Freeze between layers of waxed paper in freezer containers. Reheat waffles in a toaster on medium setting. Or microwave each waffle on high for 30-60 seconds or until heated through. If desired, serve with maple syrup.
2 waffles: 299 cal., 19g fat (3g sat. fat), 34mg chol., 266mg sod., 26g carb. (8g sugars, 2g fiber), 8g pro.

HAM & FETA OMELET

Any excuse to have feta cheese and balsamic vinaigrette is a good one! I pile this Italian-inspired omelet with tomatoes for a great get-started breakfast.
—Brittany Beus, College Station, TX

Takes: 20 min. • **Makes:** 2 servings

- **4 large eggs**
- **1 green onion, chopped**
- **1 Tbsp. 2% milk**
- **¼ tsp. dried basil**
- **¼ tsp. dried oregano**
- **Dash garlic powder**
- **Dash salt**
- **Dash pepper**
- **1 Tbsp. butter**
- **¼ cup crumbled feta cheese**
- **3 slices deli ham, chopped**
- **1 plum tomato, chopped**
- **2 tsp. balsamic vinaigrette**

1. In a small bowl, whisk eggs, green onion, milk and seasonings until blended. In a large nonstick skillet, heat butter over medium-high heat. Pour in egg mixture. Mixture should set immediately at edge.
2. As eggs set, push cooked portions toward the center, letting the uncooked eggs flow underneath. When eggs are thickened and no liquid egg remains, top 1 side with cheese and ham.
3. Fold omelet in half; cut into 2 portions. Slide onto plates; top with tomato. Drizzle with vinaigrette before serving.
½ omelet: 289 cal., 20g fat (9g sat. fat), 410mg chol., 749mg sod., 5g carb. (3g sugars, 1g fiber), 21g pro.

BOUNTIFUL THANKSGIVING

Few things warm hearts more than the comforting goodness found at a Thanksgiving table. Whether you're hosting at your house or bringing a dish to share at someone else's, start here to create a holiday favorite, or two, that everyone will love. You'll find familiar staples here—roasted turkey and stuffing—along with a few new ideas to spice things up.

Thanksgiving Day Countdown

It's among the most joyous holidays of the year, but Thanksgiving is also one of the busiest in the kitchen. Refer to our timeline to help plan the big feast. Many of the dishes in this menu are perfect for preparing ahead, leaving more time for those that need party-day attention. From turkey to trimmings, we have you covered.

A FEW WEEKS BEFORE

☐ Prepare two grocery lists—one for nonperishable items to buy now and one for perishable items to buy a few days before Thanksgiving.

☐ Prepare the Spicy Beet Relish. Store canning jars in a cool, dry place until ready to use.

TWO DAYS BEFORE

☐ Buy remaining grocery items.

☐ Bake the Sweet Milk Dinner Rolls. Store in an airtight container.

☐ Bake the Oatmeal-Chip Cranberry Bars. Store in an airtight container.

☐ Wash china, stemware and table linens.

THE DAY BEFORE

☐ Mix ingredients for the brine for the Juicy Roast Turkey. Refrigerate turkey with brine overnight.

☐ Make filling for Rye Party Puffs. Cover and refrigerate.

☐ Prepare Apple Ladyfinger Dessert, but do not sprinkle with cinnamon. Cover and refrigerate until serving.

☐ Bake Southern Sweet Potato Tart. Cover and refrigerate until serving.

☐ Prepare the Almond Broccoli Salad. Cover and refrigerate until serving.

☐ Set the table.

THANKSGIVING DAY

☐ About 4 hours before dinner, remove the turkey from the refrigerator. Roast the turkey and let stand 20 minutes before carving. If desired, prepare homemade gravy from the pan drippings. Keep turkey warm until ready to serve.

☐ About 3-4 hours before dinner, bake the Cranberry-Orange Meatballs. After baking, place meatballs in the slow cooker. Cover and cook on low for 3-4 hours.

☐ Bake Rye Party Puffs. Allow to cool and fill with with prepared filling.

☐ About an hour before dinner, prepare the Moist Turkey Sausage Stuffing, and Hot Cider. Keep warm until serving.

☐ About 30-40 minutes before dinner, prepare the Rosemary Mashed Potatoes. Keep warm until serving.

☐ About 20 minutes before dinner, prepare the Herbed Corn. Keep warm until serving.

☐ Open one of the beet relish canning jars. Serve on baguettes for an appetizer or use relish to garnish turkey.

☐ Just before dinner, warm the dinner rolls in the oven.

☐ After dinner, remove the desserts from the refrigerator. Sprinkle the Apple Ladyfinger Dessert with cinnamon. If desired, slightly warm the Southern Sweet Potato Tart or serve cold. Serve alongside Oatmeal-Chip Cranberry Bars.

CRANBERRY-ORANGE MEATBALLS

I only make these meatballs on holidays. It's a special request every year from my son, so I can't refuse!
—Delsia Lathrop, Westminster, CO

Prep: 45 min. • **Cook:** 3 hours
Makes: about 6 dozen

- **2 large eggs, lightly beaten**
- **1½ cups dry bread crumbs**
- **1 cup chopped dried cranberries**
- **1 small onion, finely chopped**
- **1 small green pepper, finely chopped**
- **¼ cup all-purpose flour**
- **2 Tbsp. grated orange zest**
- **2 tsp. onion powder**
- **½ tsp. salt**
- **½ tsp. rubbed sage**
- **½ tsp. pepper**
- **2 lbs. bulk pork sausage**
- **1 lb. ground beef**
- **2 cans (15 oz. each) tomato sauce**
- **1 can (14 oz.) whole-berry cranberry sauce**

1. Preheat oven to 400°. In a large bowl, combine the first 11 ingredients. Add pork and ground beef; mix lightly but thoroughly. Shape into 1½-in. balls. Place the meatballs on a greased rack in 15x10x1-in. baking pan. Bake until browned, 18-22 minutes.
2. In a 6-qt. slow cooker, combine tomato sauce and cranberry sauce. Add meatballs and gently stir to coat. Cook, covered, on low until meatballs are cooked through, 3-4 hours.
1 meatball: 73 cal., 4g fat (1g sat. fat), 16mg chol., 172mg sod., 7g carb. (3g sugars, 1g fiber), 3g pro.

TEST KITCHEN TIP

You can freeze meatballs to enjoy later. After they're out of the oven, let them cool down completely before freezing. Or prep the meatballs and put them in an airtight container in the fridge to cook later in the week—just be sure to cook them within 3 days.

ALMOND BROCCOLI SALAD

ALMOND BROCCOLI SALAD

This colorful salad is easy to make, and I like that it can be made ahead. Add the almonds and bacon just before serving so they stay nice and crunchy.
—Margaret Garbade, Tulsa, OK

Prep/Total: 25 min. • **Makes:** 12 servings

- **1 bunch broccoli (about 1½ lbs.)**
- **1 cup mayonnaise**
- **¼ cup red wine vinegar**
- **2 Tbsp. sugar**
- **¼ tsp. salt**
- **½ tsp. freshly ground pepper**
- **1 pkg. (7 oz.) mixed dried fruit**
- **¼ cup finely chopped red onion**
- **1 pkg. (2¼ oz.) slivered almonds, toasted**
- **4 bacon strips, cooked and crumbled**

1. Cut florets from broccoli, reserving stalks; cut florets into 1-in. pieces. Using a paring knife, remove peel from thick stalks; cut stalks into ½-in. pieces.
2. In a small bowl, mix the mayonnaise, wine vinegar, sugar, salt and pepper. In a large bowl, combine broccoli, dried fruit, and onion. Add mayonnaise mixture; toss to coat. Refrigerate until serving.
3. Just before serving, sprinkle with almonds and bacon.
¾ cup: 236 cal., 17g fat (3g sat. fat), 1mg chol., 180mg sod., 21g carb. (15g sugars, 3g fiber), 3g pro.

▲
How to Remove Beet Skin

1. On a cutting board, cut the beet greens to 1 in. and cut off the tail (root end).

2. Place trimmed beets in a Dutch oven or baking dish; add enough water to cover, and then cook according to recipe directions.

3. With a slotted spoon, carefully remove beets to a bowl of cold water.

4. When beets are cool enough to handle, trim off what's left of the stem. Grab a couple of paper towels and hold 1 in each hand. Pick up a beet with both hands, hold firmly, and twist your hands in opposite directions. The skin will slide right off and your hands will stay clean.

SPICY BEET RELISH

We love the taste of this relish with any type meat or bean dish. You can adjust the pepper and horseradish to taste.
—Norma Leatherwood, Sevierville, TN

Prep: 1 hour • **Process:** 15 min.
Makes: 3 pints

- **4 lbs. fresh beets**
- **1 cup sugar**
- **1 cup cider vinegar**
- **2 Tbsp. grated peeled horseradish**
- **2 tsp. canning salt**
- **½ tsp. cayenne pepper**
- **¼ tsp. pepper**
- **Optional: Sliced baguette and grated lemon zest**

1. Scrub beets and trim tops to 1 in. Place in a Dutch oven; add water to cover. Bring to a boil. Reduce heat; simmer, covered, until tender, 45-60 minutes. Remove from water; cool. Peel and shred beets.
2. In a Dutch oven, combine the sugar and vinegar; cook and stir over medium heat until sugar is dissolved. Stir in the shredded beets, horseradish, salt, cayenne and pepper; bring to a boil.
3. Ladle hot beet mixture into hot 1-pint jars, leaving ½-in. headspace. Remove air bubbles and adjust headspace, if necessary, by adding hot relish. Wipe the rims. Center lids on jars; screw on bands until fingertip tight.
4. Place jars into canner, ensuring that they are completely covered with water. Bring to a boil; process for 15 minutes. Remove jars and cool. If desired, serve on baguette and sprinkle with lemon zest.
¼ cup: 70 cal., 0 fat (0 sat. fat), 0 chol., 256mg sod., 17g carb. (15g sugars, 2g fiber), 1g pro.

ROSEMARY MASHED POTATOES

These special-occasion mashed potatoes call for whipping cream instead of milk. I must admit that I was a little shocked when a good friend suggested this substitution. Now I agree that it certainly makes mashed potatoes taste exceptional.
—Sue Gronholz, Beaver Dam, WI

Takes: 30 min. • **Makes:** 12 servings

- **8 large potatoes (about 4 lbs.), peeled and quartered**
- **1½ tsp. salt, divided**
- **¾ cup heavy whipping cream**
- **¼ cup butter, cubed**
- **½ tsp. minced fresh rosemary**
- **¼ tsp. ground nutmeg**
- **¼ tsp. pepper**

1. Place potatoes in a Dutch oven; add 1 tsp. salt. Cover with water. Bring to a boil. Reduce heat; cover and simmer for 15-20 minutes or until tender. Drain.
2. Place potatoes in a large bowl. Add the cream, butter, rosemary, nutmeg, pepper and remaining salt; mash until desired consistency.
¾ cup: 280 cal., 10g fat (6g sat. fat), 30mg chol., 342mg sod., 45g carb. (4g sugars, 4g fiber), 5g pro.

MOIST TURKEY SAUSAGE STUFFING

With tangy apricots and turkey sausage, this stuffing is a terrific mix of sweet and savory.
—Priscilla Gilbert, Indian Harbour Beach, FL

Prep: 20 min. • **Cook:** 20 min.
Makes: 16 servings

- **1 pkg. (19½ oz.) Italian turkey sausage links, casings removed**
- **4 celery ribs, chopped**
- **1 large onion, chopped**
- **1½ cups chopped dried apricots**
- **¼ cup minced fresh parsley**
- **1 Tbsp. minced fresh sage or 1 tsp. dried sage**
- **1 tsp. poultry seasoning**
- **¼ tsp. pepper**
- **3¼ cups chicken stock**
- **1 pkg. (12 oz.) crushed cornbread stuffing**
- **1 cup fresh or frozen cranberries, chopped**

1. In a Dutch oven, cook turkey sausage, celery and onion over medium heat until meat is no longer pink and vegetables are tender; drain. Stir in the apricots, parsley, sage, poultry seasoning and pepper; cook 3 minutes longer.
2. Add stock; bring to a boil. Stir in cornbread stuffing; cook and stir until liquid is absorbed. Gently stir in cranberries; heat through.
⅔ cup: 176 cal., 3g fat (1g sat. fat), 13mg chol., 540mg sod., 30g carb. (8g sugars, 3g fiber), 7g pro. **Diabetic exchanges:** 2 starch, 1 lean meat.

MOIST TURKEY
SAUSAGE STUFFING

JUICY ROAST TURKEY

I can't wait to serve this amazingly juicy turkey at Thanksgiving—so I make it several times a year. The aroma that wafts through the house during baking is almost as mouthwatering as the turkey dinner itself.

—Terrie Herman, North Myrtle Beach, SC

Prep: 20 min. + chilling
Bake: 3½ hours + standing
Makes: 12 servings

- **¼ cup ground mustard**
- **2 Tbsp. Worcestershire sauce**
- **2 Tbsp. olive oil**
- **½ tsp. white vinegar**
- **1 tsp. salt**
- **⅛ tsp. pepper**
- **1 turkey (10 to 12 lbs.)**
- **1 medium onion, quartered**
- **2 celery ribs, quartered lengthwise**
- **Fresh parsley sprigs**
- **2 bacon strips**
- **¼ cup butter, softened**
- **2 cups chicken broth**
- **1 cup water**

1. In a small bowl, combine first 6 ingredients. Brush brine over turkey. Place turkey on a platter. Cover and refrigerate for 1-24 hours.
2. Preheat oven to 325°. Place turkey on a rack in a shallow roasting pan, breast side up. Add the onion, celery and parsley to turkey cavity. Tuck the wings under turkey; tie the drumsticks together. Arrange bacon over top of turkey breast. Spread butter over turkey. Pour broth and water into pan.
3. Bake, uncovered, until a thermometer inserted in thickest part of thigh reads 170°-175°, 3½-4 hours, basting occasionally. Remove turkey from oven. If desired, remove and discard bacon. Tent with foil; let stand 20 minutes before carving. If desired, skim fat and thicken pan drippings for gravy. Serve with turkey.

8 oz. cooked turkey: 535 cal., 29g fat (9g sat. fat), 219mg chol., 594mg sod., 2g carb. (1g sugars, 0 fiber), 62g pro.

JUICY ROAST TURKEY

RYE PARTY PUFFS

I can't go anywhere without taking along my puffs. They're pretty enough for a wedding reception yet hearty enough for snacking while watching football on television. A big platter of these will disappear even with a small group.
—Kelly Williams, Forked River, NJ

Prep: 30 min. • **Bake:** 20 min. + cooling
Makes: 4½ dozen

- **1 cup water**
- **½ cup butter, cubed**
- **½ cup all-purpose flour**
- **½ cup rye flour**
- **2 tsp. dried parsley flakes**
- **½ tsp. garlic powder**
- **¼ tsp. salt**
- **4 large eggs**
- **Caraway seeds**

CORNED BEEF FILLING

- **2 pkg. (8 oz. each) cream cheese, softened**
- **2 pkg. (2 oz. each) thinly sliced deli corned beef, chopped**
- **½ cup mayonnaise**
- **¼ cup sour cream**
- **2 Tbsp. minced chives**
- **2 Tbsp. diced onion**
- **1 tsp. spicy brown or horseradish mustard**
- **⅛ tsp. garlic powder**
- **10 small pimiento-stuffed olives, chopped**

1. Preheat oven to 400°. In a large saucepan over medium heat, bring water and butter to a boil. Add the flours, parsley, garlic powder and salt all at once; stir until a smooth ball forms. Remove from the heat; let stand for 5 minutes. Add eggs, 1 at a time, beating well after each addition until smooth. Continue beating until the mixture is smooth and shiny.
2. Drop batter by rounded teaspoonfuls 2 in. apart onto greased baking sheets. Sprinkle with caraway seeds. Bake until golden brown, 18-20 minutes. Remove to wire racks and Immediately cut a slit in each puff to allow the steam to escape; let puffs cool.
3. In a large bowl, combine the first 8 filling ingredients. Stir in olives. Split puffs; add filling. Refrigerate.
1 appetizer: 78 cal., 7g fat (3g sat. fat), 29mg chol., 108mg sod., 2g carb. (0 sugars, 0 fiber), 2g pro.

SWEET MILK DINNER ROLLS

A hint of sweetness in these tender buns brings in many compliments. Served warm with butter or jam, they're a big hit at any meal. They reheat nicely, too.
—Merle Dyck, Elkford, BC

Prep: 20 min. + rising • **Bake:** 35 min.
Makes: 16 rolls

- **1 pkg. (¼ oz.) active dry yeast**
- **2 cups warm 2% milk (110° to 115°)**
- **½ cup sugar**
- **2 Tbsp. butter, melted**
- **1 tsp. salt**
- **4 to 5 cups all-purpose flour**

1. In a large bowl, dissolve yeast in warm milk. Add the sugar, butter, salt and 3 cups flour. Beat until smooth. Add enough remaining flour to form a soft dough.
2. Turn onto a floured surface; knead until smooth and elastic, 6-8 minutes. Place in a greased bowl, turning once to grease top. Cover and let rise in a warm place until doubled, about 1 hour.
3. Punch dough down. Turn onto a floured surface; divide into 16 pieces. Shape each into a ball. Place 2 in. apart on greased baking sheets. Cover and let rise until doubled, about 30 minutes.
4. Bake at 350° until golden brown, 35-40 minutes. Remove from pans to wire racks. Serve warm.
1 roll: 168 cal., 2g fat (1g sat. fat), 6mg chol., 174mg sod., 32g carb. (8g sugars, 1g fiber), 4g pro.

Brush the tops of the rolls with melted butter after baking to produce a pretty sheen.

Apple Cider Mix-Ins

Looking for a new way to enjoy apple cider? Try one of these fun add-ons and mix-ins for fall's most iconic drink.

CARAMEL
Caramel and apple is a match made in heaven. Next time you heat up your favorite apple cider recipe to enjoy next to the fire, stir in some caramel sauce, a sprinkle of cinnamon and top with whipped cream. Trust us, this one is too tasty to pass up.

CRUSHED ICE
Summer and fall tend to overlap. You're craving fall flavors, but it still might be warm outside, especially if you live in the South. Combine ice, apple cider and a dash of cinnamon in the blender for a drink that will keep you cool.

MAPLE SYRUP
Maple and apple go so well together. Have this combo cold—just add a teaspoon or so of syrup to cider and top with sparkling water. If you prefer warm cider, just stir in a bit of syrup while heating the cider.

GINGER BEER
Want to give your apple cider an extra kick? A splash of spicy ginger beer is just the thing. This ginger drink gives cider a bit of spice and some fizz. This combo is great on its own as a mocktail. If you want to make an Apple Cider Mule (a take on a Moscow Mule), add a splash of vodka to the mix.

WINE
Turn apple cider into a fall sangria with just a few ingredients. Mix a favorite bottle of white wine with 2-3 cups of cider, a splash of brandy and a cinnamon stick. Stir together in a pitcher and garnish with orange and apple slices.

CRANBERRY JUICE
Cranberry juice has some excellent detoxifying ingredients. On its own, apple cider packs a good dose of iron and potassium. Why not combine the two into a super drink?

MULLING SPICES
This one's a classic! Combine classic warming spices like clove, allspice and cinnamon in your cider for an especially autumnal treat.

HOT CIDER

I dress up classic apple cider using lemonade, orange juice, honey and spices. It's a new version of a classic fall beverage.
—Glenna Tooman, Boise, ID

Prep: 5 min. • **Cook:** 45 min.
Makes: 18 servings (4½ qt.)

- **4 cups water**
- **2 tsp. ground allspice**
- **1 cinnamon stick (3 in.)**
- **Dash ground cloves**
- **1 gallon apple cider or unsweetened apple juice**
- **1 can (12 oz.) frozen lemonade concentrate, thawed**
- **¾ cup orange juice**
- **⅓ cup honey**
- **1 tea bag**

1. In a large stockpot, combine the water, allspice, cinnamon stick and cloves. Bring to a boil. Reduce heat; simmer, uncovered, for 30 minutes.
2. Add the remaining ingredients. Return just to a boil. Discard cinnamon stick and tea bag. Stir and serve warm.
1 cup: 168 cal., 0 fat (0 sat. fat), 0 chol., 24mg sod., 42g carb. (38g sugars, 0 fiber), 0 pro.

HERBED CORN

A pleasant blend of herbs dresses up this buttery, fresh-flavored corn dish that I often take to carry-in dinners. It's a must for my family's Thanksgiving meals.
—Edna Hoffman, Hebron, IN

Takes: 20 min. • **Makes:** 12 servings

- **12 cups frozen corn**
- **1 cup water**
- **½ cup butter, cubed**
- **2 Tbsp. minced fresh parsley**
- **2 tsp. salt**
- **1 tsp. dill weed**
- **½ tsp. garlic powder**
- **½ tsp. Italian seasoning**
- **¼ tsp. dried thyme**

In a large saucepan, combine corn and water. Bring to a boil. Reduce heat; cover and simmer until corn is tender, 3-4 minutes. Drain; stir in the remaining ingredients.
¾ cup: 212 cal., 9g fat (5g sat. fat), 20mg chol., 476mg sod., 34g carb. (3g sugars, 4g fiber), 5g pro.

HOT CIDER

APPLE LADYFINGER DESSERT

This recipe is adapted from a German dessert, special to the region where I grew up. I like to use unsweetened applesauce because I love the combination of tart and creamy, but if you prefer your desserts a bit sweeter, you can use sweetened applesauce.
—Marly Chaland, Maple, ON

Prep: 40 min. + chilling • **Makes:** 16 servings

1 carton (8 oz.) mascarpone cheese
1 pkg. (7 oz.) crisp ladyfinger cookies
¼ cup apple brandy
2 cups unsweetened applesauce
⅓ cup sugar
1 tsp. vanilla extract
1 cup heavy whipping cream
Ground cinnamon

1. Stir mascarpone cheese; let stand at room temperature 30 minutes. Meanwhile, arrange ladyfingers in a single layer in a 13x9-in. dish, breaking to fit as needed (save remaining for another use). Brush ladyfingers generously with apple brandy; spread applesauce over ladyfingers.
2. Beat mascarpone cheese, sugar and vanilla on low speed until blended. Gradually add heavy whipping cream, increasing speed to high. Beat until soft peaks form. Spread the cheese mixture over the applesauce layer; refrigerate at least 2 hours. Before serving, sprinkle lightly with cinnamon.
1 piece: 187 cal., 12g fat (7g sat. fat), 45mg chol., 28mg sod., 16g carb. (12g sugars, 0 fiber), 2g pro.

SOUTHERN SWEET POTATO TART

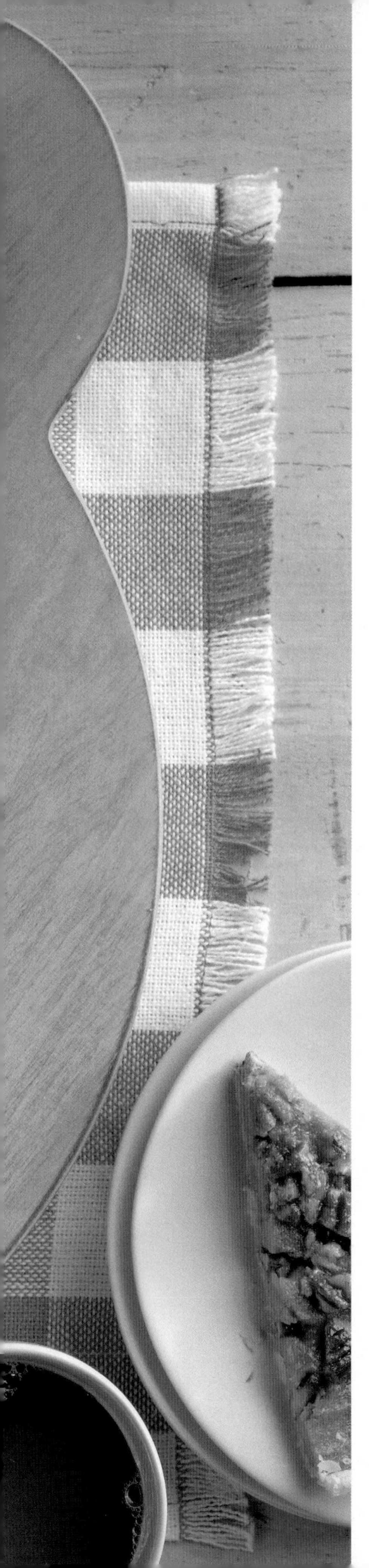

SOUTHERN SWEET POTATO TART

We love sweet potatoes, so I try to add them in as many dishes as I can, including desserts. My secret ingredient is the bourbon—it's what makes it so delicious.

—Marie Bruno, Greensboro, GA

Prep: 20 min. • **Bake:** 25 min.
Makes: 8 servings

- **1 lb. sweet potatoes (about 2 small)**
- **Pastry for single-crust pie (See p. 184 for recipe)**
- **¼ cup butter, softened**
- **½ cup packed dark brown sugar**
- **2 Tbsp. all-purpose flour**
- **1 tsp. pumpkin pie spice**
- **¼ tsp. salt**
- **1 large egg**
- **¼ cup heavy whipping cream**
- **1 Tbsp. bourbon or 1 Tbsp. whipping cream plus ½ tsp. vanilla extract**

TOPPING

- **2 Tbsp. butter, softened**
- **2 Tbsp. dark brown sugar**
- **2 Tbsp. dark corn syrup**
- **½ cup chopped pecans**

1. Preheat oven to 400°. Place potatoes on a foil-lined baking sheet. Bake until tender, 40-50 minutes.
2. On a lightly floured surface, roll the pastry dough to a ⅛-in.-thick circle; transfer to a 9-in. tart pan with removable bottom. Press onto bottom and sides of pan; trim edges to edge of pan. Refrigerate while preparing filling.
3. Remove potatoes from oven; increase oven setting to 425°. When the potatoes are cool enough to handle, remove peel and place pulp in a large bowl; beat until smooth (you will need 1 cup mashed). Add the butter, brown sugar, flour, pie spice and salt; beat until blended. Beat in the egg, cream and bourbon. Pour mixture into crust. Bake on a lower oven rack 15 minutes.
4. Meanwhile, for topping, mix the butter, brown sugar and corn syrup until blended. Stir in the pecans.
5. Remove pie; reduce oven setting to 350°. Spoon topping evenly over pie. Bake until a knife inserted in the center comes out clean, 8-10 minutes.
6. Cool on a wire rack. Serve within 2 hours or refrigerate, covered, and serve cold.

1 piece: 477 cal., 29g fat (15g sat. fat), 85mg chol., 326mg sod., 52g carb. (27g sugars, 3g fiber), 5g pro.

Optional pecan topping: Mix ½ cup pecan pieces, 2 Tbsp. butter, 2 Tbsp. Dark Karo Syrup and 2 Tbsp. dark brown sugar in small bowl. Sprinkle mixture over the top of tart during the last 15 minutes of baking.

OATMEAL-CHIP CRANBERRY BARS

These bars are a family favorite. The simple icing dresses them up and adds a touch of extra sweetness.

—Lee Roberts, Racine, WI

Prep: 15 min. • **Bake:** 30 min. + cooling
Makes: 2 dozen

- **1 cup butter, softened**
- **1 cup packed brown sugar**
- **½ cup sugar**
- **2 large eggs, room temperature**
- **1 tsp. vanilla extract**
- **3 cups old-fashioned oats**
- **1½ cups all-purpose flour**
- **1 tsp. baking soda**
- **1 tsp. ground cinnamon**
- **½ tsp. salt**
- **1 cup dried cranberries**
- **1 cup (6 oz.) semisweet chocolate chips**
- **1 cup confectioners' sugar**
- **2 Tbsp. 2% milk**

1. Preheat oven to 350°. In a large bowl, cream butter and sugars until light and fluffy. Beat in eggs and vanilla. Combine the oats, flour, baking soda, cinnamon and salt; gradually add to creamed mixture and mix well. Stir in cranberries and chocolate chips.
2. Press into a greased 13x9-in. baking pan. Bake until golden brown, 30-35 minutes. Cool on a wire rack. Combine confectioners' sugar and milk; drizzle over bars.

1 bar: 266 cal., 11g fat (6g sat. fat), 36mg chol., 173mg sod., 41g carb. (27g sugars, 2g fiber), 3g pro.

FARMHOUSE THANKSGIVING

Celebrate Thanksgiving with a meal inspired by the traditions of the farmhouse kitchen. Whether you live on a farm or simply love wholesome foods that capture the essence of country cooking, you won't have to look any further for a comforting holiday meal from start to finish. Our rustic yet modern menu features fresh ingredients, homey touches and an heirloom charm the whole family will adore. Get ready to dig in!

Brined Grilled Turkey Breast (p. 101)
Cider Baked Squash (p. 96) **Buttermilk Biscuits** (p. 98)

CIDER BAKED SQUASH

I'm a freelance writer who sometimes needs a break from a long session of working on a story. That's when I escape to the kitchen to whip up something that's good to eat, yet easy to prepare. This squash is one of my favorites!
—*Christine Gibson, Fontana, WI*

Prep: 10 min. • **Bake:** 45 min.
Makes: 6 servings

- **2 medium acorn squash, cut into 1-in. slices, seeds removed**
- **½ cup apple cider or juice**
- **¼ cup packed brown sugar**
- **½ tsp. salt**
- **⅛ tsp. ground cinnamon**
- **⅛ tsp. ground mace**

Preheat oven to 325° Arrange squash in a 15x10x1-in. baking pan. Pour cider over squash. Combine the brown sugar, salt, cinnamon and mace; sprinkle over squash. Cover with foil. Bake until squash is tender, 40-45 minutes.

2 slices: 137 cal., 0 fat (0 sat. fat), 0 chol., 208mg sod., 35g carb. (16g sugars, 3g fiber), 2g pro. **Diabetic exchanges:** 2 starch.

When buying, look for squash that feel heavy for their size and have hard, deep-colored rind free of blemishes. Unwashed winter squash can be stored in a dry, cool, well-ventilated place up to 1 month.

CIDER BAKED SQUASH

PARMESAN SESAME CRACKERS

These rustic crackers are crispy, crunchy and topped with cheese and plenty of seeds. They are perfect for parties and have none of the preservatives and additives of store-bought alternatives.
—Elena Iorga, Helena, MT

Prep: 25 min. • **Bake:** 15 min. + cooling
Makes: 4 dozen

- **2 cups all-purpose flour**
- **⅓ cup sesame seeds**
- **⅓ cup shredded Parmesan cheese**
- **2 Tbsp. poppy seeds**
- **1 tsp. baking powder**
- **½ tsp. salt**
- **⅔ cup plus 2 Tbsp. warm water, divided**
- **⅓ cup canola oil**
- **1 large egg white**

TOPPING
- **2 Tbsp. shredded Parmesan cheese**
- **1 Tbsp. sesame seeds**
- **1 Tbsp. poppy seeds**

1. Preheat oven to 400°. In a bowl, combine the first 6 ingredients. Gradually add ⅔ cup water and oil, tossing with a fork until dough forms a ball. Turn onto a lightly floured surface; knead 8-10 times.
2. Divide dough in half. Roll each ball directly on a baking sheet coated with cooking spray into a 12x9-in. rectangle. Pierce each dough rectangle with a fork.
3. Whisk together egg white and remaining water; brush over dough. Combine topping ingredients; sprinkle over tops.
4. Score each pan of dough into 24 pieces. Bake until golden brown, 15-18 minutes. Immediately cut along the scored lines; cool in pans on wire racks. Store crackers in an airtight container.
1 cracker: 44 cal., 3g fat (0 sat. fat), 1mg chol., 47mg sod., 4g carb. (0 sugars, 0 fiber), 1g pro.

CREAMY SUN-DRIED TOMATO SPREAD

This creamy, bubbly spread is sure to please. Baked to a golden brown, it gets its richness from cream cheese and mayonnaise.
—Valerie Elkinton, Gardner, KS

Prep: 15 min. • **Bake:** 20 min.
Makes: 28 servings

- **2 pkg. (8 oz. each) cream cheese, softened**
- **2 cups mayonnaise**
- **¼ cup finely chopped onion**
- **4 garlic cloves, minced**
- **1 jar (7 oz.) oil-packed sun-dried tomatoes, drained and chopped**
- **⅔ cup chopped roasted sweet red peppers**
- **2 cups shredded part-skim mozzarella cheese**
- **2 cups shredded Italian cheese blend**
- **1 cup shredded Parmesan cheese, divided**
- **Assorted crackers**

1. Preheat oven to 350°. In a large bowl, combine cream cheese, mayonnaise, onion and garlic until blended. Stir in tomatoes and red peppers. Stir in mozzarella cheese, Italian cheese blend and ¾ cup Parmesan cheese.
2. Transfer to a greased 13x9-in. baking dish. Sprinkle with remaining ¼ cup Parmesan cheese. Bake, uncovered, until edges are bubbly and lightly browned, 18-22 minutes or until edges are bubbly and lightly browned. Serve with crackers.
¼ cup: 244 cal., 23g fat (8g sat. fat), 36mg chol., 382mg sod., 2g carb. (1g sugars, 0 fiber), 6g pro.

ROASTED MUSHROOM & COUSCOUS SOUP

I love including mushrooms in soup. They add an earthy richness and roasting them makes them even more flavorful.
—Robin Haas, Hyde Park, MA

Prep: 15 min. • **Cook:** 30 min.
Makes: 6 servings (2 qt.)

- **1 lb. medium fresh mushrooms, quartered**
- **Cooking spray**
- **2 tsp. dried oregano**
- **½ tsp. kosher salt**
- **1 Tbsp. butter**
- **1 large onion, finely chopped**
- **2 medium carrots, diced**
- **2 cups diced fennel bulb**
- **2 cloves garlic, minced**
- **1 cup uncooked pearl (Israeli) couscous**
- **6 cups chicken or vegetable broth**
- **1 Tbsp. minced fresh parsley**
- **Lemon wedges, optional**

1. Preheat oven to 425°. Arrange mushrooms in a greased 15x10x1-in. baking pan. Spritz mushrooms with cooking spray. Sprinkle with oregano and salt; toss to coat. Roast until tender and lightly browned, 15-20 minutes, stirring occasionally.
2. Meanwhile, in a large saucepan, heat butter over medium heat; saute onion, carrots and fennel until tender, 4-6 minutes. Add garlic and couscous; cook and stir 2 minutes. Stir in broth and mushrooms; bring to a boil. Reduce heat; simmer, covered, until couscous is tender, 7-8 minutes. Sprinkle with parsley. Serve with lemon wedges, if desired.
1⅓ cups: 182 cal., 4g fat (1g sat. fat), 10mg chol., 1187mg sod., 31g carb. (4g sugars, 2g fiber), 7g pro.

DID YOU KNOW?

You may not always have time to let soup sit for 24 hours, but it really does tastes better the next day. If you really want your soup to shine, make it ahead of time. Resting your soup allows proteins to break down, release amino acids and, as the ingredients continue to sit together, their flavors will meld together, too.

BUTTERMILK BISCUITS

These biscuits are made from a recipe that's been in our family for years. They're simple to make and smell so good when baking! The wonderful aroma takes me back to those days when Mom made this meal—it's like I'm there in our family's kitchen again, with her busy at the stove.
—Jean Parsons, Sarver, PA

Prep: 25 min. • **Bake:** 15 min.
Makes: 1½ dozen

- **2 cups all-purpose flour**
- **1 Tbsp. sugar**
- **1 tsp. baking powder**
- **½ tsp. salt**
- **½ tsp. baking soda**
- **¼ cup cold shortening**
- **¾ cup buttermilk**

1. Preheat oven to 450°. In a large bowl, combine the flour, sugar, baking powder, salt and baking soda. Cut in shortening until mixture resembles coarse crumbs. Add the buttermilk; stir just until the dough clings together.
2. Turn onto a lightly floured surface; knead gently, 10-12 times. Roll to ½-in. thickness; cut with a floured 2-in. round biscuit cutter. Place 1 in. apart on a greased baking sheets. Bake until lightly browned, 11-12 minutes. Serve warm.
1 biscuit: 82 cal., 3g fat (1g sat. fat), 0 chol., 147mg sod., 12g carb. (1g sugars, 0 fiber), 2g pro.

ROASTED MUSHROOM
& COUSCOUS SOUP

BUTTER LETTUCE & AVOCADO SALAD

The tangy Dijon vinaigrette pairs nicely with sweet apple and rich avocado in this simple, but elegant salad. Make the dressing ahead for super fast assembly right before serving.
—JoAnn Augustine, Grafton, WI

Takes: 20 min. • **Makes:** 6 servings

- **¼ cup olive oil**
- **2 Tbsp. white wine vinegar**
- **1 Tbsp. minced fresh tarragon or 1 tsp. dried tarragon**
- **1 Tbsp. chopped green onion**
- **1 Tbsp. Dijon mustard**
- **⅛ tsp. pepper**
- **8 cups torn Bibb or Boston lettuce**
- **1 medium ripe avocado, peeled and cubed**
- **1 medium red apple, sliced**
- **1 small red onion, sliced**
- **¼ cup chopped pecans, toasted**

In a small bowl, whisk the first 6 ingredients. Divide the lettuce, avocado, apple, onion and pecans among 6 plates; drizzle each salad with vinaigrette.

1 serving: 179 cal., 16g fat (2g sat. fat), 0 chol., 67mg sod., 9g carb. (4g sugars, 4g fiber), 2g pro. **Diabetic exchanges:** 3 fat, 1 vegetable, ½ starch.

GARLIC GREEN BEANS

Standard green beans get a boost from onions and garlic. Their fresh flavor comes shining though.
—Jane Walker, Dewey, AZ

Takes: 20 min. • **Makes:** 6 servings

- **2 lbs. fresh or frozen green beans, cut into 2-in. pieces**
- **1 medium onion, finely chopped**
- **1 Tbsp. olive oil**
- **2 garlic cloves, minced**

1. Place beans in a saucepan and cover with water; bring to a boil. Cook, uncovered, until crisp-tender, 8-10 minutes.

2. Meanwhile, in a large skillet, heat olive oil over medium heat. Add onion; cook and stir until tender, 3-5 minutes. Add garlic; cook 1 minute longer. Drain beans; add to onion mixture. Cook and stir until heated through, 2-3 minutes.

¾ cup: 76 cal., 2g fat (0 sat. fat), 0 chol., 10mg sod., 13g carb. (5g sugars, 5g fiber), 3g pro **Diabetic exchanges:** 2 vegetable, ½ fat.

SAUSAGE & SWISS MINI QUICHES

I created these miniature quiches for a holiday party. They were so tasty and pretty that my family and friends ask for them by name. I find the mascarpone makes the quiches extra rich, but you can substitute cream cheese if you like.
—Lisa Renshaw, Kansas City, MO

Prep: 20 min. • **Bake:** 15 min.
Makes: 4 dozen

- **1 pkg. (17.3 oz.) frozen puff pastry, thawed**
- **1 pkg. (16 oz.) bulk pork sausage**
- **4 green onions, finely chopped**
- **½ cup finely chopped sweet red pepper**
- **1 garlic clove, minced**
- **4 large eggs**
- **1 carton (8 oz.) Mascarpone cheese**
- **1 tsp. salt**
- **1 tsp. crushed red pepper flakes**
- **1 tsp. Worcestershire sauce**
- **½ tsp. dried sage leaves**
- **½ tsp. dried thyme**
- **¼ tsp. ground mustard**
- **½ cup shredded Swiss cheese**

1. Preheat oven to 400°. Roll puff pastry to ⅛-in. thickness. Cut out twenty-four 2½-in. circles from each sheet. Press pastry onto the bottoms and up the sides of greased miniature muffin cups.

2. In a large skillet, cook the sausage, onions, red pepper and garlic over medium heat until meat is no longer pink; drain. Spoon mixture into pastry cups.

3. In a small bowl, combine eggs, Mascarpone cheese, salt, pepper flakes, Worcestershire sauce, sage, thyme and mustard. Spoon over tops and sprinkle with Swiss cheese.

4. Bake until a knife inserted in the center comes out clean, 10-12 minutes. Serve warm.

1 quiche: 101 cal., 7g fat (3g sat. fat), 28mg chol., 134mg sod., 6g carb. (0 sugars, 1g fiber), 3g pro.

Make ahead: Prepare and bake quiches as directed. Allow to cool completely and freeze in a single layer on a waxed paper-lined baking sheet. Once frozen, package in airtight freezer containers and freeze up to 1 month. To use, place frozen quiches on an ungreased baking sheet. Bake at 350° until heated through, 15-20 minutes.

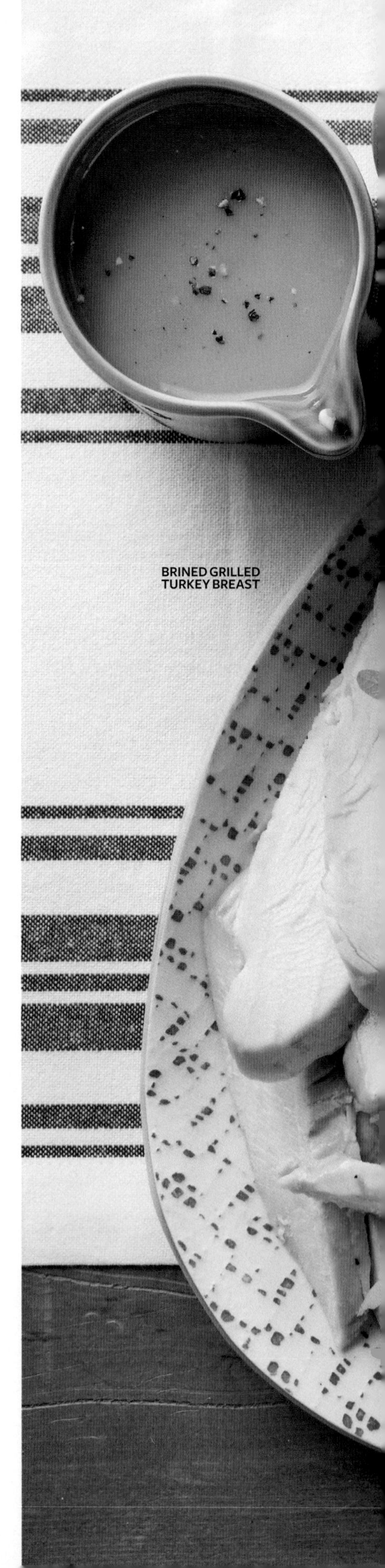

BRINED GRILLED TURKEY BREAST

BRINED GRILLED TURKEY BREAST

You'll want to give thanks for this mouthwatering turkey! Moist and slightly sweet, with just a hint of spice, it's one of our best turkey recipes ever.

—Tina Mirilovich, Johnstown, PA

Prep: 20 min. + marinating
Grill: 1¼ hours + standing
Makes: 6 servings

- **2 qt. cold water, divided**
- **½ cup kosher salt**
- **½ cup packed brown sugar**
- **1 Tbsp. whole peppercorns**
- **1 boneless skinless turkey breast half (2 to 3 lbs.)**

BASTING SAUCE

- **¼ cup canola oil**
- **¼ cup sesame oil**
- **¼ cup reduced-sodium soy sauce**
- **3 Tbsp. lemon juice**
- **2 Tbsp. honey**
- **3 garlic cloves, minced**
- **¼ tsp. dried thyme**
- **¼ tsp. crushed red pepper flakes**

1. In a large saucepan, combine 1 qt. water, salt, brown sugar and peppercorns. Bring to a boil. Cook and stir until the salt and sugar are dissolved. Pour into a large bowl. Add the remaining 1 qt. cold water to cool the brine to room temperature. Add turkey breast; turn to coat. Cover and refrigerate 4-6 hours, turning occasionally.

2. Prepare grill for indirect medium heat. Place a drip pan on grill. Meanwhile, combine basting sauce ingredients. Grill turkey breast, covered, until a thermometer reads 170°, for 1¼-1½ hours, basting occasionally with sauce. Remove to a cutting board. Cover and let stand 10 minutes before slicing.

5 oz. cooked turkey: 364 cal., 19g fat (2g sat. fat), 94mg chol., 553mg sod., 8g carb. (6g sugars, 0 fiber), 38g pro.

BOURBON BRIOCHE
BREAD PUDDING

BOURBON BRIOCHE BREAD PUDDING

My husband wasn't a fan of bread pudding until he tried a bite of mine from a local restaurant. I replicated it with some added bourbon, walnuts and a different type of bread. It's a keeper!
—Cindy Worth, Lapwai, ID

Prep: 25 min. + standing • **Bake:** 40 min.
Makes: 6 servings

- **½ cup bourbon, divided**
- **½ cup raisins**
- **2½ cups brioche bread, toasted**
- **⅓ cup finely chopped walnuts**
- **4 large eggs**
- **1¾ cups heavy whipping cream**
- **⅓ cup sugar**
- **1 tsp. ground cinnamon**
- **1 tsp. vanilla extract**
- **½ tsp. ground nutmeg**
- **¼ tsp. salt**
- **Confectioners' sugar and whipped cream, optional**

1. Preheat oven to 375°. Pour ¼ cup bourbon over raisins in a bowl; let stand for 5 minutes. Place toasted bread in a greased 8-in. square baking dish. Top with walnuts, raisins and soaking liquid.
2. In a large bowl, whisk eggs, cream, sugar, cinnamon, vanilla, nutmeg, salt and remaining bourbon until blended. Pour mixture over bread; let stand until bread is softened, about 15 minutes.
3. Bake, uncovered, until puffed, golden and a knife inserted in the center comes out clean, 35-40 minutes. Serve warm. If desired, serve with confectioners' sugar and whipped cream.
1 serving: 469 cal., 34g fat (19g sat. fat), 213mg chol., 218mg sod., 30g carb. (22g sugars, 1g fiber), 9g pro.

Brioche bread is a type of yeast-raised French bread. But unlike regular sandwich bread, brioche is enriched with lots of butter and eggs, which means the dough contains a high portion of fat. This enriched formula yields a bread with a flaky, tender, almost pastrylike texture with a dark golden crust. Brioche is great for recipes where you want to add extra richness, such as bread pudding. Try it for French toast, too.

CRAN-ORANGE GINGER COOKIES

This is a spin-off of a basic ginger cookie. Even though it's a slice-and-bake, the texture is more like a drop cookie.
—Robert Bosley, Auburn, WA

Prep: 20 min. + chilling
Bake: 10 min. + cooling
Makes: 2 dozen

- **1½ cups unsalted butter, softened**
- **1 cup packed dark brown sugar**
- **2 large eggs, room temperature**
- **¼ tsp. orange extract**
- **1¾ cups almond flour**
- **1 cup all-purpose flour**
- **½ tsp. baking powder**
- **½ tsp. baking soda**
- **¼ tsp. salt**
- **2½ tsp. ground ginger**
- **¼ tsp. Chinese five-spice powder**
- **1 cup dried cranberries, chopped**

1. Cream butter and brown sugar until light and fluffy. Beat in eggs and extract. Whisk together almond flour, all-purpose flour, baking powder, baking soda, salt and spices; gradually beat into creamed mixture. Stir in cranberries.
2. Shape dough into a 10-in.-long roll; wrap and refrigerate until firm, about 4 hours.
3. Preheat oven to 375°. Unwrap and cut dough crosswise into ½-in. slices. Place 2 in. apart on greased baking sheets. Bake until edges are set, 8-10 minutes. Remove from pans to wire racks to cool.
1 cookie: 230 cal., 16g fat (8g sat. fat), 46mg chol., 74mg sod., 20g carb. (14g sugars, 1g fiber), 3g pro.

SQUASH HARVEST

It's easy to elevate a simple ingredient like squash to a dish worthy of a special occasion. These hardy vegetables, members of the gourd family, are available year-round but are at their peak from October through December, making them perfect for a fall meal. Whether they're mashed, stuffed, roasted or baked into a casserole, squash varieties will add color and variety to your meal.

Roasted Acorn Squash & Brussels Sprouts (p. 108)

SPAGHETTI SQUASH
CASSEROLE BAKE

MAPLE-GLAZED SQUASH

Squash draws pleasantly sweet and spicy flavors from the maple syrup and cinnamon in this recipe.

—Betty Kay Sitzman, Wray, CO

Prep: 15 min. • **Bake:** 50 min.
Makes: 6 servings

- **2 medium acorn squash**
- **¼ tsp. salt**
- **⅛ tsp. pepper**
- **1 cup maple syrup**
- **1 medium tart apple, peeled and chopped**
- **2 Tbsp. raisins, optional**
- **1 tsp. ground cinnamon**

1. Preheat oven to 350°. Cut the squash lengthwise in half; remove and discard seeds. Cut halves crosswise into 1-in. slices; discard ends. Place squash in a greased 13x9-in. baking dish; sprinkle with salt and pepper.
2. In a small bowl, mix remaining ingredients; pour over squash. Bake, covered, until squash is tender, 50-60 minutes.
1 serving: 242 cal., 0 fat (0 sat. fat), 0 chol., 112mg sod., 63g carb. (43g sugars, 4g fiber), 2g pro.

SPAGHETTI SQUASH CASSEROLE BAKE

One of our daughters passed this recipe on to us, along with squash from her first garden.

—Glenafa Vrchota, Mason City, IA

Prep: 25 min. • **Bake:** 1 hour
Makes: 6 servings

- **1 medium spaghetti squash (about 8 in.)**
- **1 Tbsp. butter**
- **½ lb. sliced fresh mushrooms**
- **1 large onion, chopped**
- **2 garlic cloves, minced**
- **1 tsp. dried basil**
- **½ tsp. dried oregano**
- **½ tsp. salt**
- **¼ tsp. dried thyme**
- **¼ tsp. pepper**
- **2 medium tomatoes, chopped**
- **1 cup dry bread crumbs**
- **1 cup ricotta cheese**
- **¼ cup minced fresh parsley**
- **¼ cup grated Parmesan cheese**

1. Cut the squash in half lengthwise and scoop out the seeds. Place squash, cut side down, in a baking dish. Add ½ in. water and cover tightly with foil. Bake at 375° until squash can be easily pierced with a fork, 20-30 minutes.
2. Meanwhile, melt butter in a large skillet. Add the mushrooms, onion, garlic, basil, oregano, salt, thyme and pepper; saute until onion is tender. Add tomatoes; cook until most of the liquid has evaporated. Set aside.
3. Scoop out the flesh of squash, separating strands with a fork. Combine the flesh, tomato mixture, bread crumbs, ricotta cheese and parsley.
4. Transfer to a greased 2-qt. baking dish. Sprinkle with Parmesan cheese. Bake, uncovered, at 375° until heated through and top is golden brown, about 40 minutes.
¾ cup: 263 cal., 9g fat (5g sat. fat), 24mg chol., 528mg sod., 37g carb. (6g sugars, 5g fiber), 12g pro.

HUBBARD SQUASH PIE

My mom made this pie—never pumpkin—each Thanksgiving, and everyone looked forward to it. I have fond memories of my dad cutting up a hulking big blue Hubbard squash on the kitchen counter and cooking it in order for Mom to make the pies. A more manageable butternut squash will deliver an equally delicate-tasting pie.

—Patti Ann Christian, Ararat, NC

Prep: 15 min. • **Bake:** 55 min.
Makes: 8 servings

- **1 sheet refrigerated pie crust**
- **1 large egg**
- **1½ cups mashed cooked Hubbard or butternut squash**
- **1 can (12 oz.) evaporated milk**
- **1 cup sugar**
- **2 Tbsp. molasses**
- **1 Tbsp. cornstarch**
- **½ tsp. salt**
- **¼ tsp. ground nutmeg**
- **Optional: Sweetened whipped cream and additional ground nutmeg**

1. Preheat oven to 400°. Unroll crust into a 9-in. pie plate; flute edge. In a large bowl, whisk together egg, squash, milk, sugar, molasses, cornstarch and salt. Pour into the crust; sprinkle with nutmeg.
2. Bake pie on a lower oven rack 10 minutes. Reduce oven setting to 325°; bake until a knife inserted in the center comes out clean, 45-50 minutes. Cool on a wire rack; serve or refrigerate within 2 hours. If desired, top with sweetened whipped cream and additional ground nutmeg.
1 piece: 316 cal., 10g fat (5g sat. fat), 42mg chol., 300mg sod., 51g carb. (34g sugars, 1g fiber), 5g pro.

BUTTERNUT SQUASH ROLLS

With their cheery yellow color and delicious aroma, these appealing rolls will brighten your buffet table. This recipe is a wonderful way to utilize homegrown squash.

—Bernice Morris, Marshfield, MO

Prep: 30 min. + rising • **Bake:** 20 min.
Makes: 2 dozen

- **1 pkg. (¼ oz.) active dry yeast**
- **1 cup warm 2% milk (110° to 115°)**
- **¼ cup warm water (110° to 115°)**
- **3 Tbsp. butter, softened**
- **2 tsp. salt**
- **½ cup sugar**
- **1 cup mashed cooked butternut squash**
- **5 to 5½ cups all-purpose flour, divided**

1. In a large bowl, dissolve yeast in milk and water. Add the butter, salt, sugar, squash and 3 cups flour; beat until smooth. Add enough remaining flour to form a soft dough.
2. Turn onto a floured surface; knead until smooth and elastic, 6-8 minutes. Place in a greased bowl, turning once to grease top. Cover and let rise in a warm place until doubled, about 1 hour.
3. Punch dough down. Form into rolls; place in 2 greased 10-in. cast-iron skillets or 9-in. round baking pans. Cover and let rise until doubled, about 30 minutes.
4. Bake at 375° for 20-25 minutes or until golden brown.
1 roll: 135 cal., 2g fat (1g sat. fat), 5mg chol., 213mg sod., 26g carb. (5g sugars, 1g fiber), 3g pro.

ROASTED ACORN SQUASH & BRUSSELS SPROUTS

I love creating dishes with few ingredients and easy steps, including this squash with Brussels sprouts. Maple syrup adds a slight sweetness, and pecans give it a toasty crunch.
—Angela Lemoine, Howell, NJ

Prep: 15 min. • **Bake:** 30 min.
Makes: 8 servings

- **1 medium acorn squash**
- **1 lb. fresh Brussels sprouts**
- **2 Tbsp. olive oil**
- **½ tsp. salt**
- **¼ tsp. pepper**
- **1¾ cups pecan halves**
- **¼ cup maple syrup**
- **3 Tbsp. butter**

1. Preheat oven to 375°. Cut acorn squash lengthwise into quarters; remove and discard the seeds. Cut each quarter crosswise into ½-in. slices; discard ends. Trim and halve Brussels sprouts.
2. Place squash and Brussels sprouts in a large bowl. Drizzle with oil; sprinkle with salt and pepper, and toss to coat. Transfer to 2 foil-lined 15x10x1-in. baking pans. Roast 30-35 minutes or until vegetables are tender, stirring occasionally.
3. Meanwhile, in a dry large skillet, toast the pecans over medium-low heat until lightly browned, 6-8 minutes, stirring frequently. Add syrup and butter; cook and stir until butter is melted.
4. Sprinkle vegetables with pecan mixture; gently toss to combine.
¾ cup: 300 cal., 24g fat (5g sat. fat), 11mg chol., 198mg sod., 23g carb. (11g sugars, 5g fiber), 4g pro.

ROASTED BUTTERNUT SQUASH PANZANELLA

Squash was a hard sell with my family until I paired it with pumpkin seeds, cranberries and horseradish. Now they love it!
—Devon Delaney, Westport, CT

Prep: 25 min. • **Bake:** 45 min.
Makes: 8 servings

- **4 cups cubed sourdough bread**
- **5 Tbsp. olive oil, divided**
- **1 medium butternut squash (about 3 lbs.), peeled and cut into 1-in. cubes**
- **½ tsp. each salt, ground ginger, ground cumin and pepper**
- **1 cup salted shelled pumpkin seeds or pepitas**
- **1 cup dried cranberries**
- **4 shallots, finely chopped (about ½ cup)**

DRESSING

- **⅓ cup red wine vinegar**
- **¼ cup maple syrup**
- **2 Tbsp. prepared horseradish**
- **½ tsp. salt**
- **½ tsp. pepper**
- **¼ tsp. dried rosemary, crushed**
- **¼ cup olive oil**

1. Preheat oven to 425°. Place bread cubes in a 15x10x1-in. baking pan; toss with 2 Tbsp. oil. Bake 10-15 minutes or until toasted, stirring twice.
2. Place squash in a greased 15x10x1-in. baking pan. Mix seasonings and remaining 3 Tbsp. oil; drizzle over squash and toss to coat. Roast for 35-45 minutes or until tender and lightly browned, stirring occasionally.
3. In a large bowl, combine the bread cubes, squash, pumpkin seeds, cranberries and shallots. In a small saucepan, combine the first 6 dressing ingredients; heat through, stirring to blend. Remove from heat; gradually whisk in oil until blended.
4. Drizzle ½ cup dressing over salad and toss to combine. (Save remaining dressing for another use.)
1 cup: 407 cal., 20g fat (3g sat. fat), 0 chol., 387mg sod., 54g carb. (19g sugars, 8g fiber), 9g pro.

WILD RICE STUFFED SQUASH

I made this recipe when we invited both our families to celebrate our first Thanksgiving in our new home. There were 37 of us, and everyone who tried this dish raved about it.
—Robin Thompson, Roseville, CA

Prep: 45 min. • **Bake:** 50 min.
Makes: 8 servings

- **4 medium acorn squash (about 22 oz. each)**
- **3 Tbsp. olive oil, divided**
- **1 pkg. (6 oz.) long grain and wild rice mix**
- **2⅓ cups vegetable or chicken broth**
- **1 tsp. rubbed sage**
- **1 tsp. dried thyme**
- **2 celery ribs, chopped**
- **1 medium onion, chopped**
- **¾ cup dried cranberries**
- **½ cup coarsely chopped pecan halves, toasted**
- **2 Tbsp. minced fresh parsley**

1. Preheat oven to 400°. Cut each squash crosswise in half; remove and discard seeds. Cut a thin slice from bottom of each half to allow each to lie flat. Place on baking sheets, hollow side up; brush tops with 2 Tbsp. olive oil. Bake until almost tender, 30-35 minutes.
2. In a large saucepan, combine rice with contents of seasoning mix, broth, sage and thyme. Bring to a boil. Reduce heat; simmer, covered, until the rice is tender and liquid is almost absorbed, 23-25 minutes. Meanwhile, in a large skillet, saute celery and onion in remaining oil until tender. Stir in cranberries, pecans and parsley. Remove from heat. Stir in rice mixture.
3. Fill each squash half with about ½ cup rice mixture. Return to oven, uncovered, until rice is heated through and squash is tender, 12-15 minutes.

1 stuffed squash half: 275 cal., 7g fat (1g sat. fat), 0 chol., 593mg sod., 53g carb. (16g sugars, 6g fiber), 6g pro.

Spotlight: Winter Squash

Winter squashes are members of the gourd family. They have a hard, inedible shell and fully mature seeds. Harvested in the fall, these hardy veggies keep well through the cold months of winter, as their name suggests. As an added bonus, they are a low-calorie food and a good source of fiber and vitamins.

ACORN SQUASH
Aptly named since it resembles an acorn. Its ridged shell can be dark green, cream-colored or golden orange. The orange flesh is mild.

BUTTERNUT SQUASH
Bell-shaped with a pale tan shell. The shell can be peeled before cooking. The orange flesh is sweet and flavorful.

HUBBARD SQUASH
A larger squash, growing up to 25 lbs., sometimes sold in pieces because of its size. Its hard, bumpy shell can be orange, gray-blue or green. The orange flesh is sweet and rich.

SPAGHETTI SQUASH
Watermelon-shaped with a thin yellow shell. Once cooked, its mild and slightly nutty-flavored flesh separates into strands like spaghetti.

HONEY-THYME BUTTERNUT SQUASH

Instead of potatoes, try whipping up mashed butternut squash with honey, butter and thyme. More than a festive Thanksgiving side, this 30-minute dish will be a new fall favorite for weeknight meals, too.
—Bianca Noiseux, Bristol, CT

Takes: 30 min. • **Makes:** 10 servings

- **1 large butternut squash (about 5 lbs.), peeled and cubed**
- **¼ cup butter, cubed**
- **3 Tbsp. half-and-half cream**
- **2 Tbsp. honey**
- **2 tsp. dried parsley flakes**
- **½ tsp. salt**
- **⅛ tsp. dried thyme**
- **⅛ tsp. coarsely ground pepper**

1. In a large saucepan, bring 1 in. water to a boil. Add butternut squash; cover and cook for 10-15 minutes or until tender.
2. Drain. Mash squash with the remaining ingredients.
¾ cup: 145 cal., 5g fat (3g sat. fat), 14mg chol., 161mg sod., 26g carb. (9g sugars, 7g fiber), 2g pro. **Diabetic exchanges:** 1½ starch, 1 fat.

BUTTERNUT SQUASH MAC & CHEESE

I created this dish after my father had triple bypass surgery. He loves comfort food, and I wanted him to be able to enjoy a rich and tasty dish like mac and cheese without all the fat and butter. It's also a perfect way to sneak in some veggies.
—Megan Schwartz, New York, NY

Prep: 35 min. • **Bake:** 15 min.
Makes: 6 servings

- **8 oz. uncooked whole wheat elbow macaroni**
- **1 medium butternut squash (about 3 lbs.), seeded and cubed**
- **¼ cup plain Greek yogurt**
- **1 cup fat-free milk**
- **1 tsp. salt**
- **¼ tsp. pepper**
- **Dash ground nutmeg**
- **1½ cups shredded sharp cheddar cheese**
- **½ cup shredded Parmesan cheese**
- **½ cup soft whole wheat bread crumbs**

1. Preheat oven to 400°. Cook the pasta according to package directions for al dente. Place squash in a large saucepan; add water to cover. Bring to a boil. Cook, covered, for 8-10 minutes or until tender.
2. Meanwhile, place yogurt, milk, salt, pepper and nutmeg in a blender. Drain squash and transfer to blender; cover and process until pureed. Return mixture to saucepan; heat through. Stir in the cheeses until melted.
3. Drain pasta; add to squash mixture. Toss to coat. Transfer to a greased 8-in. square baking dish. Sprinkle with bread crumbs.
4. Bake, uncovered, until golden brown, 15-20 minutes.
1¼ cups: 422 cal., 13g fat (7g sat. fat), 36mg chol., 750mg sod., 60g carb. (10g sugars, 12g fiber), 20g pro.

ROASTED HERBED SQUASH WITH GOAT CHEESE

Cooking for my family is a hobby that brings me so much joy. My young daughter (and all our holiday party guests) heartily approved of this new favorite. Any type of winter squash would work well in this standout recipe.
—Lindsay Oberhausen, Lexington, KY

Prep: 25 min. • **Cook:** 30 min.
Makes: 10 servings

- **2 medium acorn squash (about 1½ lbs. each), peeled and cut into 2-in. cubes**
- **1 large butternut squash (5 to 6 lbs.), peeled and cut into 2-in. cubes**
- **3 Tbsp. olive oil**
- **2 Tbsp. minced fresh thyme**
- **2 Tbsp. minced fresh rosemary**
- **1 Tbsp. kosher salt**
- **1 tsp. coarsely ground pepper**
- **1 log (11 oz.) fresh goat cheese, crumbled**
- **2 Tbsp. coarsely chopped fresh parsley**
- **1 Tbsp. maple syrup, warmed slightly**

1. Preheat oven to 425°. Toss squashes with oil and seasonings. Transfer to 2 foil-lined 15x10x1-in. baking pans.
2. Roast squash, stirring once, until soft and some pieces are caramelized, 30-35 minutes. Switch position of the pans midway through roasting to ensure even doneness. If a darker color is desired, broil 3-4 in. from heat for 2-4 minutes.
3. Cool slightly. To serve, add goat cheese to squash; gently toss. Sprinkle with parsley; drizzle with maple syrup.
1 cup: 251 cal., 8g fat (3g sat. fat), 21mg chol., 715mg sod., 43g carb. (10g sugars, 10g fiber), 7g pro.

To save time, first cut squash into rings, then peel each ring.

ROASTED HERBED SQUASH
WITH GOAT CHEESE

EASTER GATHERINGS

Warmer weather brings spring fever and the glorious freshness of a new start. Each delicate bud that raises its head to the sky is a sign that the drab, bleak winter is over, and another season is upon us. Springtime menus are a breeze when you turn to these offerings. Refresh your cooking routine and let your light shine with a bounty of fresh and seasonal favorites, including homemade breads, herb-infused creations and retro-inspired Easter classics worthy of a comeback.

BREAKING BREAD

It just isn't Easter without a basket of fresh-baked favorites to complement the feast. Here's a whole day's worth of ideas, from fruit-filled biscuits and cinnamon coffee cakes for brunch to lovely braids and hot cross buns for dinner. Some are so golden and beautiful they can even serve as an edible centerpiece.

Grandma Nardi's Italian Easter Bread (p. 119)

LEMON BLUEBERRY BISCUITS

LEMON BLUEBERRY BISCUITS

Lemon and blueberries make such a fresh, flavorful combination in all kinds of baked goods, especially these delightful biscuits.
—Taste of Home *Test Kitchen*

Prep: 30 min. • **Bake:** 15 min.
Makes: 1 dozen

- **2 cups all-purpose flour**
- **½ cup sugar**
- **2 tsp. baking powder**
- **½ tsp. baking soda**
- **¼ tsp. salt**
- **1 cup lemon yogurt**
- **1 large egg, room temperature**
- **¼ cup butter, melted**
- **1 tsp. grated lemon zest**
- **1 cup fresh or frozen blueberries**

GLAZE

- **½ cup confectioners' sugar**
- **1 Tbsp. lemon juice**
- **½ tsp. grated lemon zest**

1. Preheat oven to 400°. In a large bowl, whisk the first 5 ingredients. In another bowl, whisk yogurt, egg, melted butter and lemon zest until blended. Add to flour mixture; stir just until moistened. Fold in blueberries.
2. Drop batter by ⅓ cupfuls 1 in. apart onto a greased baking sheet. Bake 15-18 minutes or until light brown.
3. In a small bowl, combine glaze ingredients; stir until smooth. Drizzle over warm biscuits.
1 biscuit: 193 cal., 5g fat (3g sat. fat), 29mg chol., 223mg sod., 35g carb. (18g sugars, 1g fiber), 4g pro.

TEST KITCHEN TIP

Keep biscuits fresh by storing them in an airtight container at room temperature. Biscuits will be at their best if eaten within 1-2 days. Can't eat them that quickly? Put them in the freezer—they will keep for up to 3 months.

ALMOND STREUSEL ROLLS

Try my prize-winning pastry this Easter. These rolls are so popular that they often don't even cool completely before the pan is empty.
—*Perlene Hoekema, Lynden, WA*

Prep: 40 min. + rising • **Bake:** 35 min. + cooling
Makes: 1 dozen

- **2 pkg. (¼ oz. each) active dry yeast**
- **¾ cup warm water (110° to 115°)**
- **¾ cup warm 2% milk (110° to 115°)**
- **¼ cup butter, softened**
- **½ cup sugar**
- **2 large eggs, room temperature**
- **1 tsp. salt**
- **5¼ to 5½ cups all-purpose flour**

FILLING

- **½ cup almond paste**
- **¼ cup butter, softened**
- **½ cup packed brown sugar**
- **¼ tsp. almond extract**

TOPPING

- **3 Tbsp. sugar**
- **1 Tbsp. all-purpose flour**
- **1 Tbsp. butter**

ICING

- **1½ cups confectioners' sugar**
- **¼ tsp. almond extract**
- **1 to 2 Tbsp. 2% milk**

1. In a large bowl, dissolve yeast in warm water. Add the milk, butter, sugar, eggs, salt and 2 cups flour. Beat until smooth. Stir in enough remaining flour to form a soft dough.
2. Turn onto a floured surface; knead until smooth and elastic, 6-8 minutes. Place in a greased bowl, turning once to grease top. Cover and let rise in a warm place until doubled, about 1 hour.
3. Punch dough down; roll out to a 15x10-in. rectangle. In a bowl, beat filling ingredients until smooth. Spread over dough.
4. Roll up jelly-roll style, starting with a short side; seal seams. Cut into 12 slices. Place in a greased 12-in. ovenproof skillet or 13x9-in. baking pan. Cover and let rise in a warm place until doubled, about 30 minutes.
5. Combine topping ingredients; sprinkle over rolls. Bake at 350° for 35-40 minutes or until golden brown. Cool on a wire rack.
6. In a small bowl, combine confectioners' sugar, extract and enough milk to achieve drizzling consistency; drizzle over rolls.
1 roll: 482 cal., 13g fat (6g sat. fat), 61mg chol., 308mg sod., 83g carb. (37g sugars, 2g fiber), 8g pro.

▲
Proofing Active Dry Yeast

To determine—or proof—active yeast, dissolve 1 package active dry yeast and 1 tsp. sugar in ¼ cup warm (110°-115°) water. Let stand 5-10 minutes. If there is foam on the top of the mixture, the yeast is alive and active. If there is no foam, the yeast should be discarded. Note that this method is for active dry yeast; do not try with quick-rise yeast.

CINNAMON COFFEE CAKE

I love the excellent texture of this vintage streusel-topped coffee cake. It's always a crowd-pleaser, and its lovely spiced flavor is enriched by sour cream.
—*Eleanor Harris, Cape Coral, FL*

Prep: 20 min. • **Bake:** 1 hour + cooling
Makes: 20 servings

- **1 cup butter, softened**
- **2¾ cups sugar, divided**
- **4 large eggs, room temperature**
- **2 tsp. vanilla extract**
- **3 cups all-purpose flour**
- **1 tsp. baking soda**
- **1 tsp. salt**
- **2 cups sour cream**
- **2 Tbsp. ground cinnamon**
- **½ cup chopped walnuts**

1. In a large bowl, cream butter and 2 cups sugar until light and fluffy. Add 1 egg at a time, beating well after each addition. Beat in vanilla. Combine the flour, baking soda and salt; add alternately with sour cream, beating just enough after each addition to keep batter smooth.
2. Spoon a third of batter into a greased 10-in. tube pan. Combine the cinnamon, nuts and remaining sugar; sprinkle a third over batter in pan. Repeat the layers 2 more times. Bake at 350° until a toothpick inserted in the center comes out clean, 60-65 minutes. Cool for 15 minutes before removing from pan to a wire rack to cool completely.
1 piece: 340 cal., 16g fat (9g sat. fat), 83mg chol., 299mg sod., 44g carb. (28g sugars, 1g fiber), 5g pro.

BACON-RANCH MINI LOAVES

Need to round out your Easter brunch menu? Add these savory miniature loaves that bake up tender and golden brown. Slices are divine alongside vegetable omelets, breakfast bakes, frittatas or any favorite egg dish.
—*Brandon Norton, Auburn, KY*

Prep: 25 min. • **Bake:** 30 min. + cooling
Makes: 4 mini loaves (6 slices each)

- **½ lb. bacon strips, diced**
- **1 cup chopped green onions**
- **3 cups all-purpose flour**
- **2 Tbsp. sugar**
- **2 tsp. baking powder**
- **2 tsp. ranch salad dressing mix**
- **1½ tsp. garlic powder**
- **1 tsp. baking soda**
- **1 tsp. pepper**
- **2 large eggs, room temperature**
- **1½ cups 2% milk**
- **3 Tbsp. butter, melted**
- **2 cups shredded sharp cheddar cheese**

1. In a large skillet, cook bacon over medium heat until crisp. Using a slotted spoon, remove to paper towels. Drain, reserving 1 Tbsp. drippings. Saute onions in reserved drippings until tender; cool.
2. Preheat oven to 350°. In a large bowl, combine flour, sugar, baking powder, ranch dressing mix, garlic powder, baking soda and pepper. In a small bowl, whisk the eggs, milk and butter. Stir into dry ingredients just until moistened. Fold in cheese, bacon and onions.
3. Transfer to 4 greased 5¾x3x2-in. loaf pans. Bake until a toothpick inserted in the center comes out clean, 30-35 minutes. Cool for 10 minutes before removing from pans to wire racks.
1 slice: 167 cal., 9g fat (5g sat. fat), 39mg chol., 293mg sod., 15g carb. (2g sugars, 1g fiber), 6g pro.
Note: Bread can also be baked in 2 greased 8x4-in. loaf pans for 35-40 minutes.

GRANDMA NARDI'S ITALIAN EASTER BREAD

My Grandma Nardi's bread with dyed eggs is a family tradition. I have fond memories of her teaching me to make it when I was a young girl. *—Pat Merkovich, South Milwaukee, WI*

Prep: 35 min. + rising • **Bake:** 30 min. + cooling
Makes: 1 loaf (16 slices)

- **3 large eggs**
- **Assorted food coloring**

BREAD

- **⅔ cup warm 2% milk (70° to 80°)**
- **2 large eggs, room temperature**
- **2 Tbsp. butter, melted**
- **2 Tbsp. sugar**
- **1½ tsp. salt**
- **3 cups bread flour**
- **1 pkg. (¼ oz.) quick-rise yeast**
- **1 Tbsp. canola oil**

EGG WASH

- **1 large egg**
- **1 Tbsp. water**
- **1 Tbsp. sesame seeds or poppy seeds**

1. Place 3 eggs in a single layer in a small saucepan; add enough cold water to cover by 1 in. Cover and quickly bring to a boil. Remove from heat. Let stand 15 minutes.
2. Rinse the eggs in cold water and place in ice water until completely cooled. Drain; dye the hard-boiled eggs with food coloring, following package directions. Let the eggs stand until completely dry.
3. In bread machine pan, place the first bread ingredients in order suggested by manufacturer. Select dough setting. Check the dough after 5 minutes of mixing; add 1-2 Tbsp. additional milk or flour if needed.
4. When cycle is completed, turn dough onto a lightly floured surface. Punch down dough; divide into thirds. Roll each into a 15-in. rope. Place ropes on a greased baking sheet and braid. Shape into a ring. Pinch ends to seal. Lightly coat dyed eggs with oil; arrange on braid, tucking them carefully between ropes. For egg wash, whisk egg with water. Brush over dough; sprinkle with sesame seeds.
5. Cover with a kitchen towel; let rise in a warm place until almost doubled, about 30 minutes. Preheat oven to 350°.
6. Bake until golden brown, 30-35 minutes. Remove from pan to a wire rack to cool. Refrigerate leftovers.

1 slice: 157 cal., 5g fat (2g sat. fat), 75mg chol., 264mg sod., 21g carb. (2g sugars, 1g fiber), 6g pro.

CRANBERRY ORANGE
ALMOND QUICK BREAD

CRANBERRY ORANGE ALMOND QUICK BREAD

The beauty of this bread is that you can customize it to your family's specific tastes. Try it with dried apricots and pecans, or dried blueberries and hazelnuts.
—Taste of Home *Test Kitchen*

Prep: 15 min. • **Bake:** 40 min. + cooling
Makes: 1 loaf (12 slices)

- **3 cups all-purpose flour**
- **3 Tbsp. sugar**
- **1 Tbsp. baking powder**
- **½ tsp. salt**
- **1 cup dried cranberries**
- **½ cup sliced almonds, toasted**
- **1 large egg, room temperature**
- **1 cup fat-free milk**
- **⅓ cup canola oil**
- **¾ tsp. grated orange zest**
- **¾ tsp. almond extract**

1. Preheat oven to 350°. In a large bowl, whisk together first 4 ingredients; stir in cranberries and almonds. In another bowl, whisk together egg, milk, oil, zest and extract. Add to flour mixture; stir just until moistened.
2. Transfer to a 9x5-in. loaf pan coated with cooking spray. Bake until a toothpick inserted in center comes out clean, 40-50 minutes. Cool in pan 10 minutes before removing to a wire rack to cool.
1 slice: 258 cal., 9g fat (1g sat. fat), 16mg chol., 234mg sod., 40g carb. (14g sugars, 2g fiber), 5g pro.

TEST KITCHEN TIP

To bake this bread in a cast-iron skillet, prepare batter as directed. Spoon the batter into a greased 8-in. skillet and bake at 350° until a toothpick inserted in center comes out clean, 45-50 minutes. For muffins, prepare batter as directed. Spoon batter into 9 greased muffin cups and bake at 350° until a toothpick inserted in the center comes out clean, 25-30 minutes.

TRADITIONAL HOT CROSS BUNS

On Easter morning, our family always looked forward to a breakfast of dyed hard-boiled eggs and Mom's hot cross buns. I still serve these for special brunches or buffets.
—*Barbara Jean Lull, Fullerton, CA*

Prep: 25 min. + rising • **Bake:** 15 min. + cooling
Makes: 2½ dozen

- **2 pkg. (¼ oz. each) active dry yeast**
- **2 cups warm whole milk (110° to 115°)**
- **2 large eggs, room temperature**
- **⅓ cup butter, softened**
- **¼ cup sugar**
- **1½ tsp. salt**
- **1 tsp. ground cinnamon**
- **¼ tsp. ground allspice**
- **6 to 7 cups all-purpose flour**
- **½ cup dried currants**
- **½ cup raisins**
- **1 large egg yolk**
- **2 Tbsp. water**

ICING

- **1½ cups confectioners' sugar**
- **4 to 6 tsp. whole milk**

1. In a small bowl, dissolve yeast in warm milk. In a large bowl, combine eggs, butter, sugar, salt, spices, yeast mixture and 3 cups flour; beat on medium speed until smooth. Stir in currants, raisins and enough remaining flour to form a soft dough (dough will be sticky).
2. Turn onto a floured surface; knead until dough is smooth and elastic, 6-8 minutes. Place in a greased bowl, turning once to grease the top. Cover and let rise in a warm place until doubled, about 1 hour.
3. Punch down dough. Turn onto a lightly floured surface; divide and shape into 30 balls. Place 2 in. apart on greased baking sheets. Cover with kitchen towels; let rise in a warm place until doubled, 30-45 minutes. Preheat oven to 375°.
4. Using a sharp knife, cut a cross on top of each bun. In a small bowl, whisk egg yolk and water; brush over tops. Bake 15-20 minutes or until golden brown. Remove from pans to wire racks to cool slightly.
5. For icing, in a small bowl, mix confectioners' sugar and enough milk to reach the desired consistency. Pipe a cross on top of each bun. Serve warm.
1 bun: 171 cal., 3g fat (2g sat. fat), 28mg chol., 145mg sod., 31g carb. (12g sugars, 1g fiber), 4g pro.

TENDER CRESCENT ROLLS

My family's holiday dinner consists of a variety of soups and breads. These rolls are one of our favorites to enjoy during that meal.
—*Bonnie Myers, Callaway, NE*

Prep: 45 min. + rising • **Bake:** 10 min./batch
Makes: 4 dozen

- **2 envelopes (¼ oz. each) active dry yeast**
- **1 cup warm water (110° to 115°)**
- **1 cup warm 2% milk (110° to 115°)**
- **3 large eggs, room temperature**
- **½ cup sugar**
- **6 Tbsp. shortening**
- **1 tsp. salt**
- **6½ to 7 cups all-purpose flour**

1. In a small bowl, dissolve yeast in warm water. In a large bowl, combine the milk, eggs, sugar, shortening, salt, yeast mixture and 3 cups flour; beat on medium speed for 3 minutes until smooth. Stir in enough remaining flour to form a soft dough (dough will be sticky).
2. Turn dough onto a floured surface; knead until smooth and elastic, 6-8 minutes. Place in a greased bowl, turning once to grease the top. Cover with a kitchen towel and let rise in a warm place until doubled, about 1 hour.
3. Punch down dough. Turn onto a lightly floured surface; divide into 4 portions. Roll each portion into a 12-in. circle; cut each into 12 wedges. Roll up wedges from the wide ends. Place 2 in. apart on greased baking sheets, point side down; curve to form crescents.
4. Cover crescents with kitchen towels; let rise in a warm place until doubled, about 30 minutes. Preheat oven to 350°.
5. Bake until golden brown, 8-10 minutes. Remove from pans to wire racks; serve warm.
1 roll: 92 cal., 2g fat (1g sat. fat), 14mg chol., 56mg sod., 15g carb. (3g sugars, 1g fiber), 2g pro. **Diabetic exchanges:** 1 starch.

Tips for Successful Quick Breads

READ the entire recipe before starting.

ARRANGE the oven racks in the ideal positions before preheating. Preheat the oven for 10-15 minutes.

USE fats like butter, stick margarine with at least 80% oil, or shortening. Unless a recipe specifically calls for it, do not use whipped, tub, soft, liquid or reduced-fat butter or margarine.

ALLOW butter or margarine to soften at room temperature, so it is pliable before you begin creaming it with other ingredients.

MEASURE ingredients accurately.

MIX liquid and dry ingredients together just until moistened. A few lumps in the batter are fine. Overmixing leads to a tough and coarse texture.

REMEMBER that a pan's material and finish can affect cook time and browning. Aluminum pans with a dull finish give the best results. Dark finishes may cause overbrowning. Shiny finishes or air-cushioned pans may result in lightly colored products or longer baking times.

GREASE pans if the recipe dictates, and fill them only two-thirds full.

BAKE quick breads shortly after combining ingredients.

ALLOW for good air circulation during baking. Leave at least an inch of space between pans and sides of the oven. If baking more than 1 pan at a time, switch pan positions and rotate halfway through baking time.

ITALIAN RICOTTA EASTER BREAD

I tweaked our family's traditional Easter bread by adding ricotta and a few other ingredients. The almond flavoring works wonders!
—Tina Mirilovich, Johnstown, PA

Prep: 30 min. • **Bake:** 45 min.
Makes: 18 servings

- **¾ cup plain or butter-flavored shortening, room temperature**
- **1½ cups sugar**
- **3 large eggs, room temperature**
- **3 large egg yolks, room temperature**
- **1 cup whole-milk ricotta cheese**
- **1 tsp. almond extract (or flavor of choice)**
- **6 cups all-purpose flour**
- **1 Tbsp. baking powder**
- **1 tsp. salt**
- **½ cup 2% milk**

GLAZE

- **1½ cups confectioners' sugar**
- **3 Tbsp. 2% milk**
- **½ tsp. almond extract (or flavor of choice)**
- **Sliced toasted almonds or assorted sprinkles**

1. Preheat oven to 350°. Cream shortening and sugar until light and fluffy. Add eggs and egg yolks, 1 at a time, beating well after each addition. Beat in ricotta and extract. In another bowl, whisk flour, baking powder and salt; add to creamed mixture alternately with milk, beating well after each addition, stirring in final 1 cup flour by hand.
2. Turn onto a lightly floured surface; divide into thirds. Roll each into an 18-in. rope. Place ropes on a parchment-lined baking sheet and braid. Pinch ends to seal; tuck under braid. Bake until a toothpick inserted in center comes out clean, 45-55 minutes (do not overbake). Remove to wire racks to cool.
3. Meanwhile, beat the confectioners' sugar, milk and extract until smooth. Brush on warm bread; top with sliced almonds or sprinkles.
1 piece: 376 cal., 11g fat (4g sat. fat), 68mg chol., 247mg sod., 60g carb. (28g sugars, 1g fiber), 8g pro.

CHEESY GARLIC HERB QUICK BREAD

Herby skillet bread complements just about any main dish. The sharp cheddar cheese makes it irresistible.
—Taste of Home *Test Kitchen*

Prep: 15 min. • **Bake:** 25 min.
Makes: 1 loaf (12 slices)

- **3 cups all-purpose flour**
- **3 Tbsp. sugar**
- **1 Tbsp. baking powder**
- **2 tsp. Italian seasoning**
- **1 tsp. garlic powder**
- **½ tsp. salt**
- **1 large egg, room temperature**
- **1 cup fat-free milk**
- **⅓ cup canola oil**
- **1 cup shredded sharp cheddar cheese**

1. Preheat oven to 350°. In a large bowl, whisk together the first 6 ingredients. In another bowl, whisk together the egg, milk and oil. Stir in cheese and add to flour mixture; stir just until moistened.
2. Spoon batter into greased 9-in. cast-iron skillet and bake at 350° until a toothpick inserted in the center comes out clean, 25-30 minutes.
1 slice: 233 cal., 10g fat (2g sat. fat), 25mg chol., 175mg sod., 29g carb. (4g sugars, 1g fiber), 7g pro.

If you use your cast-iron skillet on a regular basis, you might notice food starting to stick, even if you clean it daily. That means it's time to re-season the pan. Seasoning is the process of adhering oil to the surface to create a nonstick coating. Simply line the lower oven rack with aluminum foil and preheat the oven to 350°. Scrub the pan with hot, soapy water and a stiff brush to remove any rust. Towel-dry and apply a thin coat of vegetable oil to the entire pan—outside and handle included. Place on top oven rack, upside down; bake for 1 hour. Turn off the oven and leave the pan inside to cool. Now you're ready to cook.

CHEESY GARLIC
HERB QUICK BREAD

VINTAGE EASTER

Relive treasured childhood memories—and the flavors behind them—with this retro holiday spread that will make you feel nostalgic for Easter at Grandma's house. After all, her recipes have stood the test of time, so what better way to honor this special lady and please your family than with a warm and hearty meal inspired by her delicious home cooking.

Maple-Peach Glazed Ham (p. 128) **Grandma's Rosemary Dinner Rolls** (p. 128)

Easter Day Countdown

This year, make Easter reminiscent of dinner at Grandma's. But don't stress over all the details. Refer to this handy cooking and prep timeline to help you create a modern, elegant gathering with a retro flair.

A FEW WEEKS BEFORE

☐ Prepare two grocery lists—one for nonperishable items to buy now and one for perishable items to buy a few days before Easter.

☐ Bake Grandma's Rosemary Dinner Rolls. Wrap securely in an airtight container and store in the freezer.

TWO DAYS BEFORE

☐ Buy remaining grocery items.

☐ Prepare and decorate the Peanut Butter Easter Eggs. Store in airtight containers in the refrigerator.

☐ Wash china, stemware and table linens.

THE DAY BEFORE

☐ Bake the cake layers for the Incredible Coconut Cake, but do not assemble. Store in an airtight container.

☐ Prepare the Olive-Stuffed Celery. Cover and store in the refrigerator.

☐ Prepare the Spring Rhubarb Salad. Keep in refrigerator until serving time.

☐ Mix together the ingredients for the vinaigrette for the Snap Pea Salad. Cover and store in the refrigerator.

☐ Set the table.

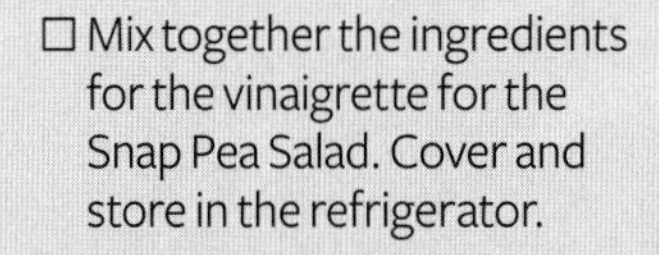

EASTER DAY

☐ In the morning, remove the dinner rolls from the freezer to thaw.

☐ About 3-4 hours before dinner, mix together the ingredients for the Springtime Punch, but do not add the ginger ale. Chill in the refrigerator.

☐ About 3-4 hours before dinner, prepare the Snap Pea Salad. Add vinaigrette. Cover salad and refrigerate until serving.

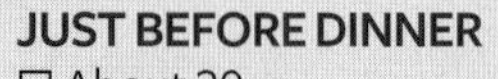

☐ About 2-3 hours before dinner, prepare and bake the Maple-Peach Glazed Ham. Keep warm until serving.

☐ About 2 hours before dinner, prepare the Schaum Strawberry Torte. Let cool. Keep covered until ready to serve.

☐ About 1 hour before dinner, prepare the New Potatoes. Cover and keep warm until serving.

☐ About an hour before dinner, prepare and bake the Poppy Seed Squares. Keep warm until guests arrive and serve as appetizers.

JUST BEFORE DINNER

☐ About 20 minutes before dinner, assemble and frost coconut cake. Remove peanut butter cups from the refrigerator.

☐ As guests arrive, remove the Olive-Stuffed Celery sticks from the refrigerator and serve as appetizers.

☐ Remove the punch from the refrigerator and stir in the ginger ale. Serve with appetizers or as a beverage with dinner.

☐ Warm the dinner rolls in the oven. Serve warm.

☐ Following dinner, serve desserts. Serve torte with strawberries and whipped cream.

SPRING RHUBARB SALAD

In our part of Iowa, we know spring is coming when we see the first rhubarb peeking out of the ground. We enjoy it so much that it's hard to wait for the stalks to grow large enough to be picked! I've collected lots of recipes for this sweet-tart fruit, but this classic gelatin mold is one of our family's favorites.
—Joy Hansmeier, Waukon, IA

Prep: 10 min. • **Cook:** 10 min. + chilling
Makes: 10 servings

- **4 cups diced fresh rhubarb**
- **1½ cups water**
- **½ cup sugar**
- **1 pkg. (6 oz.) strawberry gelatin**
- **1 cup orange juice**
- **1 tsp. grated orange zest**
- **1 cup sliced fresh strawberries**

Combine the rhubarb, water and sugar in a saucepan. Cook and stir over medium heat until rhubarb is tender. Remove from heat; add gelatin and stir until dissolved. Add the orange juice and zest. Chill until syrupy. Add strawberries. Pour mixture into 6-cup mold; chill until set.

1 serving: 127 cal., 0 fat (0 sat. fat), 0 chol., 41mg sod., 31g carb. (29g sugars, 1g fiber), 2g pro.

OLIVE-STUFFED CELERY

My grandma taught both me and my mom how to make this appetizer. We always serve it on holidays. The filling is so yummy that even if you don't normally care for the ingredients on their own, you'll love the end result.
—Stacy Powell, Santa Fe, TX

Takes: 25 min. • **Makes:** 2 dozen

- **1 dill pickle spear plus 1 tsp. juice**
- **3 sweet pickles plus 1 tsp. juice**
- **6 pitted ripe olives plus 1 tsp. juice**
- **6 pimiento-stuffed olives plus 1 tsp. juice**
- **1 pkg. (8 oz.) cream cheese, softened**
- **⅓ cup Miracle Whip**
- **¼ tsp. salt**
- **¼ cup finely chopped pecans, toasted**
- **6 celery ribs, cut into 2-in. pieces**

1. Finely chop the pickles and olives; set aside. In a bowl, beat the cream cheese, Miracle Whip, juices and salt until blended. Stir in the pickles, olives and pecans.
2. Pipe or stuff filling into celery sticks. Store in the refrigerator.

1 piece: 61 cal., 5g fat (2g sat. fat), 12mg chol., 228mg sod., 2g carb. (1g sugars, 0 fiber), 1g pro.

SNAP PEA SALAD

SNAP PEA SALAD

A quick and easy dressing amps up the flavor of sugar snap peas for this change-of-pace salad. Crunchy, colorful and unique, it adds a bit of fun to family dinners.
—Jean Ecos, Hartland, WI

Takes: 20 min.
Makes: 12 servings

- **¼ cup white wine vinegar**
- **¼ cup Dijon mustard**
- **2 Tbsp. minced fresh parsley**
- **2 Tbsp. olive oil**
- **2 Tbsp. honey**
- **1 Tbsp. lemon juice**
- **1 tsp. salt**
- **½ tsp. pepper**
- **3 lbs. fresh sugar snap peas**
- **Grated lemon zest, optional**

1. For vinaigrette, in a small bowl, whisk the first 8 ingredients until blended. In a 6-qt. stockpot, bring 16 cups water to a boil. Add snap peas; cook, uncovered, 2-3 minutes or just until peas turn bright green. Remove the peas and immediately drop into ice water. Drain and pat dry; place in a large bowl.
2. Drizzle with vinaigrette and toss to coat. Serve immediately or refrigerate, covered, up to 4 hours before serving. If desired, sprinkle with lemon zest.

¾ cup: 84 cal., 3g fat (0 sat. fat), 0 chol., 322mg sod., 12g carb. (7g sugars, 3g fiber), 4g pro. **Diabetic exchanges:** 1 vegetable, ½ starch, ½ fat.

GRANDMA'S ROSEMARY DINNER ROLLS

GRANDMA'S ROSEMARY DINNER ROLLS

My grandma, whom I affectionately called Baba, made these in her coal oven. How she regulated the temperature is beyond me! She always made extra rolls for the neighbors to bake in their own ovens. At lunchtime, my mom and aunts delivered the formed rolls.
—Charlotte Hendershot, Hudson, PA

Prep: 35 min. + rising • **Bake:** 20 min.
Makes: 1 dozen

- **1 pkg. (¼ oz.) active dry yeast**
- **¼ cup warm water (110° to 115°)**
- **3 cups bread flour**
- **2 Tbsp. sugar**
- **1 Tbsp. minced fresh rosemary, divided**
- **¾ tsp. salt**
- **⅔ cup warm 2% milk (110° to 115°)**
- **1 large egg, room temperature**
- **¼ to ⅓ cup canola oil**

EGG WASH
- **1 large egg yolk**
- **2 Tbsp. 2% milk**

1. In a small bowl, dissolve the yeast in warm water. Place the flour, sugar, 2 tsp. rosemary and salt in a food processor; pulse until blended. Add the warm milk, egg and yeast mixture; cover and pulse 10 times or until almost blended.
2. While processing, gradually add oil just until dough pulls away from sides and begins to form a ball. Process 2 minutes longer to knead dough (dough will be very soft).
3. Transfer dough to a greased bowl, turning once to grease the top. Cover and let rise in a warm place until doubled, about 1 hour.
4. Punch down dough. Turn onto a lightly floured surface; divide and shape into 12 balls. Roll each into a 15-in. rope. Starting at 1 end, loosely wrap dough around itself to form a coil. Tuck end under; pinch to seal.
5. Place 2 in. apart on greased baking sheets. Cover and let rise until doubled, about 30 minutes.
6. For egg wash, in a small bowl, whisk egg yolk and milk; brush over rolls. Sprinkle with remaining rosemary. Bake at 350° until golden brown, 18-22 minutes. Remove from pans to wire racks; serve warm.
1 roll: 194 cal., 6g fat (1g sat. fat), 32mg chol., 163mg sod., 28g carb. (3g sugars, 1g fiber), 6g pro.

MAPLE-PEACH GLAZED HAM

This is one of my husband's favorite recipes. He makes it regularly for his group of friends on the weekends because it's so good and so easy. The chili pepper adds a little heat.
—Bonnie Hawkins, Elkhorn, WI

Prep: 5 min. • **Bake:** 2 hours
Makes: 16 servings (about 2 cups sauce)

- **1 fully cooked bone-in ham (7 to 9 lbs.)**
- **2 cups peach preserves or orange marmalade**
- **½ cup maple syrup**
- **⅓ cup orange juice**
- **2 Tbsp. ground ancho chili pepper, optional**

1. Preheat oven to 325°. Place ham on a rack in a shallow roasting pan. Cover and bake 1¾-2¼ hours or until a thermometer reads 130°.
2. Meanwhile, in a small saucepan, mix the preserves, syrup, orange juice and, if desired, chili pepper until blended. Remove ¾ cup mixture for glaze.
3. Remove ham from oven; brush with some of the glaze. Bake, uncovered, 15-20 minutes longer or until a thermometer reads 140°, brushing occasionally with remaining glaze.
4. In a medium saucepan over medium heat, bring the preserves mixture to a boil, stirring occasionally. Cook and stir until the mixture is slightly thickened, 1-2 minutes. Serve as a sauce with the ham.
4 oz. cooked ham with 2 Tbsp. sauce: 294 cal., 5g fat (2g sat. fat), 87mg chol., 1040mg sod., 34g carb. (31g sugars, 0 fiber), 29g pro.

MAPLE-PEACH
GLAZED HAM

SPRINGTIME PUNCH

I use this punch to start off a party. Its blend of lemon, orange and pineapple juices defines the sunny color and fruity flavor, while ginger ale adds a zesty fizz. I add fresh strawberries in the punch bowl for extra flair.
—Janet Mooberry, Peoria, IL

Prep: 15 min. + chilling
Makes: 12 servings (3 qt.)

- **2 cups sugar**
- **2½ cups water**
- **1 cup lemon juice (3 to 4 lemons)**
- **1 cup orange juice (2 to 3 oranges)**
- **¾ cup thawed pineapple juice concentrate**
- **2 qt. ginger ale, chilled**

In a large saucepan, bring sugar and water to a boil. Boil for 10 minutes; remove from the heat. Stir in the lemon, orange and pineapple juices. Refrigerate. Just before serving; transfer to a punch bowl; stir in ginger ale.
1 cup: 231 cal., 0 fat (0 sat. fat), 0 chol., 12mg sod., 59g carb. (58g sugars, 0 fiber), 0 pro.

NEW POTATOES

When I was growing up, we were always eager to taste those first fresh vegetables from the garden—especially with Sunday dinner. These new potatoes, showered with freshly picked parsley, remain a standout among other spring delights such as rhubarb pie and asparagus.
—Marilyn Kutzli, Preston, IA

Prep: 15 min. • **Cook:** 40 min.
Makes: 12 servings

- **4 lb. small red potatoes**
- **½ cup butter, cubed**
- **½ cup minced fresh parsley**

Cook potatoes in boiling salted water for 20-30 minutes or until tender; drain. Cool for 5 minutes. Remove skins. In a large skillet over medium heat, cook and stir potatoes in butter until lightly browned, about 20 minutes. Stir in fresh parsley.
¾ cup: 177 cal., 8g fat (5g sat. fat), 20mg chol., 88mg sod., 24g carb. (2g sugars, 3g fiber), 3g pro.

INCREDIBLE COCONUT CAKE

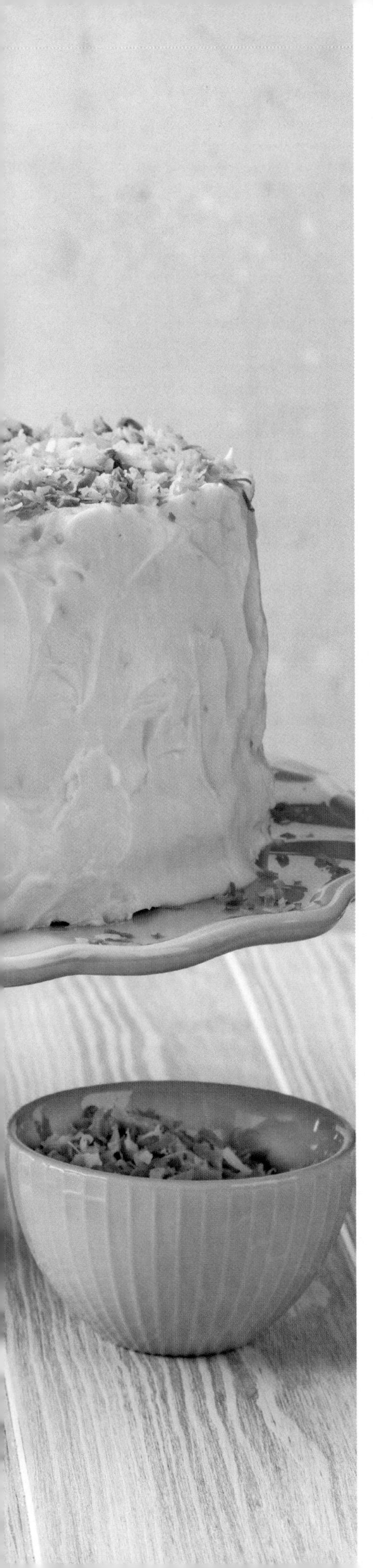

SCHAUM STRAWBERRY TORTE

My German grandmother took great pride in serving this delicate, low-fat dessert, handing down the recipe. Whenever I make it, I'm filled with warm memories of my childhood. The strawberries add a boost of nutrition, too.
—Diane Krisman, Hales Corners, WI

Prep: 15 min. • **Bake:** 50 min. + cooling
Makes: 12 servings

- **8 large egg whites**
- **1 Tbsp. white vinegar**
- **1 tsp. vanilla extract**
- **¼ tsp. salt**
- **2 cups sugar**
- **3 cups sliced fresh strawberries**
- **1½ cups whipped cream**

1. Place egg whites in a large bowl and let stand at room temperature for 30 minutes.
2. Preheat oven to 300°. Add vinegar, vanilla and salt to egg whites; beat on medium speed until soft peaks form. Gradually beat in sugar, about 2 Tbsp. at a time, on high until stiff glossy peaks form and sugar is dissolved.
3. Spread into a greased 10-in. springform pan. Bake 50-60 minutes or until lightly browned. Remove to a wire rack to cool (meringue will fall).
4. Serve with strawberries and whipped cream. Store leftovers in the refrigerator.
1 piece: 206 cal., 6g fat (3g sat. fat), 20mg chol., 92mg sod., 37g carb. (36g sugars, 1g fiber), 3g pro.

INCREDIBLE COCONUT CAKE

This recipe lives up to its name! I found it in a newspaper many years ago and modified it to suit my taste. This is my all-time favorite cake, and my family and friends absolutely love it.
—Lynne Bassler, Indiana, PA

Prep: 35 min.
Bake: 25 min. + chilling
Makes: 16 servings

- **5 eggs, separated, room temperature**
- **2 cups sugar**
- **½ cup butter, softened**
- **½ cup canola oil**
- **2¼ cups cake flour**
- **1 tsp. baking powder**
- **½ tsp. baking soda**
- **¼ tsp. salt**
- **1 cup buttermilk**
- **2 cups sweetened shredded coconut, chopped**
- **1 tsp. coconut extract**
- **½ tsp. vanilla extract**
- **¼ tsp. almond extract**
- **¼ tsp. cream of tartar**

FROSTING

- **11 oz. cream cheese, softened**
- **⅔ cup butter, softened**
- **4⅓ cups confectioners' sugar**
- **1¼ tsp. coconut extract**
- **2 cups sweetened shredded coconut, toasted**

1. Place the egg whites in a large bowl; let stand at room temperature for 30 minutes.
2. Preheat oven to 325°. In another large bowl, beat sugar, butter and oil until well blended. Add egg yolks, 1 at a time, beating well after each addition.
3. Combine flour, baking powder, baking soda and salt; add to creamed mixture alternately with buttermilk, beating well after each addition. Stir in coconut and extracts.
4. Add cream of tartar to egg whites; with clean beaters, beat on medium until stiff peaks form. Fold a fourth of the egg whites into batter, then fold in remaining whites.
5. Transfer to 3 greased and floured 9-in. round baking pans. Bake 25-30 minutes or until a toothpick inserted in center comes out clean. Cool 10 minutes before removing from pans to wire racks to cool completely.
6. For frosting, in a bowl, beat cream cheese and butter until fluffy. Add the confectioners' sugar and extract; beat until smooth.
7. Place 1 cake layer on a serving plate; spread with ½ cup frosting and sprinkle with ⅓ cup coconut. Repeat. Top with remaining cake layer. Spread remaining frosting over top and sides of cake; sprinkle with remaining coconut. Refrigerate for 2 hours before cutting. Store in the refrigerator.
1 slice: 689 cal., 37g fat (21g sat. fat), 123mg chol., 353mg sod., 85g carb. (64g sugars, 1g fiber), 6g pro.

TEST KITCHEN TIP

This cake recipe offers the convenience of using bagged sweetened shredded coconut. To toast shredded coconut for the topping, bake in a shallow pan in a 350° oven for 5-10 minutes or cook in a skillet over low heat until golden brown, stirring occasionally.

PEANUT BUTTER
EASTER EGGS

POPPY SEED SQUARES

When I came across the recipe for this unique appetizer, I couldn't wait to try it. I prepare these savory squares every holiday. They're so tasty, no one tires of them.
—Jo Baden, Independence, KS

Prep: 35 min. • **Bake:** 25 min.
Makes: about 8 dozen

- **1 lb. ground beef**
- **1½ cups finely chopped fresh mushrooms**
- **1 medium onion, finely chopped**
- **1 can (10¾ oz.) condensed cream of celery or mushroom soup, undiluted**
- **1 Tbsp. prepared horseradish**
- **1 tsp. salt**
- **½ tsp. pepper**

CRUST

- **3 cups all-purpose flour**
- **2 Tbsp. poppy seeds**
- **¾ tsp. baking powder**
- **¾ tsp. salt**
- **1 cup shortening**
- **½ cup cold water**

1. In a large skillet, cook the beef, mushrooms and onion over medium heat until meat is no longer pink. Add the soup, horseradish, salt and pepper. Remove from the heat; set aside.
2. In a bowl, combine the flour, poppy seeds, baking powder and salt. Cut in the shortening until the mixture resembles coarse crumbs. Gradually add water, tossing with a fork until a ball forms. Divide dough in half. Roll out 1 portion into a 15x10-in. rectangle; transfer to an ungreased 15x10x1-in. baking pan.
3. Spoon meat mixture over crust. Roll out the remaining dough into 15x10-in. rectangle; place over filling. Bake at 425° until golden brown, about 25 minutes. Cut into small squares to serve.

1 piece: 43 cal., 3g fat (1g sat. fat), 3mg chol., 50mg sod., 3g carb. (0 sugars, 0 fiber), 1g pro.

TEST KITCHEN TIP

When offering finger foods, have tongs, scoops or other utensils available for guests to serve themselves without touching the food. Once the appetizers are on their own plate, they can use their fingers for eating.

PEANUT BUTTER EASTER EGGS

Get the kids or grandkids involved in making these treats. The memories are well worth the sticky fingers!
—Mary Joyce Johnson, Upper Darby, PA

Prep: 35 min. + chilling • **Cook:** 5 min.
Makes: 16 eggs

- **¾ cup creamy peanut butter**
- **½ cup butter, softened**
- **½ tsp. vanilla extract**
- **2⅓ cups confectioners' sugar**
- **1 cup graham cracker crumbs**
- **1½ cups dark chocolate chips**
- **2 Tbsp. shortening**
- **Optional: Confectioners' sugar icing and sprinkles**

1. In a large bowl, beat peanut butter, butter and vanilla until blended. Gradually beat in confectioners' sugar and cracker crumbs. Shape mixture into 16 eggs; place on waxed paper-lined baking sheets. Refrigerate for 30 minutes or until firm.
2. In a microwave, melt chocolate chips and shortening; stir until smooth. Dip eggs in chocolate mixture; allow excess to drip off.
3. Return eggs to baking sheets. Refrigerate 30 minutes.
4. If desired, decorate eggs with icing and sprinkles. Let stand until set. Store in airtight containers in refrigerator.

1 egg: 346 cal., 21g fat (10g sat. fat), 15mg chol., 128mg sod., 37g carb. (29g sugars, 1g fiber), 5g pro.

Confectioners' sugar icing: In a bowl, mix 2 cups confectioners' sugar, 4 tsp. corn syrup, 1 tsp. almond extract and 1-2 Tbsp. milk until smooth. Tint frosting with paste food coloring if desired. Yield: ⅔ cup.

To decorate eggs with bunny ears: Cut decorative paper into bunny ears. Tape each ear to a toothpick; insert into top of eggs. Remove ears before eating.

Blueberry cake
1/2 cup sugar
1/4 " shortening
1 egg
3/4 cup blueberries
3/4 cups milk
2 cups flour
2 1/2 tsp baking powder
salt nutmeg
400° 25 to 30 min

Culinary Arts

This project is a great way to turn a favorite recipe card into a decorative piece. Start by arranging reclaimed wood planks together to create a rectangular base. Line the back of the planks with a few wood strips, perpendicular to the seams between the planks. Nail the strips to the planks, securing them in place. Enlarge the recipe card on a color copier, so the print picks up time-earned stains and illustrations. Choose a size slightly smaller than the base. Apply decoupage glue on the back of the print and press it into place on the wood. Brush another layer of glue over entire front side to seal it. Dry thoroughly. Drill holes in the upper corners of wood base and thread twine through the holes, knotting the ends to secure it.

EASTER EGG DECORATING PARTY

Invite friends and little ones over for an Easter egg decorating party. Here you'll find fun new ways to decorate eggs, a springy menu and cute-as-can-be sweet treats. Let's decorate!

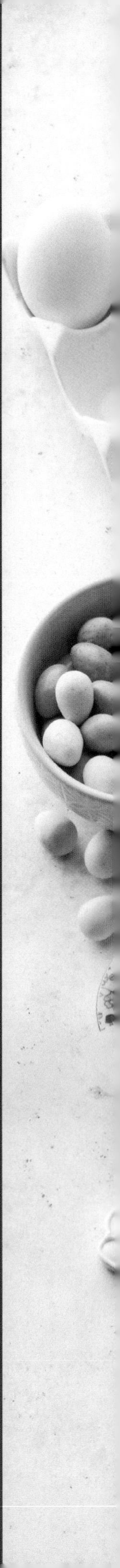

Easter Sugar Cookies (p. 141) **Cupcake Easter Baskets** (p. 137)

MARSHMALLOW
EASTER EGGS

MARSHMALLOW EASTER EGGS

I've been making this wonderful Easter candy for years. These eggs are a big hit with everyone who loves marshmallows.
—Betty Claycomb, Alverton, PA

Prep: 45 min. + standing • **Cook:** 15 min.
Makes: 3 dozen

- **25 cups all-purpose flour (about 8 lbs.)**
- **1 large egg**
- **2 Tbsp. unflavored gelatin**
- **½ cup cold water**
- **2 cups sugar**
- **1 cup light corn syrup, divided**
- **¾ cup hot water**
- **2 tsp. vanilla extract**
- **1 lb. dark chocolate candy coating, melted**
- **Candy coating disks, multiple colors**

1. Spread 7 cups all-purpose flour in each of three 13x9-in. pans and 4 cups flour in a 9-in. square pan. Carefully wash the egg in a mild bleach solution (1 tsp. chlorine bleach to 1 qt. warm water); dry. Press washed egg halfway into the flour to form an impression. Repeat 35 times, 2 in. apart; set aside.
2. In a small bowl, sprinkle the gelatin over cold water; set aside. In a large saucepan, combine the sugar, ½ cup corn syrup and hot water. Bring to a boil over medium heat, stirring constantly, until a candy thermometer reads 238° (soft-ball stage). Remove from the heat; stir in remaining corn syrup.
3. Pour into a large bowl. Add the reserved gelatin, 1 Tbsp. at a time, beating on high speed until candy is thick and has cooled to lukewarm, about 10 minutes. Beat in vanilla.
4. Spoon lukewarm gelatin mixture into egg depressions; dust with flour. Let stand for 3-4 hours or until set.
5. Brush excess flour off marshmallow eggs. Dip each in chocolate candy coating. Place flat side down on waxed paper. Let stand until set. Drizzle candy coating over eggs.
1 piece: 147 cal., 4g fat (4g sat. fat), 0 chol., 7mg sod., 28g carb. (28g sugars, 0 fiber), 1g pro.

TEST KITCHEN TIP

Silicone egg molds are available and can be used instead of the flour.

CUPCAKE EASTER BASKETS

CUPCAKE EASTER BASKETS

These pastel beauties have a mild orange flavor and fun candy elements on top. Bake up a batch of "baskets" for the next church potluck, classroom party or bake sale.
—Julie Johnston, Shaunavon, SK

Prep: 20 min. • **Bake:** 20 min. + cooling
Makes: 1½ dozen

- **½ cup butter, softened**
- **1 cup sugar**
- **1 large egg, room temperature**
- **1 tsp. grated orange zest**
- **2 cups cake flour**
- **¾ tsp. baking soda**
- **½ tsp. baking powder**
- **¼ tsp. salt**
- **⅔ cup buttermilk**

FROSTING

- **¾ cup butter, softened**
- **6 oz. cream cheese, softened**
- **1 tsp. vanilla extract**
- **3 cups confectioners' sugar**
- **1 tsp. water**
- **4 drops green food coloring**
- **1½ cups sweetened shredded coconut**
- **Chocolate licorice twists**
- **Chocolate egg candy**

1. Preheat oven to 350°. In a large bowl, cream butter and sugar. Beat in the egg and orange zest. Combine the flour, baking soda, baking powder and salt; add to creamed mixture alternately with buttermilk.
2. Fill 18 paper-lined muffin cups two-thirds full. Bake until a toothpick comes out clean, 20-25 minutes. Cool for 10 minutes; remove from pans to wire racks to cool completely.
3. In a small bowl, beat butter, cream cheese and vanilla until smooth. Gradually beat in confectioners' sugar; spread over cupcakes. Combine water and food coloring in a large bowl; add coconut. Stir to coat. Sprinkle colored coconut over cupcakes.
4. Using a metal or wooden skewer, poke a hole in the top on opposite sides of each cupcake. Cut licorice into 6-in. strips for handles; insert each end into a hole. Decorate with candy eggs.
1 cupcake: 351 cal., 18g fat (11g sat. fat), 51mg chol., 273mg sod., 47g carb. (33g sugars, 1g fiber), 3g pro.

HAM & CHEESE LOAF

This golden loaf starts with convenient refrigerated dough—and stuffs it with deli ham and three types of cheese. I created the recipe by experimenting with ingredients my family loves. It makes a delicious hot sandwich in hardly any time.
—Gloria Lindell, Welcome, MN

Prep: 15 min. • **Bake:** 30 min.
Makes: 6 servings

- **1 tube (13.8 oz.) refrigerated pizza crust**
- **10 slices deli ham**
- **¼ cup sliced green onions**
- **1 cup shredded part-skim mozzarella cheese**
- **1 cup shredded cheddar cheese**
- **4 slices provolone cheese**
- **1 Tbsp. butter, melted**

1. Preheat oven to 350°. Unroll dough onto a greased baking sheet; top with the ham, onions and cheeses. Roll up tightly jelly-roll style, starting with a long side; pinch seam to seal and tuck ends under. Brush with butter.
2. Bake until golden brown, 30-35 minutes. Let stand for 5 minutes; cut into 1-in. slices.
Freeze option: Cool unsliced loaf on a wire rack. Spray a large piece of foil with cooking spray. Wrap loaf in prepared foil and freeze for up to 3 months. To use, thaw at room temperature for 2 hours. Preheat oven to 350°. Unwrap and place on a greased baking sheet. Bake 15-20 minutes or until heated through. Let loaf stand 5 minutes; cut into 1-in. slices.
2 slices: 406 cal., 18g fat (10g sat. fat), 65mg chol., 1151mg sod., 34g carb. (5g sugars, 1g fiber), 26g pro.

STRAWBERRY RICOTTA BRUSCHETTA

Here's an sweet spin on bruschetta. A creamy ricotta cheese spread is the ideal complement to the sweet, minty strawberry topping.
—Laura Stricklin, Jackson, MS

Takes: 25 min. • **Makes:** 2 dozen

- **24 slices French bread baguette (½ in. thick)**
- **3 Tbsp. butter, melted**
- **3 cups fresh strawberries, chopped**
- **3 Tbsp. minced fresh mint**
- **3 Tbsp. honey**
- **½ cup ricotta cheese**
- **2 Tbsp. seedless strawberry jam**
- **1½ tsp. grated lemon zest**

1. Brush bread slices with butter; place on an ungreased baking sheet. Bake at 375° until lightly browned, 8-10 minutes .
2. Meanwhile, in a small bowl, combine the strawberries, mint and honey; set aside. In another bowl, combine the ricotta, jam and lemon zest. Spread ricotta mixture over toast; top with strawberry mixture.
1 piece: 89 cal., 3g fat (1g sat. fat), 6mg chol., 88mg sod., 14g carb. (4g sugars, 1g fiber), 2g pro. **Diabetic exchanges:** 1 starch, ½ fat.

RANCH SNACK MIX

Looking for a fast-to-fix munchie for your next party? This recipe makes a generous 24 cups and doesn't involve any cooking. It's a cinch and guests go crazy for it.
—Linda Murphy, Pulaski, WI

Takes: 15 min. • **Makes:** 32 servings (6 qt.)

- **1 pkg. (12 oz.) miniature pretzels**
- **16 cups Bugles (about 12 oz.)**
- **1 can (10 oz.) salted cashews**
- **1 pkg. (6 oz.) Goldfish cheddar crackers**
- **1 envelope ranch salad dressing mix**
- **¾ cup canola oil**

In 2 large bowls, combine the pretzels, Bugles, cashews and crackers. Sprinkle with dressing mix; toss gently to combine. Drizzle with oil; toss until well coated. Store in airtight containers.
¾ cup: 185 cal., 11g fat (2g sat. fat), 2mg chol., 357mg sod., 19g carb. (1g sugars, 1g fiber), 4g pro.

STRAWBERRY RICOTTA BRUSCHETTA

EDAMAME HUMMUS

We love hummus at our house. This recipe is a scrumptious and refreshing twist on an old favorite, and it's a tasty way to add healthy soy to our diets.
—Marla Clark, Albuquerque, NM

Takes: 15 min. • **Makes:** 3 cups

- **1 pkg. (16 oz.) frozen shelled edamame, thawed**
- **½ cup tahini**
- **½ cup water**
- **⅓ to ½ cup lemon juice**
- **2 garlic cloves, minced**
- **1 tsp. sea salt**
- **¼ cup olive oil**
- **¼ cup minced fresh mint**
- **2 jalapeno peppers, seeded and chopped**
- **Assorted fresh vegetables**
- **Rice crackers**

Microwave edamame, covered, on high until tender, 2-3 minutes. Transfer to a food processor; add the remaining ingredients. Process until smooth, 1-2 minutes. Serve with assorted fresh vegetables and rice crackers.

¼ cup: 167 cal., 13g fat (2g sat. fat), 0 chol., 167mg sod., 7g carb. (1g sugars, 2g fiber), 7g pro.

TEST KITCHEN TIP

Edamame—soybeans that are harvested early, before the beans become hard—are a popular Asian food. The young beans are parboiled and frozen to retain their freshness. Look for them in the freezer section of grocery and health food stores. Known as a good source of fiber, protein, calcium and vitamin C, edamame are a tasty addition to soups, salads and main dishes. They are also delicious eaten alone as a healthy snack.

EASTER
SUGAR COOKIES

EASTER SUGAR COOKIES

Cream cheese contributes to the rich taste of these melt-in-your-mouth cookies. They have such nice flavor, you can skip the frosting and sprinkle them with colored sugar for a change.
—Julie Brunette, Green Bay, WI

Prep: 15 min. + chilling • **Bake:** 10 min./batch
Makes: 4 dozen

- **1 cup butter, softened**
- **3 oz. cream cheese, softened**
- **1 cup sugar**
- **1 large egg yolk, room temperature**
- **½ tsp. vanilla extract**
- **¼ tsp. almond extract**
- **2¼ cups all-purpose flour**
- **½ tsp. salt**
- **¼ tsp. baking soda**
- **Tinted frosting or colored sugar**

1. In a bowl, cream butter, cream cheese and sugar. Beat in egg yolk and extracts. Combine the flour, salt and baking soda; gradually add to creamed mixture. Cover and refrigerate for 3 hours or until easy to handle.
2. Preheat oven to 375°. On a lightly floured surface, roll out dough to ⅛-in. thickness. Cut with 2½-in. cookie cutters dipped in flour. Place 1 in. apart on ungreased baking sheets. Bake until the edges begin to brown, 8-10 minutes. Cool for 2 minutes before removing from pans to wire racks. Decorate as desired.
1 cookie: 79 cal., 5g fat (3g sat. fat), 16mg chol., 67mg sod., 9g carb. (4g sugars, 0 fiber), 1g pro.

PBJ ON A STICK

Take the classic peanut butter and jelly sandwich on the go, if you'd like, with this recipe. They also make easy treats for parties.
—Sara Martin, Brookfield, WI

Takes: 10 min. • **Makes:** 4 skewers

- **2 peanut butter and jelly sandwiches**
- **4 wooden skewers (5 to 6 in.)**
- **1 cup seedless red or green grapes**
- **1 small banana, sliced**

Cut sandwiches into 1-in. squares. Alternately thread grapes, sandwich squares and banana slices onto each skewer. Serve immediately.
2 skewers: 415 cal., 14g fat (3g sat. fat), 0 chol., 368mg sod., 63g carb. (30g sugars, 7g fiber), 13g pro.

SPECIAL STUFFED STRAWBERRIES

SPECIAL STUFFED STRAWBERRIES

These sweet bites can be made ahead of time...and they look gorgeous on a platter. I sometimes sprinkle the piped filling with finely chopped pistachio nuts.
—Marcia Orlando, Boyertown, PA

Takes: 20 min. • **Makes:** 2 dozen

- **24 large fresh strawberries**
- **½ cup spreadable strawberry cream cheese**
- **3 Tbsp. sour cream**
- **Graham cracker crumbs**

1. Place strawberries on cutting board and cut off tops; remove bottom tips so they sit flat. Using a small paring knife, hull out the center of each berry.
2. In a small bowl, beat the cream cheese and sour cream until smooth. Pipe or spoon filling into each berry. Top with crushed graham crackers. Refrigerate until serving.
1 strawberry: 18 cal., 1g fat (1g sat. fat), 4mg chol., 22mg sod., 1g carb. (1g sugars, 0 fiber), 1g pro.

FAVORITE CABBAGE SALAD

This cabbage salad has been a favorite for decades. It is easy to make and travels well for potluck suppers. Toss in some shredded carrots or pine nuts for extra crunch.
—Edna Culbertson, Jenison, MI

Prep: 10 min. + chilling • **Makes:** 6 servings

- **1 small head cabbage, shredded**
- **½ cup chopped green pepper**
- **½ cup chopped onion**
- **3 Tbsp. mayonnaise**
- **2 Tbsp. white vinegar**
- **1 Tbsp. sugar**
- **¼ tsp. salt**
- **4 bacon strips, cooked and crumbled**

In a large bowl, combine cabbage, green pepper and onion. In a small bowl, combine mayonnaise, vinegar, sugar and salt. Pour over cabbage mixture and toss to coat. Cover and refrigerate at least 4 hours. Stir in bacon just before serving.
¾ cup: 90 cal., 6g fat (1g sat. fat), 5mg chol., 169mg sod., 8g carb. (5g sugars, 2g fiber), 2g pro.

DIY Easter Egg Dye

In a glass cup, mix ½ cup boiling water, 1 tsp. white vinegar and drops of food coloring to reach desired color.

GARLIC CUCUMBER DIP

Creamy and full of fresh cucumber flavor, this classic dip always makes a popular appetizer. Serve it with pita bread, crackers or veggies.
—Lisa Stavropoulos, Stouffville, ON

Prep: 20 min. + chilling • **Makes:** 2 cups

- **1 large cucumber**
- **¾ cup plain yogurt**
- **¾ cup sour cream**
- **3 Tbsp. olive oil**
- **4½ tsp. minced fresh dill**
- **4½ tsp. red wine vinegar**
- **3 garlic cloves, minced**
- **¼ tsp. salt**
- **Pita bread wedges**

1. Peel cucumber; cut in half lengthwise and scoop out seeds. Grate cucumber; squeeze shreds between paper towels several times to remove excess moisture.
2. Place cucumber in a small bowl; stir in the yogurt, sour cream, oil, dill, vinegar, garlic and salt. Refrigerate until chilled. If desired, drizzle with additional oil and sprinkle with additional dill. Serve with pita wedges.
¼ cup: 111 cal., 10g fat (4g sat. fat), 8mg chol., 93mg sod., 4g carb. (2g sugars, 0 fiber), 2g pro.

EASTER BUNNY TREATS

Our family had fun making these bunny-riffic treats together. They are easy to assemble and almost too adorable to eat!
—Holly Jost, Manitowoc, WI

Takes: 15 min. • **Makes:** 1 dozen

- **⅓ cup vanilla frosting**
- **36 large marshmallows**
- **36 miniature marshmallows**
- **Red and pink heart-shaped decorating sprinkles**
- **Small black nonpareils**
- **White jimmies**
- **Pink colored sugar**

Place frosting in piping bag. Cut 2 mini marshmallows in half and attach to a large marshmallow using frosting to form arms and legs. For face, attach 2 mini marshmallow halves for cheeks. Use white jimmies, black nonpareils and heart-shaped sprinkles to form whiskers, eyes and nose. For the ears, cut a large marshmallow in half diagonally and dip each sticky side in colored sugar; use frosting to attach to the top of the large marshmallow. Use frosting to join the 2 large marshmallows, let stand until dry.
1 treat: 128 cal., 2g fat (1g sat. fat), 0 chol., 48mg sod., 27g carb. (20g sugars, 0 fiber), 0 pro.

EASTER BUNNY TREATS

▲

Easy Egg Designs

Embrace your inner artist with one of these easy techniques to decorate eggs.

1. For a marbled effect, add a few drops of food coloring to a bowl of whipped cream, and swirl using a toothpick. Roll eggs in the rainbow mixture and let sit for 45 minutes to an hour before rinsing in water.

2. To add a message, dip eggs in your choice of homemade or store-bought egg dyes. Let dry, then write words, draw a picture or add a pattern on the egg using an opaque white food-safe marker.

3. To stamp a pattern, use mini rubber stamps—like the flower ones shown here—dipped in food dye poured onto a paper towel or napkin. Make sure you choose tiny stamps so you can see the entire shape.

SPRING HERB PARTY

If you've been considering starting a kitchen herb garden, kick off the project by inviting your favorite gal pals over for an herb swap party. Grab some planters, set out the snacks and dig in. It's so much fun you'll barely be able to herb your enthusiasm!

Rosemary Strawberry Daiquiri (p. 147) **Lime & Dill Chimichurri Shrimp** (p. 149)
Lavender & Lemon Biscochitos (p. 151)

ROSEMARY STRAWBERRY DAIQUIRI

ROSEMARY STRAWBERRY DAIQUIRI

This strawberry daiquiri is a standout with its herbal twist! I used to teach herb classes at our local technical college and everyone enjoyed my segment on herbal cocktails like this one.
—Sue Gronholz, Beaver Dam, WI

Prep: 20 min. + cooling • **Makes:** 8 servings

- **1 cup sugar**
- **1 cup water**
- **4 fresh rosemary sprigs**

EACH SERVING

- **1 cup frozen unsweetened sliced strawberries**
- **1½ oz. white rum**
- **2 Tbsp. lime juice**
- **Whole fresh strawberries**

1. In a small saucepan, bring sugar and water to a boil. Reduce heat; simmer 10 minutes. Remove from heat; add rosemary. Steep, covered, 10-15 minutes according to taste. Discard rosemary. Cool completely. Store in an airtight container in the refrigerator up to 1 month.
2. For each serving, in a blender, combine frozen strawberries, rum, lime juice and 2 Tbsp. rosemary syrup; cover and process until smooth. Pour into chilled glasses; garnish each with a whole strawberry and additional rosemary sprig.
1 serving: 251 cal., 0 fat (0 sat. fat), 0 chol., 1mg sod., 41g carb. (32g sugars, 3g fiber), 0 pro.

TEST KITCHEN TIP

Almost any herb will work in place of the rosemary. Mint, basil and thyme are some of our favorites.

GREEN SALAD WITH TANGY BASIL VINAIGRETTE

GREEN SALAD WITH TANGY BASIL VINAIGRETTE

A tart and tangy dressing turns a basic salad into something special. It works for weeknight dining but is good enough for company and pairs perfectly with just about anything.
—Kristin Rimkus, Snohomish, WA

Takes: 15 min. • **Makes:** 4 servings

- **3 Tbsp. white wine vinegar**
- **4½ tsp. minced fresh basil**
- **4½ tsp. olive oil**
- **1½ tsp. honey**
- **¼ tsp. salt**
- **⅛ tsp. pepper**
- **6 cups torn mixed salad greens**
- **1 cup cherry tomatoes, halved**
- **2 Tbsp. shredded Parmesan cheese**

In a small bowl, whisk the first 6 ingredients until blended. In a large bowl, combine salad greens and tomatoes. Drizzle with vinaigrette; toss to coat. Sprinkle with cheese.
1 cup: 89 cal., 6g fat (1g sat. fat), 2mg chol., 214mg sod., 7g carb. (4g sugars, 2g fiber), 3g pro. **Diabetic exchanges:** 1 vegetable, 1 fat.

THYMED ZUCCHINI SAUTE

Simple and flavorful, this recipe is the way to use all those zucchini taking over the garden. Use your fresh thyme, too!
—Bobby Taylor, Ulster Park, NY

Takes: 15 min. • **Makes:** 4 servings

- **1 Tbsp. olive oil**
- **1 lb. medium zucchini, quartered lengthwise and halved**
- **¼ cup finely chopped onion**
- **½ vegetable bouillon cube, crushed**
- **2 Tbsp. minced fresh parsley**
- **1 tsp. minced fresh thyme or ¼ tsp. dried thyme**

In a large skillet, heat oil over medium-high heat. Add zucchini, onion and bouillon; cook and stir 4-5 minutes or until zucchini is crisp-tender. Sprinkle with herbs.
¾ cup: 53 cal., 4g fat (1g sat. fat), 0 chol., 135mg sod., 5g carb. (2g sugars, 2g fiber), 2g pro. **Diabetic exchanges:** 1 vegetable, ½ fat.

MARJORAM LENTILS

Providing 13 grams of fiber per serving, this delicious medley packs lots of nutrition. Serve with a light meat entree or keep it meatless with a side of cornbread or rice.
—Mildred Sherrer, Fort Worth, TX

Prep: 30 min. • **Cook:** 45 min.
Makes: 6 servings

- **4 medium carrots, chopped**
- **2 medium onions, chopped**
- **6 garlic cloves, minced**
- **1 Tbsp. olive oil**
- **1 can (14½ oz.) vegetable broth**
- **1 cup dried lentils, rinsed**
- **3 Tbsp. minced fresh marjoram or 1 Tbsp. dried marjoram**
- **1½ tsp. rubbed sage**
- **1 can (14½ oz.) diced tomatoes, undrained**
- **¼ cup sherry or additional vegetable broth**
- **¼ cup minced fresh parsley**
- **3 Tbsp. shredded Swiss cheese**

1. In a large nonstick saucepan, saute the carrots, onions and garlic in oil until tender. Stir in the broth, lentils, marjoram and sage. Bring to a boil. Reduce the heat; cover and simmer for 30-45 minutes or until lentils are tender.
2. Stir in the tomatoes, sherry or additional broth, and parsley; heat through. Sprinkle with cheese.
¾ cup: 216 cal., 4g fat (1g sat. fat), 3mg chol., 456mg sod., 34g carb. (9g sugars, 13g fiber), 11g pro. **Diabetic exchanges:** 2 vegetable, 1½ starch, 1 lean meat, ½ fat.

CHICKEN PICCATA WITH LEMON SAUCE

Once you've tried this tangy yet delicate chicken, you won't hesitate to make it for company. Seasoned with Parmesan and parsley, it cooks up golden brown, then is drizzled with a light lemon sauce.
—Susan Pursell, Fountain Valley, CA

Prep: 25 min. • **Cook:** 25 min.
Makes: 8 servings

- **8 boneless skinless chicken breast halves (4 oz. each)**
- **½ cup egg substitute**
- **2 Tbsp. plus ¼ cup dry white wine or chicken broth, divided**
- **5 Tbsp. lemon juice, divided**
- **3 garlic cloves, minced**
- **⅛ tsp. hot pepper sauce**
- **½ cup all-purpose flour**
- **½ cup grated Parmesan cheese**
- **¼ cup minced fresh parsley**
- **½ tsp. salt**
- **3 tsp. olive oil, divided**
- **2 Tbsp. butter**

1. Flatten chicken to ¼-in. thickness. In a shallow dish, combine the egg substitute, 2 Tbsp. wine, 2 Tbsp. lemon juice, garlic and hot pepper sauce. In another shallow dish, combine the flour, Parmesan cheese, parsley and salt. Coat chicken with flour mixture, dip in egg substitute mixture, then coat again with flour mixture.
2. In a large nonstick skillet, in 1½ tsp. oil, brown 4 chicken breast halves for 3-5 minutes on each side or until juices run clear. Remove and keep warm. Drain drippings. Repeat with the remaining chicken and oil. Remove and keep warm.
3. In the same pan, melt butter. Add remaining wine and lemon juice. Bring to a boil. Continue boiling, uncovered, until sauce is reduced by a fourth. Drizzle over chicken.
1 chicken breast half: 232 cal., 9g fat (4g sat. fat), 75mg chol., 346mg sod., 8g carb. (1g sugars, 0 fiber), 27g pro. **Diabetic exchanges:** 3 lean meat, 1 fat, ½ starch.

LIME & DILL CHIMICHURRI SHRIMP

LIME & DILL CHIMICHURRI SHRIMP

Chimichurri is a popular condiment in Argentina and Uruguay, most often used as a dipping sauce or a marinade for meats. My tasty shrimp version incorporates dill and lime, which give it a brighter flavor and makes it ideal for spring and summer entertaining.
—Bonnie Landy, Castro Valley, CA

Prep: 25 min. + standing • **Grill:** 10 min.
Makes: 4 servings

- **½ cup extra virgin olive oil**
- **½ cup packed fresh parsley sprigs**
- **¼ cup snipped fresh dill**
- **¼ cup fresh cilantro leaves**
- **3 Tbsp. lime juice**
- **3 garlic cloves, halved**
- **½ tsp. salt**
- **¼ tsp. pepper**
- **1 lb. uncooked shrimp (26-30 per lb.), peeled and deveined**
- **1 medium red onion, cut into thick wedges**
- **1 medium zucchini, cut into ½-in. pieces**
- **1 medium yellow summer squash, cut into ½-in. pieces**
- **8 cherry tomatoes**
- **Crusty bread**

1. Place the first 8 ingredients in a food processor; process until pureed. Reserve 6 Tbsp. mixture for serving. Place remaining mixture in a bowl; toss with the shrimp and vegetables. Let stand 15 minutes.
2. Alternately thread shrimp and vegetables onto 8 metal or soaked wooden skewers. Grill, covered, over medium heat or broil 4 in. from heat until shrimp turn pink, 3-4 minutes per side. Serve on bed of additional herbs with crusty bread and reserved sauce.
2 kabobs: 316 cal., 22g fat (3g sat. fat), 138mg chol., 371mg sod., 10g carb. (4g sugars, 2g fiber), 21g pro.

LAVENDER & LEMON
BISCOCHITOS

LAVENDER & LEMON BISCOCHITOS

Biscochitos are the state cookie for my home state of New Mexico. They are traditionally made with anise seeds, but I used lavender and lemon for this biscochitos recipe. The result is intriguing and delicious. I have also made these with lemon and dried thyme and they were equally scrumptious.
—Marla Clark, Albuquerque, NM

Prep: 30 min. + chilling • **Bake:** 10 min./batch
Makes: 6 dozen

- **½ cup unsalted butter, softened**
- **⅔ cup sugar**
- **1 large egg, room temperature**
- **1 Tbsp. dried lavender flowers**
- **1 Tbsp. grated lemon zest**
- **1½ cups all-purpose flour**
- **1 tsp. baking powder**
- **¼ tsp. salt**

1. In a large bowl, cream butter and sugar until light and fluffy, 5-7 minutes. Beat in egg, lavender and lemon zest. In another bowl, whisk flour, baking powder and salt; gradually beat into creamed mixture. Divide dough in half. Shape each into a disk; cover and refrigerate 30 minutes or until firm enough to roll.
2. Preheat oven to 350°. On a lightly floured surface, roll each portion of dough to ¼-in. thickness. Cut with a floured 1-in. round cookie cutter. Place cutouts 1 in. apart on parchment-lined baking sheets. Sprinkle with additional sugar.
3. Bake until the bottoms are light brown, 9-11 minutes. Remove from pans to wire racks to cool. Store in airtight containers.

Freeze option: Freeze cookies in freezer containers, separating layers with waxed paper. To use, thaw before serving.
1 cookie: 29 cal., 1g fat (1g sat. fat), 6mg chol., 16mg sod., 4g carb. (2g sugars, 0 fiber), 0 pro.

TEST KITCHEN TIP

If adding fresh herbs or lavender to the top of the cookies, brush cutouts with egg white before gently pressing on fresh herbs. Bake cookies as directed.

CILANTRO PESTO

Feel free to make this simple pesto ahead of time and freeze it. It tastes as fresh as it looks!
—Karen Deaver, Babylon, NY

Takes: 10 min. • **Makes:** 1 cup

- **1 cup fresh cilantro leaves**
- **¼ cup grated Parmesan cheese**
- **¼ cup chopped walnuts**
- **2 Tbsp. lime juice**
- **½ cup olive oil**
- **Cooked jumbo shrimp, peeled and deveined**

Place cilantro and cheese in a food processor; cover and pulse until chopped. Add chopped walnuts and lime juice; cover and process until blended. While processing, gradually add oil in a steady stream. Serve with shrimp.
2 Tbsp.: 152 cal., 16g fat (2g sat. fat), 2mg chol., 40mg sod., 1g carb. (0 sugars, 0 fiber), 1g pro.

TARRAGON BUTTER

This seasoned butter is a delicious way to add great herb flavor and a hint of color to your favorite breads and vegetables.
—Connie Moore, Medway, OH

Takes: 5 min. • **Makes:** 1 cup

- **1 cup butter, softened**
- **2 Tbsp. minced fresh tarragon or 2 tsp. dried tarragon**
- **2 Tbsp. minced fresh parsley**
- **1 tsp. minced chives**
- **1 garlic clove, minced**
- **Dash pepper**

Beat all ingredients until blended. Shape into a log. Wrap and refrigerate up to 1 week or freeze up to several months.
1 Tbsp.: 101 cal., 11g fat (7g sat. fat), 31mg chol., 116mg sod., 0 carb. (0 sugars, 0 fiber), 0 pro.

MINTY MANGO SALSA

I originally made this colorful mango salsa to garnish a smoked turkey my husband made. We have since tried it on chicken and fish. It also makes a fun snack or party appetizer scooped up with your favorite tortilla chips.
—Diane Thompson, Nutrioso, AZ

Prep: 10 min. + chilling
Makes: about 2½ cups

- **1 large ripe mango, peeled and diced**
- **1 medium sweet red pepper, diced**
- **1 can (4 oz.) chopped green chiles**
- **¼ cup chopped green onions**
- **1 Tbsp. lime juice**
- **2 tsp. minced fresh mint**
- **¼ tsp. ground ginger**
- **Tortilla chips**

In a small bowl, combine the mango, pepper, chiles, onion, juice mint and ginger. Cover and refrigerate at least 8 hours. Serve with tortilla chips.
¼ cup: 27 cal., 0 fat (0 sat. fat), 0 chol., 46mg sod., 6g carb. (5g sugars, 1g fiber), 0 pro.
Diabetic exchanges: free food.

The Herb Swap Basics

Assign your fellow green thumbs a type of herb to bring, let 'em swap and pot as they please, then send them on their way with a lush kitchen garden. From there, just add water!

ROLL down brown paper bags and fill them with soil to contain the mess and add rustic flair to your table.

SPRAY-PAINT used veggie cans for simple pots. Be sure to poke holes in the bottom for drainage.

LABEL clothespins with herb names and clip to individual pots.

A PORTABLE BAR CART doubles as a holder for finished planters, clearing table space. When the party's over, roll it to guests' cars for easy transferring.

Invite guests to make their favorite herbs into flavored butters as another take-home treat. Snip, chop and mix into softened butter.

❶ BASIL

FLAVOR: Depending on the variety, you'll notice hints of pepper, mint or anise.

HOW TO USE IT: Pair with mild cheeses, fresh tomatoes and spicy flavors. It's most commonly used in Mediterranean, Asian and Indian dishes. For best results, add at the end of cooking.

❷ CILANTRO

(AKA CORIANDER LEAF)

FLAVOR: Some find this herb bright and refreshing with a zesty flavor. Others detect a mild "soapy" taste for reasons that might be related to human genetics.

HOW TO USE IT: Enjoy cilantro raw or cooked. Its invigorating flavor brings dull sauces to life. Cilantro is a staple of Latin American and Asian cooking.

❸ DILL

FLAVOR: Delicate strands boast a strong clean, fresh earthiness, or a subtle flavor of licorice or fennel.

HOW TO USE IT: Best used in small quantities—too much can overwhelm a dish—dill works well in spring salads and pairs well with vegetables like asparagus and peas. It's also a delicious addition to homemade salad dressings.

❹ THYME

FLAVOR: This is a pungent herb with a slightly sweet and woodsy flavor. The leaves are aromatic and floral, strong but with an understated taste.

HOW TO USE IT: A staple in French cooking, thyme works well with poultry dishes and strong cheeses. Or use it in breads, desserts and drinks.

How to Preserve Herbs

Growing fresh herbs like basil, cilantro, rosemary, thyme and others is a smart idea for cost-conscious cooks. Here's how to preserve them for optimal flavor year-round—and make the most of your harvest.

STORE FRESH HERBS
Wrap fresh herbs in a slightly damp paper towel, place in an airtight container. Store in the refrigerator for 5-7 days.

FREEZE FRESH HERBS
Chop fresh herbs and fill the empty sections of an ice cube tray with them. Carefully pour water into each herb-filled compartment and freeze.

DRY FRESH HERBS
Snip healthy branches and remove the leaves from the bottom inch of each stem. Bundle several stems together with string or a rubber band, and hang upside down in a warm, airy room. Check the herbs weekly until they're completely dry. Crumble the leaves into spice jars.

SPECIAL CELEBRATIONS

We spend so much time planning the big holidays and grand parties—it's easy to forget life's smaller, but equally important, moments. This year turn every occasion into a memorable event. From festive Mardi Gras and St. Patrick's Day celebrations to casual backyard barbecues and beach picnics, there is always a reason to gather with family and friends for fun and, of course, good food!

NEW YEAR'S EVE PARTY

There's no better way to kick off another trip around the sun than with an all-out New Year's Eve bash. This year, it's all about bubbles, bling and the best bites. So load up your plate, toss some confetti and raise your glass to the most epic party yet!

Honey Champagne Fondue (p. 160) **Mango Bellini** (p. 162) **Champagne Blondies** (p. 164)

GREEK SHRIMP CANAPES

GREEK SHRIMP CANAPES

I grew up by the ocean and then moved to a land-locked state. I created this recipe to share my love of seafood with my new friends and neighbors. It quickly became a favorite. You can lighten it up by using reduced-fat cream cheese.
—Amy Harris, Springville, UT

Prep: 15 min. • **Cook:** 65 min.
Makes: about 2½ dozen

- **1½ cups olive oil**
- **¾ cup lemon juice**
- **⅔ cup dry white wine**
- **¼ cup Greek seasoning**
- **4 garlic cloves, minced**
- **1 lb. uncooked shrimp (31-40 per lb.), peeled and deveined**
- **2 large cucumbers**
- **1 pkg. (8 oz.) cream cheese, softened**
- **Minced fresh parsley**

1. In a large bowl, whisk the first 5 ingredients until blended. Pour 1½ cups marinade into a large bowl. Add shrimp and stir to coat. Cover and refrigerate 45 minutes.
2. Meanwhile, pour remaining marinade in a 4- or 5-qt. slow cooker. Cook, covered, on high, 45 minutes. Drain shrimp, discarding marinade in bowl. Add shrimp to slow cooker. Cook, covered, on high until shrimp turn pink, about 20 minutes, stirring once; drain.
3. Cut each cucumber into ¼-in.-thick slices. Scoop out centers, leaving bottoms intact. Pipe cream cheese onto each cucumber slice; top with shrimp and parsley.
1 canape: 68 cal., 6g fat (2g sat. fat), 26mg chol., 139mg sod., 1g carb. (1g sugars, 0 fiber), 3g pro.

TEST KITCHEN TIP

For a brighter flavor, garnish these canapes with fresh mint instead of parsley. Instead of plain cream cheese, use your favorite variety of flavored cream cheese. If you're in a rush, skip scooping out the centers of the cucumber slices. While creating a shallow indention is helpful, it is not essential.

CRUDITE DIP

CRUDITE DIP

Vegetable crudite is an assortment of raw, crisp veggies paired with a dipping sauce like this tangy, sour cream-based dip. To bring out the dip's full flavor, chill before serving. This will allow the flavors time to blend.
—Taste of Home *Test Kitchen*

Prep: 5 min. + chilling • **Makes:** 1½ cups

- **1 cup sour cream**
- **½ cup mayonnaise**
- **2 green onions, finely chopped**
- **1 Tbsp. lemon juice**
- **1 Tbsp. minced fresh parsley**
- **1 tsp. dill weed**
- **1 garlic clove, minced**
- **½ tsp. seasoned salt**
- **⅛ tsp. pepper**
- **Assorted fresh vegetables**

Combine the first 9 ingredients; mix well. Cover and refrigerate at least 2 hours. If desired, sprinkle with additional parsley. Serve with vegetables.
2 Tbsp.: 102 cal., 11g fat (3g sat. fat), 5mg chol., 117mg sod., 1g carb. (1g sugars, 0 fiber), 1g pro.

FRUIT & CHEESE BOARD

Who says cheese and sausage get to have all the fun? Make a party platter with a combo of seasonal fruits. It will be a new favorite!
—Taste of Home *Test Kitchen*

Takes: 25 minutes • **Makes:** 14 servings

- **10 fresh strawberries, halved**
- **8 fresh or dried figs, halved**
- **2 small navel oranges, thinly sliced**
- **12 oz. seedless red grapes (about 1½ cups)**
- **1 medium mango, halved and scored**
- **½ cup fresh blueberries**
- **1 cup fresh blackberries**
- **½ cup dried banana chips**
- **2 large kiwifruit, peeled, halved and thinly sliced**
- **12 oz. seedless watermelon (about 6 slices)**
- **½ cup unblanched almonds**
- **8 oz. Brie cheese**
- **8 oz. mascarpone cheese**
- **½ cup honey**

On a large platter or cutting board, arrange fruit, almonds and cheeses. Place honey in a small jar; tuck jar among fruit.
1 serving: 304 cal., 17g fat (8g sat. fat), 36mg chol., 116mg sod., 36g carb. (30g sugars, 4g fiber), 7g pro.

MUSHROOM & OLIVE BRUSCHETTA

I tasted this delicious bruschetta at a party and knew I had to make it. Since I couldn't find the person who brought the dish, I did my best to duplicate it from memory. The original was made on an English muffin, but party rye or baguette slices work as well.
—Lynne German, Buford, GA

Prep: 15 min. • **Bake:** 10 min. • **Makes:** 4 dozen

- **1½ cups finely shredded cheddar cheese**
- **½ cup canned mushroom stems and pieces, drained and chopped**
- **½ cup chopped green onions**
- **½ cup chopped pitted green olives**
- **½ cup chopped ripe olives**
- **½ cup mayonnaise**
- **¼ tsp. curry powder**
- **2 French bread baguettes (10½ oz. each), cut into ½-in. slices**
- **Julienned green onions, optional**

1. Preheat oven to 400°. In a large bowl, combine the first 7 ingredients. Cut each baguette into 24 slices; place on ungreased baking sheets. Bake until lightly toasted, 5 minutes.
2. Top with cheese mixture. Bake until cheese is melted, 4-5 minutes. If desired, top with julienned green onions.
Freeze option: Cover and freeze unbaked topped baguette slices on a parchment-lined baking sheet until firm. Transfer to a freezer container; return to freezer. To use, bake baguette slices on ungreased baking sheets in a preheated 400° oven until heated through, 8-10 minutes.
1 appetizer: 66 cal., 3g fat (1g sat. fat), 4mg chol., 161mg sod., 7g carb. (0 sugars, 0 fiber), 2g pro.

HONEY CHAMPAGNE FONDUE

This champagne fondue has wonderful flavor from Swiss cheese and a hint of sweetness from honey. It clings well to any kind of dipper.
—Shannon Copley, Upper Arlington, OH

Takes: 30 min. • **Makes:** 4 cups

- **1 Tbsp. cornstarch**
- **1 tsp. ground mustard**
- **¼ tsp. white pepper**
- **1¼ cups champagne**
- **1 tsp. lemon juice**
- **2 Tbsp. finely chopped shallot**
- **1 garlic clove, minced**
- **1½ lbs. Swiss cheese, shredded**
- **2 Tbsp. honey**
- **Pinch ground nutmeg**
- **Toasted French bread, asparagus, tart apple slices, endive spears or cooked shrimp**

1. In a large saucepan, combine cornstarch, ground mustard and white pepper. Whisk in champagne and lemon juice until smooth. Add shallot and garlic; bring to a boil. Reduce heat to medium-low; cook and stir until thickened, about 1 minute. Gradually stir in cheese until melted. Stir in honey. Sprinkle with nutmeg.
2. Keep warm in a fondue pot or small slow cooker. Serve with toasted French bread, asparagus, apple slices, endive or cooked shrimp as desired.
¼ cup: 256 cal., 18g fat (10g sat. fat), 53mg chol., 107mg sod., 5g carb. (3g sugars, 0 fiber), 15g pro.

HONEY CHAMPAGNE FONDUE

▲

Fondue-Making Tips

- Cheese melts faster and easier if it is shredded, grated or cut into small cubes. Cooking spray keeps the cheese from sticking to the cheese grater, making cleanup easy.
- Add a little cornstarch to the shredded cheese to help the cheese bind with the wine or broth.
- Reduce the heat to low before setting the cheese into hot liquids one handful at a time. Keep the heat at low while the cheese melts.
- Cheese fondues are often made with white wine. If you don't wish to use wine, substitute vegetable or chicken broth.
- Stir in seasonings, herbs or spices after all the cheese has melted to a smooth consistency.

MANGO BELLINI

MANGO BELLINI

Simple yet delicious, this Bellini is made with fresh mango puree and your favorite sparkling wine—Prosecco is my top choice. You can easily turn it into a mocktail by using sparkling water in place of the champagne or Prosecco.
—Ellen Folkman, Crystal Beach, FL

Takes: 5 min. • **Makes:** 6 servings

- **¾ cup mango nectar or fresh mango puree, chilled**
- **1 bottle (750 ml) champagne or other sparkling wine, chilled**

Add 2 Tbsp. mango nectar to each of 6 champagne flutes. Top with champagne; gently stir to combine.

⅔ cup: 101 cal., 0 fat (0 sat. fat), 0 chol., 1mg sod., 6g carb. (4g sugars, 0 fiber), 0 pro.

ORANGE CRANBERRY SPLASH

I created this citrusy cocktail while tending bar on the Jersey Shore. For a festive touch, garnish each glass with fresh cranberries.
—Ralph Florio, New York, NY

Takes: 10 min. • **Makes:** 6 servings

- **3 cups lemon-lime soda**
- **¾ cup orange-flavored vodka**
- **½ cup cranberry juice**
- **6 Tbsp. Triple Sec**
- **Ice cubes**

GARNISH

- **Fresh cranberries**

In a pitcher, combine the soda, vodka, juice and Triple Sec. Serve over ice. Garnish with cranberries.

¾ cup: 177 cal., 0 fat (0 sat. fat), 0 chol., 15mg sod., 22g carb. (21g sugars, 0 fiber), 0 pro.

SPICY CRAB SALAD TAPAS

I served these at a party and everyone went wild! These savory morsels have a crispy flaky exterior filled with creamy sweet crab that has a little kick. I used scalloped edge cookie cutters to cut my pastry, but a small biscuit cutter works, too.
—Vanessa Mason, Summerdale, AL

Prep: 35 min. + chilling
Bake: 20 min. + cooling
Makes: about 2 dozen

- **1 can (16 oz.) lump crabmeat, drained**
- **¼ cup finely chopped sweet red pepper**
- **¼ cup finely chopped sweet yellow pepper**
- **¼ cup finely chopped green onions**
- **1 jalapeno pepper, seeded and finely chopped**
- **1 Tbsp. minced fresh cilantro**
- **1 Tbsp. lemon juice**
- **2 garlic cloves, minced**
- **1 tsp. ground mustard**
- **½ cup mayonnaise**
- **½ tsp. salt**
- **¼ tsp. pepper**
- **1 pkg. (17.3 oz.) frozen puff pastry, thawed**
- **1 large egg**
- **1 Tbsp. water**
- **Optional: Minced fresh parsley and seafood seasoning**

1. Preheat oven to 375°. Combine the first 12 ingredients. Refrigerate, covered, at least 1 hour.
2. Meanwhile, on a lightly floured surface, unfold puff pastry. Roll each pastry into a 10-in. square; cut each into twenty-five 2-in. squares. Using a round 1½-in. cookie cutter, cut out the centers of half the puff pastry squares. Whisk egg and water; brush over pastry. Place cutout squares on top of solid squares and transfer to parchment-lined baking sheets.
3. Bake until golden brown, about 18 minutes. Cool to room temperature. Once cool, spoon 1 heaping Tbsp. crab salad into center of each cooked pastry. If desired, top with minced parsley and seasoning. Serve immediately.

1 appetizer: 145 cal., 9g fat (2g sat. fat), 25mg chol., 240mg sod., 11g carb. (0 sugars, 2g fiber), 5g pro.

SPICY CRAB SALAD TAPAS

CHAMPAGNE BLONDIES

I was looking for a recipe that incorporated champagne to take as a treat to a friend's bridal shower. I couldn't find one I liked, so I came up with this fun twist on blondies. The recipe calls for white baking chips, but feel free to use butterscotch or chocolate if you like.
—*Heather Karow, Burnett, WI*

Prep: 25 min. • **Bake:** 25 min. + cooling
Makes: 16 servings

- **½ cup butter, softened**
- **1 cup packed light brown sugar**
- **1 large egg, room temperature**
- **¼ cup champagne**
- **1¼ cups all-purpose flour**
- **1 tsp. baking powder**
- **¼ tsp. salt**
- **½ cup white baking chips**
- **½ cup chopped hazelnuts, optional**

GLAZE

- **1 cup confectioners' sugar**
- **2 Tbsp. champagne**

1. Preheat oven to 350°. Line an 8-in. square baking pan with parchment, letting ends extend up sides. In a large bowl, beat the butter and brown sugar until crumbly, about 2 minutes. Beat in the egg and champagne (batter may appear curdled). In another bowl, whisk flour, baking powder and salt; gradually add to butter mixture. Fold in the baking chips and if desired, nuts.
2. Spread into prepared pan. Bake until the edges are brown and the center is set (do not overbake), 25-30 minutes. Cool completely in pan on a wire rack.
3. Combine glaze ingredients; drizzle over blondies. Lifting with parchment, remove blondies from pan. Cut into bars. Store in an airtight container.

1 blondie: 203 cal., 8g fat (5g sat. fat), 28mg chol., 126mg sod., 32g carb. (24g sugars, 0 fiber), 2g pro.

CHAMPAGNE BLONDIES

OREO CUPCAKES WITH COOKIES & CREAM FROSTING

OREO CUPCAKES WITH COOKIES & CREAM FROSTING

Kids and adults alike won't be able to resist these cupcakes. Be sure to thoroughly crush the Oreos in the frosting so it's easy to pipe.
—Taste of Home *Test Kitchen*

Prep: 20 min. • **Bake:** 20 min. + cooling
Makes: 2 dozen

- ⅔ **cup butter, softened**
- 1¾ **cups sugar**
- 2 **large eggs, room temperature**
- 1½ **tsp. vanilla extract**
- 2½ **cups all-purpose flour**
- 2½ **tsp. baking powder**
- ½ **tsp. salt**
- 1¼ **cups 2% milk**
- 2 **cups coarsely crushed Oreo cookies**

FROSTING

- 1 **cup butter, softened**
- 3 **cups confectioners' sugar**
- 2 **Tbsp. 2% milk**
- 1 **tsp. vanilla extract**
- 1½ **cups finely crushed Oreo cookie crumbs**
- 24 **mini Oreo cookies**

1. Preheat oven to 350°. Line 24 muffin cups with paper liners.

2. In a large bowl, cream butter and sugar until light and fluffy, 5-7 minutes. Adds eggs, 1 at a time, beating well after each addition. Beat in vanilla. In another bowl, whisk flour, baking powder and salt; add to creamed mixture alternately with milk, beating well after each addition. Fold in crushed cookies.

3. Fill prepared cups three-fourths full. Bake 20-22 minutes or until a toothpick inserted in center comes out clean. Cool in pans for 10 minutes before removing to wire racks to cool completely.

4. In a large bowl, combine the butter, confectioners' sugar, milk and vanilla; beat until smooth. Fold in cookie crumbs. Pipe or spread frosting over cupcakes. If desired, sprinkle with additional cookie crumbs and garnish with mini Oreo cookies.

1 cupcake: 411 cal., 19g fat (10g sat. fat), 51mg chol., 346mg sod., 58g carb. (40g sugars, 2g fiber), 4g pro.

MARDI GRAS

Mardi Gras—translated as Fat Tuesday—is the ultimate celebration with some of the best party food around: Cajun and Creole dishes, tropical drinks, paczkis and the famous king cake—baby included! This chapter will show you how to throw your best Mardi Gras party yet.

Traditional New Orleans King Cake (p. 174)

HEARTY RED BEANS & RICE

HEARTY RED BEANS & RICE

I take this dish to many potlucks and never fail to bring home an empty pot. I learned about the mouthwatering combination of meats, beans and seasonings while working for the Navy in New Orleans. If you want to get a head start, cover the beans with the water and let soak overnight. Drain them the next day and continue with the recipe as directed.
—Kathy Jacques, Summerfield, FL

Prep: 15 min. + soaking • **Cook:** 2 hours
Makes: 10 servings

- 1 **lb. dried kidney beans**
- 2 **tsp. garlic salt**
- 1 **tsp. Worcestershire sauce**
- ¼ **tsp. hot pepper sauce**
- 1 **qt. water**
- ½ **lb. fully cooked ham, diced**
- ½ **lb. fully cooked smoked sausage, diced**
- 1 **cup chopped onion**
- ½ **cup chopped celery**
- 3 **garlic cloves, minced**
- 1 **can (8 oz.) tomato sauce**
- 2 **bay leaves**
- ¼ **cup minced fresh parsley**
- ½ **tsp. salt**
- ½ **tsp. pepper**
- **Hot cooked rice**

1. Place kidney beans in a Dutch oven; add water to cover by 2 in. Bring to a boil; boil for 2 minutes. Remove from the heat; cover and let stand until beans are softened, 1-4 hours.
2. Drain beans and discard liquid. Add the garlic salt, Worcestershire sauce, hot pepper sauce and water; bring to a boil. Reduce heat; cover and simmer for 1½ hours.
3. Meanwhile, in a large skillet, saute ham and sausage until lightly browned. Remove with a slotted spoon to bean mixture. Saute onion and celery in drippings until tender. Add garlic; cook 1 minute longer. Add to bean mixture. Stir in tomato sauce and bay leaves. Cover and simmer for 30 minutes or until the beans are tender.
4. Discard bay leaves. Measure 2 cups beans; mash and return to the bean mixture. Stir in the parsley, salt and pepper. Serve over hot cooked rice.
1 cup: 276 cal., 9g fat (3g sat. fat), 27mg chol., 1149mg sod., 32g carb. (4g sugars, 8g fiber), 18g pro.

CRAWFISH ETOUFFEE

CRAWFISH ETOUFFEE

I serve this Cajun sensation when I entertain. Etouffee is typically served with shellfish over rice and is similar to gumbo. This dish has its roots in New Orleans and the bayou country of Louisiana.
—Tamra Duncan, Lincoln, AR

Prep: 15 min. • **Cook:** 50 min.
Makes: 8 servings

- ½ **cup butter, cubed**
- ½ **cup plus 2 Tbsp. all-purpose flour**
- 1¼ **cups chopped celery**
- 1 **cup chopped green pepper**
- ½ **cup chopped green onions**
- 1 **can (14½ oz.) chicken broth**
- 1 **cup water**
- ¼ **cup minced fresh parsley**
- 1 **Tbsp. tomato paste**
- 1 **bay leaf**
- ½ **tsp. salt**
- ¼ **tsp. pepper**
- ¼ **tsp. cayenne pepper**
- 2 **lbs. frozen cooked crawfish tail meat, thawed**
- **Hot cooked rice**

1. In a large heavy skillet, melt butter; stir in flour. Cook and stir over low heat for about 20 minutes until mixture is a caramel-colored paste. Add the celery, pepper and onions; stir until coated. Add the broth, water, parsley, tomato paste, bay leaf, salt, pepper and cayenne pepper. Bring to a boil.
2. Reduce heat; cover and simmer 30 minutes, stirring occasionally. Discard bay leaf. Add the crawfish and heat through. Serve with rice.
1 cup: 250 cal., 13g fat (7g sat. fat), 187mg chol., 579mg sod., 10g carb. (1g sugars, 1g fiber), 22g pro.

TEST KITCHEN TIP

Try this etouffee with cooked penne pasta instead of rice. You can mix it all together or just serve it over the pasta. Also, you can add a bit more tomato paste for a deeper color and more cayenne pepper to raise the heat level if you like.

PACZKI

My mom used to make these when I was growing up. She filled them with apricot or raspberry jam, but I enjoy them with prune.
—Lisa Kaminski, Wauwatosa, WI

Prep: 35 min. + rising • **Cook:** 5 min./batch
Makes: 2 dozen

- **1¼ cups sugar, divided**
- **1 pkg. (¼ oz.) active dry yeast**
- **1 tsp. salt**
- **3¼ to 3¾ cups all-purpose flour**
- **¾ cup 2% milk**
- **¼ cup shortening**
- **¼ cup water**
- **1 large egg, room temperature**
- **Oil for deep-fat frying**
- **1 cup seedless raspberry jam**

1. In a large bowl, mix ¼ cup sugar, yeast, salt and 2 cups flour. In a small saucepan, heat milk, shortening and water to 120°-130°. Add to dry ingredients; beat on medium speed 2 minutes. Add the egg; beat on high 2 minutes. Stir in enough remaining flour to form a soft dough (dough will be sticky).
2. Turn dough onto a floured surface; knead until smooth and elastic, 6-8 minutes. Place in a greased bowl, turning once to grease the top. Cover and let rise in a warm place until doubled, about 1 hour.
3. Punch down dough. Turn onto a lightly floured surface; roll to ½-in. thickness. Cut with a floured 3-in. round cutter. Place 2 in. apart on greased baking sheets. Cover and let rise in a warm place until nearly doubled, about 1 hour.
4. In an electric skillet or deep fryer, heat oil to 375°. Fry doughnuts, a few at a time, until golden brown, 2-3 minutes on each side. Drain on paper towels. Cool slightly; roll doughnuts in remaining 1 cup sugar.
5. Cut a small hole in the tip of a pastry bag; insert a small pastry tip. Fill bag with jam. With a small knife, pierce a hole into the side of each doughnut; fill with jam.
1 doughnut: 183 cal., 6g fat (1g sat. fat), 8mg chol., 105mg sod., 30g carb. (17g sugars, 1g fiber), 2g pro.

MUFFULETTA

The sandwich, which originated in New Orleans, is named after the round, crusty Sicilian loaf of bread it's traditionally served on. While I favor my own olive salad, there are several very good commercially-produced versions available in most supermarkets.
—Lou Sansevero, Ferron, UT

Prep: 30 min. + chilling • **Makes:** 8 servings

- **1 cup pimiento-stuffed olives, chopped**
- **¾ cup olive oil**
- **1 celery rib, finely chopped**
- **½ cup sliced pepperoncini, chopped**
- **½ cup pitted Greek olives, chopped**
- **¼ cup cocktail onions, drained and chopped**
- **¼ cup red wine vinegar**
- **2 Tbsp. capers, drained**
- **3 garlic cloves, minced**
- **1 tsp. dried oregano**
- **1 tsp. dried basil**
- **¾ tsp. pepper**
- **½ tsp. kosher salt**
- **½ tsp. celery seed**
- **1 round loaf (1 lb.) unsliced Italian bread**
- **½ lb. thinly sliced Genoa salami**
- **½ lb. thinly sliced deli ham**
- **½ lb. sliced mortadella**
- **½ lb. sliced Swiss cheese**
- **½ lb. sliced provolone cheese**

1. In a large bowl, combine the first 14 ingredients. Cover and refrigerate at least 8 hours.
2. Cut bread in half horizontally; carefully hollow out top and bottom, leaving a 1-in. shell (discard removed bread or save for another use). Spoon half of olive mixture over bottom half of bread. Layer with salami, ham, mortadella, Swiss and provolone cheeses; top with remaining olive mixture. Replace bread top. Wrap tightly. Refrigerate at least 3 hours or overnight. Cut into 8 wedges.
1 slice: 762 cal., 59g fat (18g sat. fat), 103mg chol., 2326mg sod., 25g carb. (2g sugars, 2g fiber), 35g pro.

MUFFULETTA

Throw a Mardi Gras Party

Mardi Gras is famous for its vibrant colors and delicious Louisiana-inspired cuisine. Even if you're hundreds of miles from New Orleans, it's easy to host a Mardi Gras bash that will bring the celebration to you.

DECORATIONS

Mardi Gras is known for its bright, tricolor decorations. The traditional colors are purple to symbolize justice, green to symbolize faith and gold to symbolize power, and any good party will decorate using this color scheme. Place purple, green and gold balloons in the party area. Or look for a Mardi Gras pinata at your local party store.

Don't forget the bead necklaces. The shiny necklaces are a staple at Mardi Gras parades, and your guests will have a blast layering them on.

FOOD

Good food is a must for Mardi Gras—after all, it literally means Fat Tuesday! You'll definitely want to serve up some New Orleans flavor to pay homage to the event's cultural roots. This could be heaping platters of beans and rice, bowls of jambalaya or gumbo, or a delicious seafood dish. And, of course, you can't forget the traditional New Orleans king cake! See page 174 for more fun facts about king cake.

ACTIVITIES

Keep the party going with these fun Mardi Gras games and activities:

- **Mask Decorating:** Masquerade masks are another Mardi Gras tradition, so why not create a mask-decorating station? You'll need plain masks and decorating supplies like paint, glue, glitter and feathers.

- **Selfie contest:** Create a list of fun and silly selfies—with the King Cake baby, wearing at least 10 necklaces, etc. At the end of the party, the person who completed the most selfies gets a prize.

- **Pin the Mask on the Jester:** Put a festive twist on the old-time game of pin the tail on the donkey by purchasing or printing a cutout of a Mardi Gras jester. Blindfold guests and have them take turns pinning the mask on the jester's face.

NEW ORLEANS STYLE
STEWED CHICKEN

NEW ORLEANS STYLE STEWED CHICKEN

This spicy stew is a lot like gumbo, but boasts big chunks of meat. Don't let the long recipe trick you into thinking it's difficult to cook. Most of the ingredients are herbs and spices you likely have stocked in your pantry.
—Eric Olsson, Macomb, MI

Prep: 45 min. • **Cook:** 1 hour
Makes: 4 servings

- 1 **Tbsp. dried parsley flakes**
- 2 **tsp. salt**
- 1¼ **tsp. pepper, divided**
- 1⅛ **tsp. dried thyme, divided**
- 1 **tsp. garlic powder**
- 1 **tsp. onion powder**
- ¼ **tsp. white pepper**
- ¼ **tsp. cayenne pepper**
- ¼ **tsp. rubbed sage**
- 1 **lb. chicken drumsticks**
- 1 **lb. bone-in chicken thighs**
- 2 **Tbsp. plus ½ cup bacon drippings or olive oil, divided**
- ½ **cup all-purpose flour**
- ½ **lb. sliced fresh mushrooms**
- 1 **medium onion, chopped**
- 1 **medium green pepper, chopped**
- 1 **celery rib, chopped**
- 1 **jalapeno pepper, seeded and finely chopped**
- 4 **garlic cloves, minced**
- 4 **cups chicken stock**
- 4 **green onions, finely chopped**
- 5 **drops hot pepper sauce**
- **Hot cooked rice**

1. In a small bowl, mix parsley, salt, 1 tsp. pepper, 1 tsp. thyme, garlic powder, onion powder, white pepper, cayenne and sage; rub over chicken. In a Dutch oven, brown chicken in 2 Tbsp. bacon drippings in batches; remove chicken from pan.
2. Add remaining ½ cup bacon drippings to the same pan; stir in flour until blended. Cook and stir over medium-low heat for 30 minutes or until browned (do not burn). Add the mushrooms, onion, green pepper and celery; cook and stir for 2-3 minutes or until the vegetables are crisp-tender. Add jalapeno pepper, garlic and remaining ⅛ tsp. thyme; cook 1 minute longer.
3. Gradually add stock. Return chicken to pan. Bring to a boil. Reduce the heat; cover and simmer until the chicken is very tender, about 1 hour.
4. Skim fat. Stir in green onions, pepper sauce and remaining ¼ tsp. pepper. Serve with rice.
1 serving: 680 cal., 48g fat (17g sat. fat), 131mg chol., 1847mg sod., 23g carb. (5g sugars, 3g fiber), 38g pro.

SAZERAC

This drink was homegrown in New Orleans in the 1830s by a French Quarter pharmacist named Antione Peychaud. It was originally made with cognac, but when the French liqueur became difficult to procure, rye whiskey took its place and has been the main ingredient ever since.
—Taste of Home *Test Kitchen*

Takes: 5 min. • **Makes:** 1 serving

- **Ice cubes**
- 1 **sugar cube**
- ½ **tsp. water**
- 2 **dashes Peychaud's bitters**
- 1 **dash Angostura bitters**
- 2 **oz. rye whiskey**
- 1 **tsp. absinthe, Herbsaint or other anise-flavored liqueur**
- 1 **lemon zest strip**

Fill a rocks glass with ice; set aside. In another rocks glass, muddle sugar cube, water and bitters until sugar is dissolved. Fill with ice and stir in rye whiskey. Discard ice from other rocks glass. Swirl with absinthe; pour out excess. Strain whiskey mixture into prepared glass. Twist lemon zest over drink to release oils; add to glass.
1 serving: 148 cal., 0 fat (0 sat. fat), 0 chol., 1mg sod., 5g carb. (4g sugars, 0 fiber), 0 pro.

VIRGIN HURRICANES

Revelers of all ages can enjoy a nonalcoholic version of the punchlike refresher that's often called Mardi Gras in a glass. Adults who want a more authentic flavor can mix in rum.
—Taste of Home *Test Kitchen*

Takes: 10 min.
Makes: 9 servings

- 2 **cups passion fruit juice**
- 1 **cup unsweetened pineapple juice**
- 1 **cup orange juice**
- ¾ **cup lemon juice**
- 2 **cups carbonated water**
- **Ice cubes**
- **Pineapple wedges and maraschino cherries**

Combine the juices in a pitcher. Just before serving, stir in carbonated water. Pour into hurricane or highball glasses filled with ice. Garnish with pineapple wedges and cherries.
¾ cup: 61 cal., 0 fat (0 sat. fat), 0 chol., 6mg sod., 15g carb. (12g sugars, 0 fiber), 0 pro.
Diabetic exchanges: 1 fruit.

NEW ORLEANS BEIGNETS

These sweet French doughnuts are square instead of round and have no hole in the middle. They're a traditional part of breakfast in New Orleans.
—Beth Dawson, Jackson, LA

Prep: 25 min. + chilling • **Cook:** 5 min./batch
Makes: 4 dozen

- 1 **pkg. (¼ oz.) active dry yeast**
- ¼ **cup warm water (110° to 115°)**
- 1 **cup evaporated milk**
- ½ **cup canola oil**
- ¼ **cup sugar**
- 1 **large egg, room temperature**
- 4½ **cups self-rising flour**
- **Oil for deep-fat frying**
- **Confectioners' sugar**

1. In a large bowl, dissolve yeast in warm water. Add evaporated milk, oil, sugar, egg and 2 cups flour. Beat until smooth. Stir in enough remaining flour to form a soft dough (dough will be sticky). Do not knead. Cover and refrigerate overnight.
2. Punch dough down. Turn onto a floured surface; roll into a 16x12-in. rectangle. Cut into 2-in. squares.
3. In a deep cast-iron or electric skillet, heat 1 in. oil to 375°. Fry squares, in batches, until golden brown on both sides. Drain on paper towels. Roll warm beignets in confectioners' sugar to coat.
1 beignet: 104 cal., 5g fat (1g sat. fat), 6mg chol., 142mg sod., 14g carb. (5g sugars, 0 fiber), 2g pro.

The Meaning Behind the King Cake

A traditional Mardi Gras celebration isn't complete without a king cake. King cake—also known as three kings cake or *galette des rois* in French—is a sweet pastry made with a cinnamon swirl and coated in thick frosting decorated with colorful sugar sprinkles. But there is something special about a king cake that goes beyond its ingredients. It has a toy baby inside.

WHY IS THERE A BABY?

The baby is a symbol of good luck and prosperity in the coming year. Only one is hidden inside the cake, and the lucky finder is dubbed king or queen for the evening. Along with bragging rights, becoming king cake royalty means you're in charge of making—or buying—the cake for the next year's Fat Tuesday celebration.

THE HISTORY BEHIND THE TOY

The baby inside symbolizes baby Jesus. The tradition originated centuries ago in areas such as France and Spain, where wreath-shaped cakes were eaten on King's Day (Jan. 6) to honor the three kings in the Nativity story. They were much more simple than the elaborate green, yellow and purple creations you'd find in the French Quarter today. When European emigrants made their way to America, they brought along the recipe.

By the 19th century, king cake had become a staple dessert for Mardi Gras celebrations and would be served at the New Orleans' annual King's Ball. That's when bakers began to hide objects inside the cake, usually a fava bean but sometimes a pecan or even a gold ring. Whoever found the hidden treasure would be named the king or queen of the ball.

Fast forward to the 1940. A traveling salesman happened to have a surplus of porcelain babies while traveling in New Orleans. He suggested the idea of hiding the babies in cakes to the most successful commercial bakery at the time, McKenzie's Bakery. The idea stuck, with plastic babies later replacing porcelain figures.

So use extra care when choosing your slice of king cake this Mardi Gras. You may end up with a forkful of good luck!

TRADITIONAL NEW ORLEANS KING CAKE

Get in on the fun of king cake. Let guests know you've hidden a little toy baby in the cake. Whoever finds it has one year of good luck!
—Rebecca Baird, Salt Lake City, UT

Prep: 40 min. + rising
Bake: 25 min. + cooling
Makes: 1 cake (12 slices)

2 pkg. (¼ oz. each) active dry yeast
½ cup warm water (110° to 115°)
¾ cup sugar, divided
½ cup butter, softened
½ cup warm 2% milk (110° to 115°)
2 large egg yolks, room temperature
1¼ tsp. salt
1 tsp. grated lemon zest
¼ tsp. ground nutmeg
3¼ to 3¾ cups all-purpose flour
1 tsp. ground cinnamon
1 large egg, beaten

GLAZE

1½ cups confectioners' sugar
2 tsp. lemon juice
2 to 3 Tbsp. water
Green, purple and yellow sugars

1. In a large bowl, dissolve yeast in warm water. Add ½ cup sugar, butter, milk, egg yolks, salt, lemon zest, nutmeg and 2 cups flour. Beat until smooth. Stir in enough remaining flour to form a soft dough (dough will be sticky).
2. Turn onto a floured surface; knead until smooth and elastic, 6-8 minutes. Place in a greased bowl, turning once to grease the top. Cover and let rise in a warm place until doubled, about 1 hour.
3. Punch dough down. Turn onto a lightly floured surface. Roll dough into a 16x10-in. rectangle. Combine cinnamon and remaining sugar; sprinkle over dough to within ½ in. of edges. Roll up jelly-roll style, starting with a long side; pinch seam to seal. Place seam side down on a greased baking sheet; pinch ends together to form a ring. Cover and let rise until doubled, about 1 hour. Brush with egg.
4. Bake at 375° for 25-30 minutes or until golden brown. Cool completely on a wire rack. For glaze, combine the confectioners' sugar, lemon juice and enough water to achieve desired consistency. Spread over cake. Sprinkle with colored sugars.

1 slice: 321 cal., 9g fat (5g sat. fat), 73mg chol., 313mg sod., 55g carb. (28g sugars, 1g fiber), 5g pro.

CREOLE-SPICED SHRIMP PO'BOYS

My father is Cajun, and I grew up eating all kinds of Cajun food. This recipe makes me think of happy childhood memories. Sometimes I use oysters or crawfish instead of—or in addition to—the shrimp.
—Stacey Johnson, Bonney Lake, WA

Prep: 30 min. • **Cook:** 5 min./batch
Makes: 4 sandwiches (1 cup sauce)

- **¾ cup mayonnaise**
- **½ cup ketchup**
- **1 tsp. prepared horseradish**
- **1 tsp. hot pepper sauce**
- **Oil for frying**
- **¾ cup all-purpose flour**
- **¾ cup cornmeal**
- **1 Tbsp. Creole seasoning**
- **1 tsp. salt**
- **1 lb. uncooked medium shrimp, peeled and deveined (tails removed)**
- **4 French rolls, split**
- **2 medium tomatoes, sliced**
- **2 cups shredded lettuce**

1. In a small bowl, mix the mayonnaise, ketchup, horseradish and pepper sauce. Cover and chill until serving.
2. In an electric skillet, heat ½ in. oil to 375°. In a large shallow dish, combine the flour, cornmeal, Creole seasoning and salt.
3. Add shrimp, a few at a time; and toss to coat. Fry shrimp in oil for 2-3 minutes on each side or until golden brown. Drain on paper towels.
4. Spread rolls with some of the sauce. Layer bottoms with lettuce, shrimp and tomatoes; replace tops. Serve with remaining sauce.
1 sandwich: 847 cal., 49g fat (6g sat. fat), 153mg chol., 1889mg sod., 71g carb. (12g sugars, 5g fiber), 29g pro.

PI DAY

What do you do on National Pi Day (March 14)? Eat pie, of course! From lattice-crowned classics to fruity flavor twists, these recipes make achieving sweet, flaky perfection as easy as, well, you know. Embrace your inner math geek and get ready to calculate, eat and celebrate everyone's favorite never-ending number...with pie!

Peach, Green Chile & Cheddar Pie (p. 183) **Easy Fresh Strawberry Pie** (p. 184) **Flaky Bumbleberry Pie** (p. 179)

GOLDEN
APPLE PIE

GOLDEN APPLE PIE

Pies are the dessert I like best to prepare. This one's the favorite for family get-togethers, and it has been awarded blue ribbons at a couple of local fairs.

—Theresa Brazil, Petaluma, CA

Prep: 30 min. + cooling
Bake: 40 min. + cooling
Makes: 8 servings

- 6 **cups sliced peeled Golden Delicious apples**
- ¾ **cup plus 2 Tbsp. apple juice, divided**
- ¾ **cup sugar**
- 1 **tsp. ground cinnamon**
- ½ **tsp. apple pie spice**
- 2 **Tbsp. cornstarch**
- ¼ **tsp. vanilla extract**

CRUST

- 2½ **cups all-purpose flour**
- 1 **tsp. salt**
- 1 **cup cold butter**
- 6 **to 8 Tbsp. ice water**

1. In a large saucepan, combine the apples, ¾ cup apple juice, sugar, cinnamon and apple pie spice; bring to a boil over medium heat, stirring occasionally. Combine cornstarch and remaining apple juice; add to saucepan. Return to a boil, stirring constantly. Cook and stir 1 minute more or until thickened. Remove from the heat. Stir in vanilla. Cool to room temperature, stirring occasionally.

2. For crust, combine flour and salt; cut in the butter until mixture is crumbly. Gradually add water, 1 Tbsp. at a time, tossing with a fork until dough can be formed into a ball. Divide in 2 portions, making 1 slightly larger. On a lightly floured surface, roll out larger portion.

3. Line a 9-in. pie plate with bottom crust; trim even with edge of plate. Add filling. Roll out remaining dough to fit top of pie; place over filling. Trim, seal and flute edges. Cut slits in top.

4. Bake at 400° for 40-45 minutes or until crust is golden brown and apples are tender. Cool on a wire rack.

1 slice: 480 cal., 24g fat (15g sat. fat), 61mg chol., 480mg sod., 65g carb. (30g sugars, 2g fiber), 5g pro.

TEST KITCHEN TIP

Apple filling can sometimes be too runny. This depends on the moisture of the apples. To avoid a soggy filling, precook the apples for a few minutes. Then drain the apples and mix up the filling as normal. We recommend using firm, tart apples like Cortlands and Granny Smiths.

FLAKY BUMBLEBERRY PIE

FLAKY BUMBLEBERRY PIE

When you want to impress guests, make this pie! The recipe produces one of the flakiest crusts ever, and the combination of rhubarb and different berries in the filling is delicious.

—Suzanne Alberts, Onalaska, WI

Prep: 20 min. + chilling
Bake: 1 hour + cooling
Makes: 8 servings

- 1½ **cups all-purpose flour**
- 1 **tsp. salt**
- 1 **tsp. sugar**
- 1 **cup cold butter**
- ¼ **cup cold water**

FILLING

- 1 **medium tart apple, peeled and diced**
- 1 **cup diced fresh or frozen rhubarb, thawed**
- 1 **cup fresh or frozen raspberries, thawed and drained**
- 1 **cup fresh or frozen blueberries, thawed and drained**
- 1 **cup sliced fresh or frozen strawberries, thawed and drained**
- 1 **cup sugar**
- ½ **cup all-purpose flour**
- 1 **Tbsp. lemon juice**

1. In a small bowl, combine flour, salt and sugar. Cut in butter until mixture resembles coarse crumbs. Gradually add water, tossing with a fork until a ball forms. Cover and refrigerate 1 hour or until easy to handle.

2. Preheat oven to 400°. On a lightly floured surface, roll out half the dough to fit a 9-in. pie plate. Transfer crust to pie plate. Trim to ½ in. beyond edge of plate.

3. In a large bowl, combine filling ingredients; pour into crust. Roll out remaining dough; cut out decorative shapes with cookie cutters. Place over filling. Cover edge loosely with foil.

4. Bake for 20 minutes. Reduce heat to 350°; remove foil. Bake 40-45 minutes or until crust is golden brown and filling is bubbly. Cool on a wire rack.

1 piece: 449 cal., 23g fat (14g sat. fat), 61mg chol., 528mg sod., 58g carb. (31g sugars, 3g fiber), 4g pro.

CHERRY HAND PIES

There's nothing better than a sweet delight like traditional cherry pie. These adorable little hand pies go fast at my pie bakery.
—Allison Cebulla, Milwaukee, WI

Prep: 45 min. • **Bake:** 25 min. + cooling
Makes: 8 servings

- **6 Tbsp. water, divided**
- **2 Tbsp. sugar**
- **2 Tbsp. cherry brandy**
- **4½ tsp. cornstarch**
- **1½ tsp. lemon juice**
- **1 tsp. quick-cooking tapioca**
- **¼ tsp. grated lemon zest**
- **Dash salt**
- **2 cups fresh or frozen pitted tart cherries, thawed and halved**
- **1 cup fresh or frozen pitted dark sweet cherries, thawed and halved**
- **Pastry for double-crust pie** **(see p. 184 for recipe)**
- **1 large egg**

ICING
- **2⅔ cups confectioners' sugar**
- **3 to 4 Tbsp. hot water**
- **2 Tbsp. butter, melted**
- **½ tsp. almond extract**
- **¼ tsp. vanilla extract**
- **Dash salt**
- **Freeze-dried strawberries, crushed, optional**

1. In a large saucepan, whisk 4 Tbsp. water, sugar, brandy, cornstarch, lemon juice, tapioca, lemon zest and salt until combined. Add cherries. Bring to a boil; cook and stir until thickened, 3-5 minutes. Remove from heat. Set aside to cool.

2. Preheat oven to 400°. On a lightly floured surface, roll 1 portion of dough to a 14x9-in. rectangle. Cut eight 3½ x 4½-in. rectangles. Repeat with the remaining dough. Transfer 8 of the rectangles to parchment-lined baking sheets.

3. Spoon about 3 Tbsp. cherry mixture in center of each of 8 rectangles. Whisk egg and remaining 2 Tbsp. water. Brush edges of crust with egg wash. Top with remaining 8 rectangles; press edges with a fork to seal. Brush tops with egg wash; cut slits in tops.

4. Bake until crust is golden brown and slightly puffed, 25-30 minutes. Remove from pans to wire racks to cool. Combine icing ingredients; drizzle over pies. Garnish with freeze-dried strawberries if desired. Let stand until set.

1 pie: 589 cal., 27g fat (16g sat. fat), 91mg chol., 380mg sod., 83g carb. (49g sugars, 2g fiber), 6g pro.

MINI BLUEBERRY TARTS

I served these tarts to my family while we were on vacation and they were all amazed! The best part: I didn't spend tons of time on it, thanks to refrigerated pie crust. Watch your mini tarts around the 13-minute mark to make sure they don't brown too quickly. If you like, sprinkle the tops with coarse sugar for a pretty finishing touch.
—Allison Bell, Hillsdale, NJ

Prep: 25 min. • **Bake:** 15 min. + cooling
Makes: 6 mini tarts

- **2 cups fresh blueberries**
- **⅓ cup sugar**
- **4 tsp. cornstarch**
- **2 sheets refrigerated pie crust**
- **1 large egg yolk, lightly beaten**

1. Preheat oven to 425°. Crush half the blueberries, leaving the rest whole. Sift together sugar and cornstarch. Add whole and crushed blueberries; toss until berries are well coated. Set aside.

2. On a lightly floured surface, unroll crusts. Cut out six 4½-in. circles; press circles onto bottoms and up sides of greased muffin cups. Evenly spoon in blueberry mixture. Cut out six 2-in. circles from remaining crust; place over filling. Brush with yolk.

3. Bake until the crust is golden and filling bubbles, 13-17 minutes. Cool in pans for 10 minutes; run a knife around the sides of cups and remove tarts to a serving plate.

1 mini tart: 383 cal., 18g fat (8g sat. fat), 43mg chol., 249mg sod., 52g carb. (18g sugars, 1g fiber), 3g pro.

BUTTERSCOTCH PIE

BUTTERSCOTCH PIE

This creamy puddinglike pie filling is crowned with golden peaks of meringue.
—Cary Letsche, Brandenton, FL

Prep: 30 min. • **Bake:** 15 min. + chilling
Makes: 8 servings

- **6 Tbsp. butter**
- **6 Tbsp. all-purpose flour**
- **1½ cup packed brown sugar**
- **2 cups whole milk**
- **¼ tsp. salt**
- **3 large egg yolks, beaten**
- **1 tsp. vanilla extract**
- **1 pastry shell (9 in.), baked**

MERINGUE

- **3 large egg whites**
- **¼ tsp. cream of tartar**
- **½ cup sugar**

1. In a saucepan, melt the butter. Remove from the heat; add the flour and stir until smooth. Stir in brown sugar. Return to heat; stir in milk and salt until blended. Cook and stir over medium-high heat until thickened and bubbly. Reduce the heat; cook and stir 2 minutes longer. Remove from the heat. Stir about 1 cup hot filling into the egg yolks; return all to pan, stirring constantly. Bring to a gentle boil; cook and stir for 2 minutes longer. Remove from the heat. Gently stir in vanilla. Pour into crust.
2. For meringue, beat egg whites and cream of tartar on medium speed until soft peaks form. Gradually beat in sugar, about 1 Tbsp. at a time, on high until stiff glossy peaks form and sugar is dissolved. Spread evenly over hot filling, sealing edges to crust.
3. Bake at 350° for 12-15 minutes or until meringue is golden brown. Cool on a wire rack for 1 hour. Refrigerate for at least 3 hours before serving. Refrigerate leftovers.
1 slice: 487 cal., 20g fat (10g sat. fat), 116mg chol., 330mg sod., 73g carb. (56g sugars, 0 fiber), 6g pro.

When making meringues, use older eggs. Older eggs actually produce fluffier and higher meringues. A simple trick tests how old your eggs are: Gently place an uncracked egg in a glass of water. If it stands up on end, it's perfect for meringue. (If it floats, it's actually too old—toss it. An egg that lies on its side on the bottom is very fresh.)

PEACH, GREEN CHILE
& CHEDDAR PIE

PEACH, GREEN CHILE & CHEDDAR PIE

After tasting a fantastic green chile apple pie in a local restaurant, I wanted to try my own homemade version with peaches. The result was fantastic! The combination of flavors in this unusual pie tells you what every New Mexican knows—green chile goes well with everything!
—Rd Stendel-Freels, Albuquerque, NM

Prep: 40 min. • **Bake:** 45 min. + cooling
Makes: 8 servings

- **2½ cups all-purpose flour**
- **3 Tbsp. sugar**
- **14 Tbsp. butter, cubed**
- **½ cup shredded aged cheddar cheese**
- **1 large egg yolk**
- **6 to 8 Tbsp. ice water**

FILLING

- **3 Hatch peppers, roasted, peeled, seeded and chopped (about 1 cup)**
- **⅔ cup sugar**
- **¼ cup all-purpose flour**
- **½ tsp. ground cinnamon**
- **¼ tsp. ground nutmeg**
- **¼ tsp. salt**
- **5 cups sliced peeled peaches (about 6 medium peaches)**
- **¼ cup shredded aged cheddar cheese**
- **2 Tbsp. butter**

1. Place flour and sugar in a food processor; pulse until blended. Add butter; pulse until butter is the size of peas. Add ½ cup cheese; pulse 1-2 times. Transfer flour mixture to a large bowl. Mix together egg yolk and 6 Tbsp. ice water; gradually add to flour mixture. Toss with a fork until dough holds together when pressed, adding more water if needed. Divide dough in half. Shape each into a disk; wrap and refrigerate 30 minutes or overnight.
2. Preheat oven to 450°. Wrap chopped chiles in 3 layers of paper towel and squeeze gently to remove excess moisture. (Wear disposable gloves and do not touch face.) In a large bowl, combine the sugar, flour, spices and salt. Add peaches and green chiles; toss to coat.
3. On a lightly floured surface, roll 1 dough portion into a ⅛-in.-thick circle; transfer to a 9-in. pie plate. Trim crust even with rim. Sprinkle bottom with cheese. Add filling; dot with butter. Roll out remaining dough; make a lattice crust. Place over filling. Trim, seal and flute edge.
4. Bake on lower rack for 10 minutes. Reduce oven setting to 350°. Bake 35-40 minutes longer or until crust is golden brown and filling is bubbly. Cool on a wire rack.
1 piece: 525 cal., 27g fat (16g sat. fat), 91mg chol., 308mg sod., 65g carb. (30g sugars, 4g fiber), 8g pro.

CREAMY CHOCOLATE-BANANA PIE

You can make almost any dessert more awesome with chocolate. In this cream pie, fresh banana and chocolate make a truly irresistible combo.
—Diane Nemitz, Ludington, MI

Prep: 20 min. + chilling
Bake: 25 min. + chilling
Makes: 8 servings

- **Pastry for single-crust pie (see p. 184 for recipe)**
- **⅔ cup plus ¼ cup sugar, divided**
- **½ cup all-purpose flour**
- **1 envelope unflavored gelatin**
- **1¼ cups half-and-half cream**
- **3 large egg yolks, lightly beaten**
- **1 cup sour cream**
- **1 tsp. rum extract**
- **1 tsp. vanilla extract**
- **1 oz. unsweetened chocolate, melted**
- **4 medium bananas, sliced**
- **½ cup heavy whipping cream**
- **Shaved unsweetened chocolate, optional**

1. On a floured surface, roll pie dough to a ⅛-in.-thick circle; transfer to a 9-in. pie plate. Trim crust to ½ in. beyond rim of plate; flute edge. Refrigerate 30 minutes. Preheat oven to 425°.
2. Line crust with double thickness of foil. Fill with pie weights, dried beans or uncooked rice. Bake on a lower oven rack until edges are golden brown, 20-25 minutes. Remove foil and weights; bake until bottom is golden brown, about 4 minutes. Cool on a wire rack.
3. Meanwhile, in the top of a double boiler or a metal bowl over simmering water, mix ⅔ cup sugar, flour and gelatin. Whisk in half-and-half and egg yolks; cook, whisking constantly, until temperature reaches 160° and mixture is thick enough to coat a metal spoon. Remove from heat; whisk in sour cream and extracts. Transfer ¾ cup mixture to a small bowl; stir in melted chocolate until blended. Refrigerate both mixtures until set but not firm, about 30 minutes.
4. Spread the chocolate mixture evenly over crust. Fold bananas into the other mixture; spread over chocolate layer. Refrigerate until firm, about 2 hours.
5. Beat cream until it begins to thicken. Add remaining sugar; beat until stiff peaks form. Spread over top; if desired, sprinkle with shaved chocolate.
1 piece: 562 cal., 30g fat (19g sat. fat), 159mg chol., 201mg sod., 61g carb. (33g sugars, 3g fiber), 11g pro.

KEY LIME CREAM PIE

I am very proud of this luscious no-bake beauty. It's so cool and refreshing—perfect for any potluck or get-together. Wherever I take this pie, it quickly disappears, with everyone asking for the recipe.
—Shirley Rickis, The Villages, FL

Prep: 40 min. + chilling • **Makes:** 12 servings

- **1 pkg. (11.3 oz.) pecan shortbread cookies, crushed (about 2 cups)**
- **⅓ cup butter, melted**
- **4 cups heavy whipping cream**
- **¼ cup confectioners' sugar**
- **1 tsp. coconut extract**
- **1 pkg. (8 oz.) cream cheese, softened**
- **1 can (14 oz.) sweetened condensed milk**
- **½ cup Key lime juice**
- **¼ cup sweetened shredded coconut, toasted**
- **Optional: Maraschino cherries with stems and sliced Key limes**

1. In a small bowl, mix crushed cookies and butter. Press onto bottom and up sides of a greased 9-in. deep-dish pie plate. In a large bowl, beat cream until it begins to thicken. Add confectioners' sugar and extract; beat until stiff peaks form. In another large bowl, beat cream cheese, condensed milk and lime juice until blended. Fold in 2 cups whipped cream. Spoon into prepared crust.
2. Top with remaining whipped cream; sprinkle with coconut. Refrigerate until serving, at least 4 hours. If desired, garnish with cherries and limes.
1 piece: 646 cal., 52g fat (30g sat. fat), 143mg chol., 252mg sod., 41g carb. (29g sugars, 0 fiber), 8g pro.

EASY FRESH STRAWBERRY PIE

When making this classic pie, I use whole fresh strawberries and arrange them pointed side up in the pastry shell for a new presentation.
—Josh Carter, Birmingham, AL

Prep: 20 min. + cooling
Bake: 15 min. + chilling
Makes: 8 servings

- **1 sheet refrigerated pie crust**
- **¾ cup sugar**
- **2 Tbsp. cornstarch**
- **1 cup water**
- **1 pkg. (3 oz.) strawberry gelatin**
- **4 cups sliced fresh strawberries**
- **Whipped cream, optional**

1. Unroll crust into 9-in. pie plate. Trim edge. Line unpricked crust with a double thickness of heavy-duty foil or parchment. Bake at 450° for 8 minutes. Remove foil; bake 5 minutes longer. Cool on a wire rack.
2. In a small saucepan, combine the sugar, cornstarch and water until smooth. Bring to a boil; cook and stir until thickened, about 2 minutes. Remove from the heat; stir in the gelatin until dissolved. Refrigerate until slightly cooled, 15-20 minutes.
3. Meanwhile, arrange strawberries in the crust. Pour gelatin mixture over berries. Refrigerate until set. If desired, serve with whipped cream.
1 slice: 264 cal., 7g fat (3g sat. fat), 5mg chol., 125mg sod., 49g carb. (32g sugars, 2g fiber), 2g pro.

PASTRY FOR SINGLE-CRUST PIE

If you want to make pie pastry from scratch, try this easy and traditional recipe from our Test Kitchen.
—Taste of Home *Test Kitchen*

Takes: 10 min.
Makes: 1 pastry shell (8 servings)

- **1¼ cups all-purpose flour**
- **½ tsp. salt**
- **⅓ cup shortening**
- **4 to 5 Tbsp. cold water**

1. In a bowl, combine flour and salt; cut in the shortening until crumbly. Gradually add water, tossing with a fork until dough forms a ball. Roll out to fit a 9-in. or 10-in pie plate.
2. Transfer pastry to pie plate. Trim pastry to ½ in. beyond the edge of plate; flute edges. Fill or bake shell according to recipe directions.
1 serving: 144 cal., 8g fat (2g sat. fat), 0 chol., 148mg sod., 15g carb. (0 sugars, 1g fiber), 2g pro.

EASY FRESH STRAWBERRY PIE

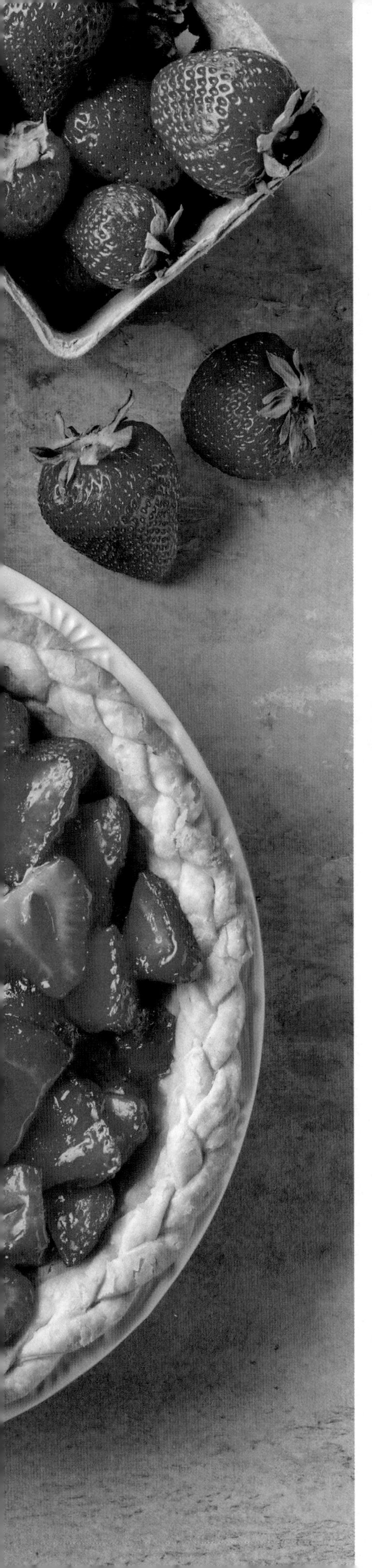

▲

Decorative Edges for Single-Crust Pies

ROLLED EDGE: Turn overhanging pastry under to form a rolled edge.

FLUTED EDGE: Trim pastry to ½ in. beyond edge for single-crust and 1 in. for double-crust pie. Position thumb and index finger about 1 in. apart on inside edge. Place index finger of the other hand between thumb and index finger and gently push the pastry toward the center in an upward direction. Continue until entire edge is fluted.

ROPE EDGE: Trim pastry to ½ in. beyond edge for single-crust and 1 in. for double-crust pie. Turn overhanging pastry under to form rolled edge. Make a fist with one hand and press thumb at an angle into the pastry. Pinch some of the pastry between the thumb and index finger. Repeat at ½-in. to 1-in. intervals.

BRAIDED EDGE: Cut twelve ¼-in.-wide strips of pastry; gently braid 3 strips. Brush edge of crust with water; place braid on edge and press lightly to secure. Repeat with remaining strips, attaching braids until entire edge is covered.

SUNFLOWER EDGE: Trim pastry even with edge of pie plate. Hold a teaspoon or tablespoon upside down and roll the tip of the spoon around the edge of the pastry, cutting it. Continue around entire edge of crust. Discard cut pieces.

LEAF TRIM: Make enough pastry for a double crust. Roll the pastry to ⅛-in. thickness. Cut shapes using a 1⅛-in. leaf cookie cutter. With a sharp knife, score leaves to create veins. Brush bottom of each leaf with water. Place leaves around the edge of crust; press lightly to secure.

ST. PATRICK'S DAY

Make your house the place to be on March 17 with this jig-worthy lineup of classic Irish dinner, dessert and drink recipes. These over-the-rainbow ideas make it as easy as pie to bring a touch o' green (and a pot o' gold) to your ultimate Irish feast!

Irish Stew Pie (p. 193)

GUINNESS FLOAT

GUINNESS FLOAT

That very first sip of a Guinness is what inspired this quick and easy dessert. The rich, creamy foam that gathers on the top of a freshly poured draft made me think of vanilla ice cream. At that point, I knew I had to combine the two in a Guinness float.
—James Schend, Pleasant Prairie, WI

Takes: 5 min. • **Makes:** 2 floats

- **1 cup vanilla ice cream, softened if necessary**
- **2 cups Guinness or other stout beer**
- **2 Tbsp. chocolate syrup**

Divide ice cream between 2 glasses. Slowly top with beer; drizzle with chocolate syrup. Serve immediately.

1 serving: 286 cal., 7g fat (4g sat. fat), 29mg chol., 68mg sod., 36g carb. (31g sugars, 1g fiber), 4g pro.

SLOW-COOKER REUBEN SPREAD

My daughter shared this recipe with me for a hearty spread that tastes just like a Reuben sandwich. Serve it from a slow cooker set to warm to keep the temperature where the dip is the most tasty.
—Rosalie Fuchs, Paynesville, MN

Prep: 5 min. • **Cook:** 2 hours • **Makes:** 3½ cups

- **1 can (14 oz.) sauerkraut, rinsed and well drained**
- **1 pkg. (8 oz.) cream cheese, cubed**
- **2 cups shredded Swiss cheese**
- **1 pkg. (3 oz.) deli corned beef, chopped**
- **3 Tbsp. prepared Thousand Island salad dressing**
- **Snack rye bread or crackers**

In a 1½-qt. slow cooker, combine the first 5 ingredients. Cover and cook on low for 2-3 hours or until cheeses are melted; stir to blend. Serve warm with bread or crackers.

2 Tbsp.: 69 cal., 6g fat (3g sat. fat), 18mg chol., 203mg sod., 1g carb. (1g sugars, 0 fiber), 3g pro.

PRESSURE-COOKER CLAM CHOWDER

If you like your chowder on the thick side, add another tablespoon of flour after it is done in a pressure cooker. Clam chowder is especially tasty when served with a sprinkle of fresh thyme, bacon crumbles and crispy oyster crackers on top.
—Taste of Home *Test Kitchen*

Prep: 20 min. • **Cook:** 25 min.
Makes: 8 servings (2 qt.)

- **4 medium potatoes, peeled and cut into ½-in. cubes (about 5 cups)**
- **1 medium onion, chopped**
- **2 celery ribs, chopped**
- **2 medium carrots, chopped**
- **4 garlic cloves, minced**
- **1 bottle (8 oz.) clam juice**
- **1 cup chicken broth**
- **1 tsp. dried thyme**
- **1 tsp. salt**
- **½ tsp. pepper**
- **2 cans (6½ oz. each) minced clams, undrained**
- **2 Tbsp. all-purpose flour**
- **1 cup heavy whipping cream**
- **4 bacon strips, cooked and crumbled**
- **Optional: Oyster crackers and fresh thyme**

1. Place first 10 ingredients in a 6-qt. electric pressure cooker. Drain and reserve liquid from clams; add reserved liquid to pressure cooker and set clams aside. Lock lid; close pressure-release valve. Adjust to pressure-cook on high for 15 minutes. Quick-release pressure.

2. Select saute setting and adjust for low heat. Mix flour and cream until smooth; stir into soup. Cook and stir until slightly thickened, 6-8 minutes. Stir in clams; heat through. Serve with bacon and, if desired, oyster crackers and fresh thyme.

1 cup: 227 cal., 13g fat (7g sat. fat), 56mg chol., 673mg sod., 21g carb. (4g sugars, 2g fiber), 8g pro.

AIR-FRYER POTATO CHIPS

I received an air fryer for Christmas one year. Crispy potato chips are an essential part of any good lunch, so I used my new appliance to make a guilt-free version. They turned out delicious, and just like when you're eating the bagged kind, you won't be able to stop at one.
—Melissa Obernesser, Utica, NY

Prep: 30 min. • **Cook:** 15 min./batch
Makes: 6 servings

- **2 large potatoes**
- **Olive oil-flavored cooking spray**
- **½ tsp. sea salt**
- **Minced fresh parsley, optional**

1. Preheat air fryer to 360°. Using a mandoline or vegetable peeler, cut potatoes into very thin slices. Transfer to a large bowl; add enough ice water to cover. Soak 15 minutes; drain. Add more ice water and soak for another 15 minutes.

2. Drain potatoes; place on towels and pat dry. Spritz potatoes with cooking spray; sprinkle with salt. In batches, place potato slices in a single layer on tray in greased air-fryer basket. Cook until crisp and golden brown, 15-17 minutes, stirring and turning every 5-7 minutes. If desired, sprinkle with minced parsley.

1 cup: 148 cal., 1g fat (0 sat. fat), 0 chol., 252mg sod., 32g carb. (2g sugars, 4g fiber), 4g pro. **Diabetic exchanges:** 2 starch.

IRISH SODA BREAD MUFFINS

Irish soda bread is traditionally prepared in a loaf shape, but these muffins have the same terrific flavor.

—Lorraine Ballsieper, Deep River, CT

Takes: 30 min. • **Makes:** 1 dozen

- **2¼ cups all-purpose flour**
- **½ cup plus 1 Tbsp. sugar, divided**
- **2 tsp. baking powder**
- **½ tsp. salt**
- **¼ tsp. baking soda**
- **1 tsp. caraway seeds**
- **1 large egg, room temperature**
- **1 cup buttermilk**
- **¼ cup butter, melted**
- **¼ cup canola oil**
- **¾ cup dried currants or raisins**

1. In a large bowl, combine the flour, ½ cup sugar, baking powder, salt, baking soda and caraway seeds. In another bowl, beat the egg, buttermilk, butter and canola oil. Stir into the dry ingredients just until moistened. Fold in the dried currants.

2. Fill greased muffin cups three-fourths full. Sprinkle with remaining sugar. Bake at 400° for 15 minutes or until a toothpick inserted in the center comes out clean. Cool 5 minutes before removing muffins from pan to wire rack. Serve warm.

1 muffin: 235 cal., 9g fat (3g sat. fat), 28mg chol., 247mg sod., 35g carb. (17g sugars, 1g fiber), 4g pro.

MINT CHOCOLATE CHEESECAKE

I created this mint chocolate cheesecake for our high school's annual fundraiser. We were told that it brought a hefty price and was one of the first desserts to be sold! If desired, you can stir the cookie pieces into the batter instead of adding them in a layer. Keep the pieces fairly small; otherwise they have a tendency to rise to the top.

—Sue Gronholz, Beaver Dam, WI

Prep: 20 min. • **Bake:** 1¼ hours + chilling
Makes: 16 servings

- **1 cup Oreo cookie crumbs**
- **3 Tbsp. sugar**
- **2 Tbsp. butter, melted**

FILLING

- **4 pkg. (8 oz. each) cream cheese, softened**
- **1 cup sugar**
- **1 cup white baking chips, melted and cooled**
- **6 Tbsp. creme de menthe**
- **¼ cup all-purpose flour**
- **2 Tbsp. creme de cacao**
- **½ tsp. peppermint extract**
- **4 large eggs, room temperature, lightly beaten**
- **1 cup coarsely crushed Oreo cookies (about 10 cookies)**

GANACHE

- **¾ cup semisweet chocolate chips**
- **6 Tbsp. heavy whipping cream**

1. Preheat oven to 325°. Place a greased 9-in. springform pan on a double thickness of heavy-duty foil (about 18 in. square). Wrap foil securely around pan. In a small bowl, mix cookie crumbs and sugar; stir in butter. Press onto bottom of prepared pan.

2. In a large bowl, beat cream cheese and sugar until smooth. Beat in cooled chips, creme de menthe, flour, creme de cacao and extract. Add eggs; beat on low speed just until blended. Pour half the batter over the crust; sprinkle with crushed Oreos. Carefully spoon remaining batter over top. Place springform pan in a larger baking pan; add 1 in. hot water to larger pan.

3. Bake until center is just set and top appears dull, 75-80 minutes. Remove springform pan from water bath. Cool cheesecake on a wire rack for 10 minutes. Loosen sides from pan with a knife; remove foil. Cool 1 hour longer. Refrigerate cake overnight, covering when completely cooled.

4. Remove rim from pan. Place chocolate chips in a small bowl. In a small saucepan, bring heavy cream just to a boil. Pour over chocolate; stir with a whisk until smooth. Spread over cheesecake.

1 slice: 518 cal., 33g fat (18g sat. fat), 116mg chol., 296mg sod., 46g carb. (38g sugars, 1g fiber), 7g pro.

IRISH SODA BREAD MUFFINS

▲
Lucky Table Decor
Small details set the scene without going overboard. Hints of green and subtle nods to Irish culture keep this celebration classy.

IRISH STEW PIE

IRISH STEW PIE

The only thing more comforting than a hearty bowl of Irish lamb stew is having it baked into a pie! This is also good with cuts of beef.
—Nicolas Hortense, Perth, Australia

Prep: 1 hour • **Bake:** 35 min. + standing
Makes: 6 servings

- **½ cup plus 1 Tbsp. all-purpose flour, divided**
- **¾ tsp. salt, divided**
- **¾ tsp. pepper, divided**
- **1 lb. boneless lamb shoulder roast, cubed**
- **2 Tbsp. canola oil**
- **2 medium carrots, finely chopped**
- **1 medium onion, halved and sliced**
- **1¼ cups beef stock**
- **2 medium Yukon Gold potatoes, peeled and cubed**
- **1 fresh thyme sprig**
- **1 bay leaf**
- **1 tsp. Worcestershire sauce**
- **1 tsp. tomato paste**
- **3 Tbsp. chopped fresh mint**
- **1 large egg yolk**
- **2 Tbsp. heavy whipping cream**
- **1 pkg. (17.3 oz.) frozen puff pastry, thawed**

1. Preheat oven to 350°. In a shallow bowl, mix ½ cup flour, ½ tsp. salt and ½ tsp. pepper. Add lamb, a few pieces at a time, and toss to coat; shake off excess. In a Dutch oven, heat oil over medium-high heat. Brown lamb in batches. Remove from pan. Add the carrots and onion to same pan; cook and stir until crisp-tender, 6-8 minutes. Stir in remaining 1 Tbsp. flour until blended; gradually whisk in beef stock. Bring to a boil, stirring to loosen browned bits from pan.
2. To the same pan, add the potatoes, thyme, bay leaf, Worcestershire sauce, tomato paste, remaining ¼ tsp. salt, ¼ tsp. pepper and lamb; return to a boil. Reduce the heat. Simmer, uncovered, until sauce is thickened and lamb is tender, 25-30 minutes. Discard thyme sprig and bay leaf. Stir in mint. Transfer mixture to a greased 9-in. deep-dish pie plate. Whisk egg yolk and cream; brush around edge of pie plate to help pastry adhere.
3. On a lightly floured surface, unfold 1 sheet puff pastry; top with remaining sheet. Roll to fit over pie plate. Carefully place over filling; trim to fit. Using a fork, press pastry firmly onto rim of pie plate to seal edge. Brush with remaining egg mixture; cut slits in top. Place on a rimmed baking sheet. Bake until golden brown, 35-40 minutes. Let stand 10 minutes.
1 serving: 731 cal., 40g fat (11g sat. fat), 75mg chol., 608mg sod., 71g carb. (4g sugars, 8g fiber), 24g pro.

COLCANNON IRISH POTATOES

COLCANNON IRISH POTATOES

My mother came from Ireland as a teen and brought this homey recipe with her. I find that it's a great way to get my family to eat cooked cabbage...hidden in Grandma's potatoes!
—Marie Pagel, Lena, WI

Takes: 30 min. • **Makes:** 10 servings

- **2½ lbs. potatoes (about 6 medium), peeled and cut into 1-in. pieces**
- **2 cups chopped cabbage**
- **1 large onion, chopped**
- **1 tsp. salt**
- **¼ tsp. pepper**
- **¼ cup butter, softened**
- **1 cup 2% milk**

1. Place potatoes in a 6-qt. stockpot; add water to cover. Bring to a boil. Reduce heat to medium; cook, covered, until potatoes are almost tender, 8-10 minutes.
2. Add cabbage and onion; cook, covered, until cabbage is tender, 5-7 minutes. Drain; return to pot. Add salt and pepper; mash to desired consistency, gradually adding butter and milk.
¾ cup: 129 cal., 5g fat (3g sat. fat), 14mg chol., 290mg sod., 19g carb. (4g sugars, 2g fiber), 3g pro. **Diabetic exchanges:** 1 starch, 1 fat.

Speak Like a Celt

Celebrate as if you just came across the pond. Try these Irish Gaelic phrases at the table.

HAPPY ST. PATRICK'S DAY TO YOU.

Lá Fhéile Pádraig sona dhuit.
(Law ale-yeh pah-drig sunna gwitch.)

CHEERS!

Sláinte!
(SLAWN-cha!)

KISS ME; I'M IRISH.

Tabhair póg dom; taím Éireannach.
(Tower pahg dum; toyme AYE-ron-okh.)

A PINT OF GUINNESS, PLEASE.

Píonta Guinness, le do thoil.
(Pyun-tah Guinness, leh duh hul.)

FAVORITE CORNED BEEF & CABBAGE

It may be the most famous dish to eat on St. Patrick's Day, but this Irish-American classic is a favorite at our table all year long.
—Evelyn Kenney, Trenton, NJ

Prep: 10 min. • **Cook:** 2¾ hours
Makes: 10 servings

- **1 corned beef brisket (about 4 lbs.) with spice packet**
- **2 Tbsp. brown sugar**
- **2 bay leaves**
- **3½ lbs. small potatoes (10-15), peeled**
- **8 medium carrots, halved crosswise**
- **1 medium head cabbage, cut into wedges**

HORSERADISH SAUCE

- **3 Tbsp. butter**
- **2 Tbsp. all-purpose flour**
- **1 to 1½ cups reserved cooking juices from corned beef**
- **1 Tbsp. sugar**
- **1 Tbsp. cider vinegar**
- **¼ cup horseradish**

MUSTARD SAUCE (OPTIONAL)

- **1 cup sour cream**
- **2 Tbsp. Dijon mustard**
- **¼ tsp. sugar**

1. Place brisket, contents of seasoning packet, brown sugar and bay leaves in a large Dutch oven or stockpot; cover with water. Bring to a boil. Reduce heat; simmer, covered, 2 hours.
2. Add potatoes and carrots; return to a boil. Reduce heat; simmer, covered, just until beef and vegetables are tender, 30-40 minutes. (If the pot is full, remove the potatoes and carrots before adding the cabbage; reheat before serving.)
3. Add the cabbage to pot; return to a boil. Reduce heat; simmer, covered, until cabbage is tender, about 15 minutes. Remove the vegetables and corned beef; keep warm.
4. For horseradish sauce, strain and reserve 1½ cups of the cooking juices; skim fat from reserved juices. Discard remaining juices. In a small saucepan, melt butter over medium heat; stir in flour until smooth. Gradually whisk in 1 cup reserved juices. Stir in sugar, vinegar and horseradish; bring to a boil, stirring constantly. Cook and stir until thickened. If desired, thin with additional juices. Season to taste with additional sugar, vinegar or horseradish.
5. If desired, mix all 3 ingredients for the mustard sauce.
6. Cut beef across the grain into slices. Serve with vegetables, horseradish sauce and, if desired, mustard sauce.

1 serving with 2 Tbsp. horseradish sauce: 564 cal., 28g fat (10g sat. fat), 134mg chol., 1616mg sod., 50g carb. (11g sugars, 8g fiber), 29g pro.

TEST KITCHEN TIP

Corned Beef and Cabbage 101

WHAT'S THE BEST CUT OF CORNED BEEF TO BUY?
It depends on your personal preference. There are two cuts of brisket for corned beef: flat cut and point cut. The flat cut is square, has less fat, slices easily and is found in grocery stores more commonly. The point cut is pointed, has more fat and is better for shredding. Another opotion would be to purchase an entire brisket, which has the point and flat cuts, or a beef round, although that is a much less common cut for corned beef.

WHAT ELSE SHOULD I SERVE WITH THE CORNED BEEF?
In addition to the vegetables and sauces, this Dutch oven corned beef is great with a hearty slice of Irish soda bread slathered with a pat of butter. Visit *tasteofhome.com* for more festive menu ideas.

WHAT'S THE BEST WAY TO COOK CORNED BEEF AND CABBAGE?
Using a Dutch oven to make corned beef will yield wonderful results. You can also make the classic dish in a slow cooker or pressure cooker. See *tasteofhome.com* for recipes.

FAVORITE CORNED BEEF & CABBAGE

ST. PATRICK'S DAY POPCORN

Everyone's eyes will be smilin' when they see this candied corn with an Irish twist. The green color gives the snack instant holiday appeal. *—Karen Weber, Salem, MO*

Prep: 15 min. + cooling • **Makes:** 6 qt.

- **4 qt. popped popcorn**
- **1 cup sugar**
- **½ cup packed brown sugar**
- **½ cup water**
- **½ cup light corn syrup**
- **1 tsp. white vinegar**
- **¼ tsp. salt**
- **½ cup butter**
- **8 to 10 drops green food coloring**

1. Place popcorn in a large roasting pan; keep warm in a 250° oven. Meanwhile, in a large heavy saucepan, combine the sugars, water, corn syrup, vinegar and salt. Cook and stir over medium heat until mixture comes to a boil. Cook, stirring occasionally, until a candy thermometer reads 260° (hard-ball stage).
2. Remove from the heat; stir in butter until melted. Stir in food coloring. Drizzle over warm popcorn and toss to coat. Cool. Break into pieces. Store in an airtight container.
1 cup: 139 cal., 6g fat (3g sat. fat), 10mg chol., 138mg sod., 22g carb. (16g sugars, 1g fiber), 1g pro.

MAY THE FOURTH BE WITH YOU

May the Fourth be with you. It's not just a pun...May 4th is a day to celebrate the most popular sci-fi movie of all time! Make it memorable by throwing an epic party that will be the talk of the galaxy. Host a movie marathon, share greetings, dress up like a character, take selfies and feast on a galactic smorgasbord of Star Wars-themed food. Party you will.

BB-8 Cake (p. 202) **Shaggy Giant Cookies** (p. 204) **Light Saber Pretzels** (p. 204)

YODA SODA

YODA SODA

It takes only three ingredients to create this jazzed-up party punch. For a tropical twist, try it with lime sherbet instead of ice cream.
—Taste of Home *Test Kitchen*

Takes: 5 min.
Makes: 36 servings

- **1 gallon green berry rush Hawaiian Punch, chilled**
- **1 bottle (2 liters) lemon-lime soda, chilled**
- **2 pints vanilla ice cream**
- **Optional: Fresh blueberries and lime wedges**

In a punch bowl, combine punch and soda. Top with scoops of ice cream. If desired, garnish each serving glass with fresh blueberries and lime wedges.
¾ cup: 82 cal., 2g fat (1g sat. fat), 6mg chol., 64mg sod., 16g carb. (15g sugars, 0 fiber), 1g pro.

Wrapping Up Baby

Guests are sure to love the Yoda green beverage—even more so all dressed up and ready to party in this decorative glass.

Wrap a linen napkin or cloth around the stem of a champagne glass or margarita glass (fold cloth over at top as needed to fit length of glass). Use a toothpick to secure cloth in the back. Fill the glass with Yoda Soda. Thread 2 blueberries onto the center of a wooden skewer to resemble eyes. Attach lime wedges on each end of skewer to resemble ears. Rest skewer on top of the glass and serve.

PRINCESS LEIA CHOCOLATE CINNAMON ROLLS

These extra-big cinnamon rolls are quickly devoured! Their spirals resemble Princess Leia's iconic side buns.
—Myrna Sippel, Thompson, IL

Prep: 30 min. + rising • **Bake:** 25 min.
Makes: 20 rolls

- **2 pkg. (¼ oz. each) active dry yeast**
- **1½ cups warm water (110° to 115°), divided**
- **½ cup butter, softened**
- **½ cup sugar**
- **1 tsp. salt**
- **4½ to 4¾ cups all-purpose flour**
- **⅔ cup baking cocoa**

FILLING

- **2 Tbsp. butter, melted**
- **⅓ cup sugar**
- **½ tsp. ground cinnamon**
- **1 cup miniature semisweet chocolate chips**
- **⅔ cup finely chopped nuts, optional**

ICING

- **2 cups confectioners' sugar**
- **½ tsp. vanilla extract**
- **2 to 3 Tbsp. 2% milk**
- **Additional miniature semisweet chocolate chips, optional**

1. In a large bowl, dissolve yeast in ½ cup warm water. Add the butter, sugar, salt and remaining water. Stir in 2½ cups flour and cocoa. Beat on medium speed for 3 minutes or until smooth. Stir in enough remaining flour to form a soft dough.
2. Turn onto a lightly floured surface; knead until smooth and elastic, 6-8 minutes. Place dough in a greased bowl, turning once to grease top. Cover and let rise in a warm place until doubled, about 1 hour.
3. Turn onto a lightly floured surface; divide in half. Roll each dough portion into a 12x10-in. rectangle; brush with melted butter. Combine the sugar, cinnamon, chocolate chips and nuts if desired; sprinkle over dough to within ½ in. of edges.
4. Roll up each jelly-roll style, starting with a long side; pinch seams to seal. Cut each into 10 slices. Place cut side down in a greased 15x10x1-in. baking pan. Cover and let rise until doubled, about 45 minutes.
5. Bake at 375° for 25-30 minutes or until lightly browned. Meanwhile, in a small bowl, combine the confectioners' sugar, vanilla and enough milk to reach desired consistency. Spread over rolls while slightly warm; sprinkle with additional chocolate chips if desired.
1 roll: 284 cal., 9g fat (5g sat. fat), 15mg chol., 161mg sod., 49g carb. (25g sugars, 2g fiber), 4g pro.

APPRENTICE POPCORN

Whenever I take this sweet mix somewhere, I bring copies of the recipe because people always ask for it. Once you start munching, it's impossible to stop!
—Cheryl Bull, Blue Grass, IA

Prep: 15 min. + chilling • **Makes:** about 6 qt.

- **14 cups popped popcorn**
- **2 cups salted peanuts**
- **2 cups crisp rice cereal**
- **2 cups miniature marshmallows**
- **1 lb. white candy coating, coarsely chopped**
- **3 Tbsp. creamy peanut butter**

1. In a large bowl, combine the popcorn, peanuts, cereal and marshmallows. In a microwave, melt candy coating and peanut butter; stir until smooth. Pour over popcorn mixture; toss to coat.
2. Spread onto waxed paper-lined baking sheets; refrigerate for 15 minutes or until set. Break into pieces. Store in an airtight container in the refrigerator.
1 cup: 241 cal., 15g fat (6g sat. fat), 0 chol., 152mg sod., 24g carb. (16g sugars, 2g fiber), 4g pro.

HANS ROLOS

Kids can help make these easy candies. Top the Rolo with a whole pecan or walnut or another kind of candy.
—Taste of Home *Test Kitchen*

Prep: 20 min. • **Bake:** 5 min. + standing
Makes: 4½ dozen

- **54 pretzel snaps or miniature pretzels**
- **54 Rolo candies (about 11 oz.)**
- **54 white candy coating disks or peanut butter M&M's**

1. Preheat oven to 250°. Place pretzels 1 in. apart on foil-lined baking sheets. Top each with a Rolo candy.
2. Bake until candies are softened, 3-4 minutes. (Rolos will still retain their shape.) Immediately top with candy coating disks or M&M's, pressing to spread candy into pretzel. Let stand until set.
1 piece: 41 cal., 2g fat (1g sat. fat), 1mg chol., 37mg sod., 6g carb. (5g sugars, 0 fiber), 0 pro.

GALAXY BITES

These perky gelatin cubes are fun to serve and eat! I vary the colors to match the occasion—pink and blue for a baby shower, school colors for a graduation party, etc. Kids of all ages snap them up.
—Deanna Pietrowicz, Bridgeport, CT

Prep: 30 min. + chilling • **Makes:** 9 dozen

- **4 pkg. (3 oz. each) assorted flavored gelatin**
- **6 envelopes unflavored gelatin, divided**
- **5¾ cups boiling water, divided**
- **1 can (14 oz.) sweetened condensed milk**
- **¼ cup cold water**

1. In a bowl, combine 1 package flavored gelatin and 1 envelope unflavored gelatin. Stir in 1 cup boiling water until dissolved. Pour into a 13x9-in. dish coated with cooking spray; refrigerate until set but not firm, about 20 minutes.
2. In small bowl, combine condensed milk and 1 cup boiling water. In another bowl, sprinkle 2 envelopes unflavored gelatin over cold water; let stand for 1 minute. Stir in ¾ cup boiling water. Add to milk mixture. Spoon 1 cup of the creamy gelatin mixture over first flavored gelatin layer. Refrigerate until set but not firm, about 25 minutes.
3. Repeat from beginning of recipe twice, alternating flavored gelatin with creamy gelatin layers. Chill each layer until set but not firm before spooning next layer on top. Make final flavored gelatin and spoon over top. Refrigerate for at least 1 hour after completing last layer before cutting into 1-in. squares.
1 piece: 25 cal., 0 fat (0 sat. fat), 1mg chol., 13mg sod., 5g carb. (5g sugars, 0 fiber), 1g pro.

STORMTROOPER TREATS

When my daughter was just 7 years old, she had the brilliant idea of adding Oreo cookies to cereal treats. Now 24, she still asks for them on occasion; they're that good.
—Tammy Phoenix, Ava, IL

Prep: 10 min. • **Cook:** 10 min. + cooling
Makes: 2 dozen

- **¼ cup butter, cubed**
- **8 cups miniature marshmallows**
- **6 cups Rice Krispies**
- **2½ cups double-stuffed Oreo cookies (about 16), chopped, divided**
- **1⅓ cups white baking chips, melted**

1. In a Dutch oven, melt butter over medium heat. Add marshmallows; cook and stir until melted. Remove from heat. Stir in cereal and 2 cups Oreos. Press into a greased 13x9-in. baking pan.
2. Spread melted baking chips over the top; sprinkle with remaining Oreos, pressing gently to adhere. Cool to room temperature. Cut into bars.
1 bar: 189 cal., 7g fat (4g sat. fat), 6mg chol., 123mg sod., 31g carb. (19g sugars, 0 fiber), 2g pro.

DARTH TATERS

Indulge in just one of these scrumptious bacon-wrapped goodies and you'll know why they're always a hit. They'll go fast, so you may want to double the recipe!
—Joni Hilton, Rocklin, CA

Prep: 30 min. • **Bake:** 15 min.
Makes: 32 appetizers

- **16 bacon strips, halved lengthwise**
- **½ cup maple syrup**
- **1 tsp. crushed red pepper flakes**
- **32 frozen Tater Tots, thawed**

1. Preheat oven to 400°. Cook bacon in a large skillet over medium heat until partially cooked but not crisp. Remove to paper towels to drain; keep warm.
2. Combine syrup and pepper flakes. Dip each bacon piece in syrup mixture, then wrap around a Tater Tot. Secure with toothpicks.
3. Place on a greased rack in a foil-lined 15x10x1-in. baking pan. Bake until bacon is crisp, 12-15 minutes.
1 appetizer: 52 cal., 3g fat (1g sat. fat), 4mg chol., 123mg sod., 6g carb. (3g sugars, 0 fiber), 2g pro.

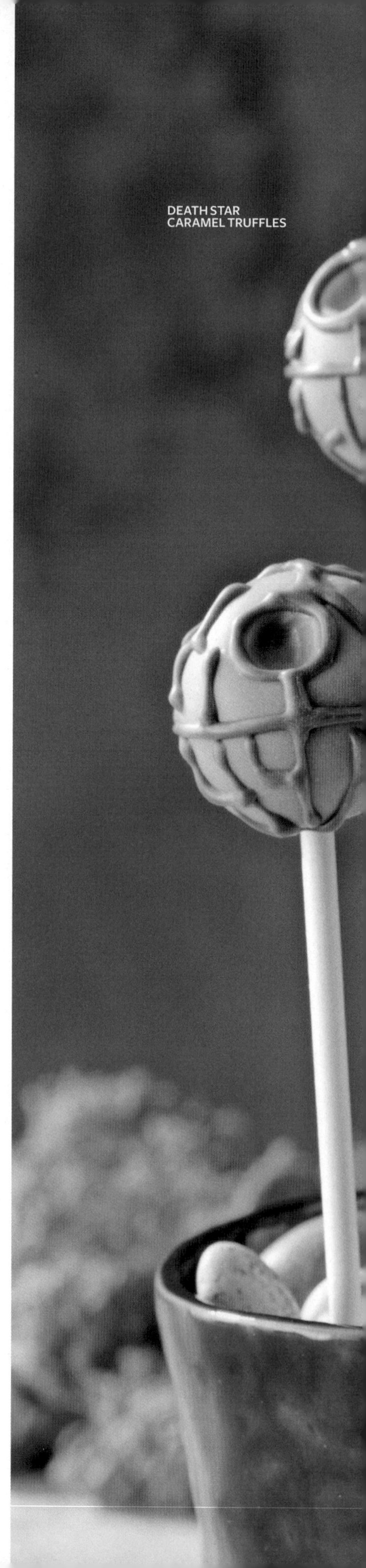

DEATH STAR CARAMEL TRUFFLES

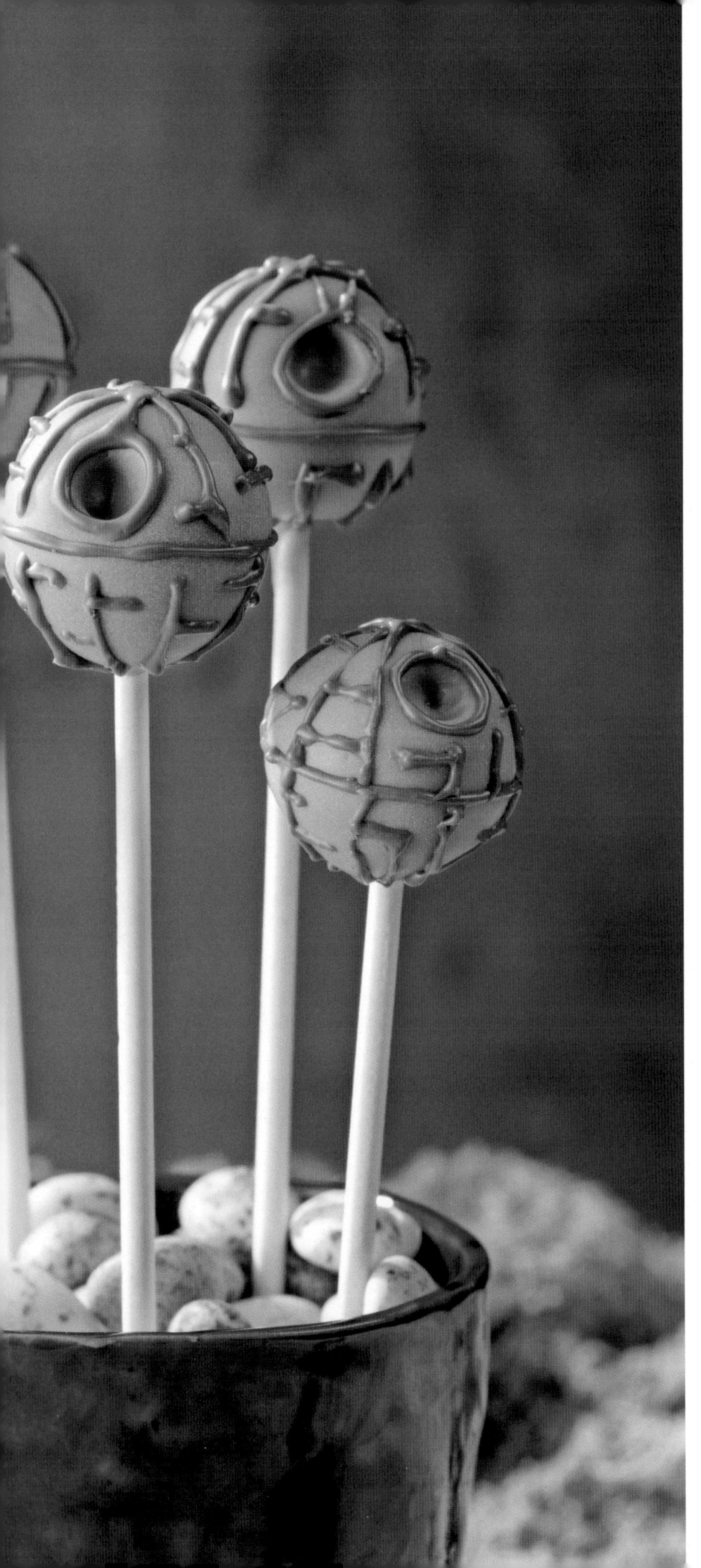

DEATH STAR CARAMEL TRUFFLES

Caramel truffles morph into Death Star candies for a fun sweet treat.
—Taste of Home *Test Kitchen*

Prep: 1 hour + chilling • **Makes:** 2½ dozen

- **26 caramels**
- **1 cup milk chocolate chips**
- **¼ cup heavy whipping cream**
- **2 cups white candy coating disks**
- **½ cup black candy coating disks**
- **30 lollipop sticks**

1. Line an 8-in. square dish with plastic wrap; set aside. In a microwave-safe bowl, combine caramels, milk chocolate chips and cream. Microwave, uncovered, on high for 1 minute; stir. Microwave 1 minute longer, stirring every 15 seconds or until caramels are melted and mixture is smooth. Spread into prepared dish; refrigerate for 1 hour or until firm.
2. Using plastic wrap, lift candy out of pan. Cut into 30 pieces; roll each piece into a 1-in. ball. Cover and refrigerate until firm, about 1 hour. Insert lollipop sticks into truffles. Press the end of a small wooden spoon into truffle to create indentation in the upper portion of each truffle. Return to refrigerator until firm.
3. In separate microwave-safe bowls, melt candy melts, stirring every 30 seconds until smooth. Tint white candy melts with black candy melts, adding 1 tsp. at a time until the desired color of gray is achieved; reserve remaining melted black candy melts. Dip caramels in gray candy melts, allowing excess to drip off; let stand until set. Tint remaining gray candy melts slightly darker with reserved black candy melts. Place in piping bag fitted with small #1 round tip; pipe onto truffles to resemble Death Star. Refrigerate until firm.
1 truffle: 158 cal., 8g fat (6g sat. fat), 5mg chol., 45mg sod., 21g carb. (20g sugars, 0 fiber), 1g pro.

Keep truffles upright and secure after dipping by placing ends of lollipop sticks into a Styrofoam block or a bowl filled with candies or uncooked rice.

BB-8 CAKE

This 3-D droid cake is easy to assemble and decorate. Using a cake mix gives you a jump start, so you can spend more time arranging the decorations.
—Taste of Home *Test Kitchen*

Prep: 40 min. • **Bake:** 1 hour + cooling
Makes: 40 servings

- 2 pkg. (16 oz. each) lb. cake mix
- 1 cup shortening
- 1 cup butter, softened
- 8 cups confectioners' sugar
- 2 tsp. vanilla extract
- 4 to 6 Tbsp. 2% milk
- 2 cups orange and 1 single brown Reese's pieces
- Silver nonpareils
- 1 mini Oreo cookie
- 2 pretzel sticks

1. Preheat oven to 350°. Prepare cake mixes according to package directions. Pour batter into 2 greased 1.5-qt. ovenproof bowls and 2 greased 10-oz. custard cups.
2. Bake until a toothpick inserted in the center of cakes comes out clean; 40-45 minutes for custard cups and 60-65 minutes for bowls. Cool in pans for 5 minutes before removing to wire racks to cool completely.
3. For frosting, beat shortening and butter in a bowl. Beat in confectioners' sugar, vanilla and just enough milk to achieve spreading consistency.
4. Use serrated knife to level the cakes. Place 1 large cake flat side up on an 8-in. serving plate. Frost top of cake. Place remaining large cake on top with the flat side down and edges even. Frost top and sides.
5. For the head, place 1 custard cup cake with flat side up on serving plate. Frost top of the cake. Place remaining custard cup cake on top with the flat side down and edges even. Frost top and sides. Trim 1 side of assembled head so it is flat, then place head above the body, using extra frosting to adhere.
6. To decorate the cake, use orange Reese's pieces to create four 3-in. circles randomly placed on the body. Arrange large silver nonpareils and additional Reese's pieces in decorative patterns inside each circle. Use additional Reese's Pieces and nonpareils to form 2 parallel lines at the top and bottom of the head. Place 1 mini Oreo and 1 brown Reese's piece outlined with nonpareils in between the lines to make the cameras. Insert pretzels rods into head for antenna, leaving 1 longer than the other.

1 piece: 318 cal., 13g fat (6g sat. fat), 22mg chol., 140mg sod., 49g carb. (39g sugars, 1g fiber), 2g pro.

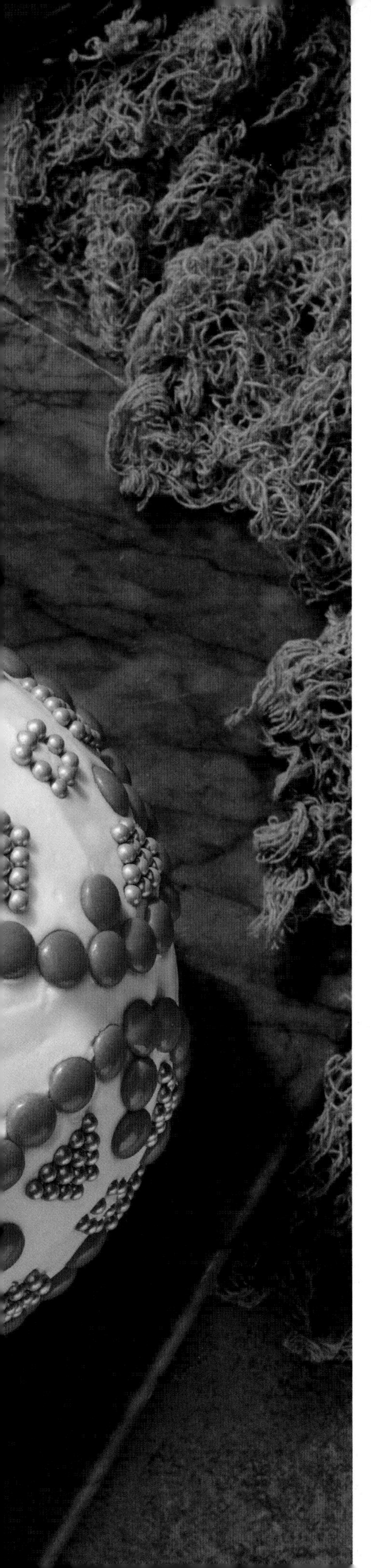

How to Host a Spectacular Star Wars-Themed Party

Get ready for the most legendary Star Wars party from here to Tatooine. Use our guide and there is no try—you can DO!

PARTY INVITATIONS
Send special invites to every last Jedi! Craft your own or download easy printable sets from the internet. They can be personalized with the time and date of the party, and the name of birthday boy or girl if this is a birthday party. Many printable sets can even be downloaded instantly—which is great when you're short on time.

SET THE SCENE
Create the atmosphere of a galaxy far, far away by decorating with Star Wars party swag. Set a perfect table with a themed tablecloth, plates and cups, table decor and confetti.

WHEN THE FORCE ASSEMBLES...
Hand out character masks to all the kids as they arrive. Use elastic and a stapler to complete the project. Then set everyone to work making simple (and safe) lightsabers using pool noodles plus electrical tape and duct tape for the handles.

PARTY GAMES
Play Star Wars-inspired party games. You can pin the lightsaber on Darth Vader, or create a plastic wrap ball (ahem, Death Star) filled with party-perfect prizes. Use printable bingo cards for some extra Star Wars birthday fun.

STAR WARS-INSPIRED FOOD
The most important part of any Star Wars party is the food! Let the Force guide you—but we'll help out, too. Guests will dig all the party favorites in this chapter.

SWEET TREATS
Any of the goodies in this chapter are sure to be winners! Or look on *tasteofhome.com* for a basic vanilla cupcake recipe, and add an adorable cupcake topper. Or use Star Wars cookie cutters with our most-loved sugar cookies and watch 'em all disappear into hyperspace.

DAZZLING DRINKS
While you can't have your party at the famous cantina, you can offer an out-of-this-world selection of drinks. Try the Yoda Soda on page 199 or check out *tasteofhome.com* for more kiddie cocktails. And why not add some Star Wars party pizazz by using printable labels to turn water or soda into Star Wars characters?

THE BEST CAKE
The cake is the crowning glory of every party, so make yours unforgettable! It's simple to use of our best cake recipes on *tasteofhome.com* and then add a custom cake topper. Or make the BB-8 cake on the opposite page to impress all the Jedi masters!

GOODY BAGS
When the guests return to their home planet, every space traveler will need treats for the road. To keep the Star Wars theme, use colorful character bag covers and pack your bags with edible party favors that they'll love.

SHAGGY GIANT COOKIES

Who wouldn't want a Chewie cookie? These adorable cutouts will be a fan favorite at any kind of Star Wars party.
—Taste of Home *Test Kitchen*

Prep: 45 min. + chilling
Bake: 10 min./batch + cooling
Makes: About 1½ dozen

- ⅓ **cup butter, softened**
- ¾ **cup packed dark brown sugar**
- ½ **cup molasses**
- 1 **large egg, room temperature**
- 2 **tsp. vanilla extract**
- 3 **cups all-purpose flour**
- 3 **tsp. ground ginger**
- 1½ **tsp. baking powder**
- 1¼ **tsp. ground cinnamon**
- ¾ **tsp. baking soda**
- ¼ **tsp. salt**
- ¼ **tsp. ground cloves**
- 1 **cup semisweet chocolate chips, melted**
- 1 **cup white baking chips, melted**

1. In a large bowl, beat butter and brown sugar until light and fluffy. Beat in molasses, egg and vanilla. In another bowl, whisk flour, ginger, baking powder, cinnamon, baking soda, salt and cloves; gradually beat into creamed mixture. Divide dough in half. Shape each into a disk. Cover and refrigerate 1 hour or until easy to handle.
2. Preheat oven to 350°. On a lightly floured surface, roll each portion to ¼-in. thickness. Cut with a floured 3-in. gingerbread man cookie cutter.
3. Place 2 in. apart on greased baking sheets. Create lines in dough with tines of a fork to look like fur. Bake until the edges are firm, 7-9 minutes. Remove from pans to wire racks to cool completely.
4. To decorate, pipe melted semisweet chocolate for eyes, nose, and weapon belt, then pipe melted white chocolate for mouth and bullets. Let stand until set.
1 cookie: 202 cal., 6g fat (4g sat. fat), 19mg chol., 154mg sod., 34g carb. (19g sugars, 1g fiber), 3g pro.

LIGHTSABER PRETZELS

Candy-coated pretzels take on a fun Star Wars theme with these sweet and salty treats.
—Taste of Home *Test Kitchen*

Total Time: 1 hour + standing
Makes: 2½ dozen

- 8 **oz. each blue, green and red candy coating disks**
- 6 **oz. each white and black candy coating disks**
- 30 **pretzel rods**
- **Blue, green and red colored sugar**
- 30 **M&M's minis**

Place each color of candy melts into separate microwave-safe bowls. Working with 1 color at a time, heat in microwave stirring every 30 seconds until smooth. Dip 10 pretzel rods each in blue, green and red melted candy coating, stopping 2 in. from end; allow excess to drip off. Immediately roll in matching colored sugar. Let stand on parchment-lined pan until set. Reheat candy coating as needed. Adding 1 tsp. at a time, stir melted black candy coating into the white, until desired shade of gray is achieved; reserve remaining melted black candy coating. Dip the uncoated end of the pretzel rods into melted gray candy coating for handle; allow excess to drip off. Return to parchment-lined pan until set. Place reserved melted black candy coating into a piping bag fitted with small round tip; pipe 3 lines onto handle. For power button, secure a M&M's minis to handle with melted black candy coating. Allow to set completely before serving. Store at room temperature in an airtight container between layers of waxed paper.
1 pretzel rod: 223 cal., 11g fat (9g sat. fat), 1mg chol., 244mg sod., 31g carb. (24g sugars, 0 fiber), 1g pro.

SHAGGY GIANT COOKIES

AMERICAN SUMMER

Relish the sunny, breezy, carefree vibe of summer with a deliciously simple menu full of seasonal ingredients. Whether you're going to a neighborhood block party, a big family reunion or just putting out a picnic spread on the grass, when it's bring-a-dish season, the fun follows.

BLT Macaroni Salad (p. 209) **Grilled Lemon Chicken** (p. 211)

SWEET & SPICY
BAKED BEANS

SWEET & SPICY BAKED BEANS

Baked beans are a must at any summer picnic or barbecue. These are sweet and simple, and someone always asks for the recipe.
—Elliot Wesen, Arlington, TX

Prep: 15 min. • **Bake:** 50 min.
Makes: 14 servings

- **2 cans (28 oz. each) baked beans**
- **1 can (20 oz.) unsweetened crushed pineapple, drained**
- **1 cup spicy barbecue sauce**
- **½ cup molasses**
- **2 Tbsp. prepared mustard**
- **½ tsp. pepper**
- **¼ tsp. salt**
- **1 can (6 oz.) french-fried onions, crushed, divided**
- **5 bacon strips, cooked and crumbled, divided**

1. In a bowl, combine the first 7 ingredients. Stir in half the onions and bacon. Transfer to a greased 13x9-in. baking dish.
2. Cover and bake at 350° for 45 minutes. Sprinkle with remaining onions and bacon. Bake, uncovered, 5-10 minutes longer or until bubbly.
¾ cup: 285 cal., 9g fat (3g sat. fat), 10mg chol., 860mg sod., 46g carb., 7g fiber, 7g pro.

CRISP ONION RELISH

I take this relish to picnics for people to use as a condiment on hamburgers and hot dogs. It adds a special zip!
—Marie Patkau, Hanley, SK

Prep: 10 min. + chilling
Makes: about 6 cups

- **4 medium sweet onions, halved and thinly sliced**
- **½ cup sugar**
- **⅓ cup water**
- **⅓ cup cider vinegar**
- **1 cup mayonnaise**
- **1 tsp. celery seed**

1. Place sliced onions in a large bowl. In a small bowl, combine the sugar, water and vinegar; stir until sugar is dissolved. Pour over onions. Cover and refrigerate at least 3 hours.
2. Drain and discard liquid from onions. Combine mayonnaise and celery seed; add to onions and mix well. Store in the refrigerator.
2 Tbsp.: 47 cal., 3g fat (1g sat. fat), 0 chol., 26mg sod., 4g carb. (3g sugars, 0 fiber), 0 pro.

BLT MACARONI SALAD

(PICTURED ON PAGE 207)

A friend served this salad, and I just had to get the recipe. My husband loves BLT sandwiches, so this has become a favorite of his. It's nice to serve on hot days, which we frequently get during summer here in Virginia.
—Hamilton Myers Jr., Charlottesville, VA

Takes: 30 min. • **Makes:** 6 servings

- **½ cup mayonnaise**
- **3 Tbsp. chili sauce**
- **2 Tbsp. lemon juice**
- **1 tsp. sugar**
- **3 cups cooked elbow macaroni**
- **½ cup chopped seeded tomato**
- **2 Tbsp. chopped green onions**
- **3 cups shredded lettuce**
- **4 bacon strips, cooked and crumbled**

In a large bowl, combine first 4 ingredients. Add the macaroni, tomatoes and onions; toss to coat. Cover and refrigerate. Just before serving, add lettuce and bacon; toss to coat.
¾ cup: 259 cal., 17g fat (3g sat. fat), 10mg chol., 287mg sod., 21g carb. (4g sugars, 2g fiber), 5g pro.

GRILLED BURGERS

Sour cream makes these burgers delightfully moist, and thyme and black pepper give them zip. They're a terrific taste of summer.
—Jesse and Anne Foust, Bluefield, WV

Takes: 20 min. • **Makes:** 10 servings

- **¼ cup sour cream**
- **2 tsp. dried parsley flakes**
- **1 tsp. dried thyme**
- **1 tsp. salt**
- **½ tsp. pepper**
- **2½ lbs. ground beef**
- **10 hamburger buns, split**
- **Optional: Lettuce leaves, sliced tomato and onion**

1. In a large bowl, combine first 5 ingredients; add beef and mix gently. Shape into 10 patties.
2. Grill, uncovered, over medium heat for 4-5 minutes on each side or until the meat is no longer pink. Serve on buns with lettuce, tomato and onion if desired.
1 burger: 358 cal., 17g fat (7g sat. fat), 79mg chol., 534mg sod., 22g carb. (3g sugars, 1g fiber), 26g pro.

SWEET CORN-TOMATO SALAD

I make this for family events and parties. Using fresh corn and basil make a huge difference in the flavor and texture.
—Jessica Kleinbaum, Plant City, FL

Prep: 15 min. • **Cook:** 10 min. + chilling
Makes: 10 servings

- **8 medium ears sweet corn, husked**
- **1 large sweet red pepper, chopped**
- **2 cups cherry tomatoes, halved**
- **1 small red onion, finely chopped**
- **¼ cup coarsely chopped fresh basil**

DRESSING

- **½ cup canola oil**
- **¼ cup rice vinegar**
- **2 Tbsp. lime juice**
- **1¼ tsp. salt**
- **½ to 1 tsp. hot pepper sauce**
- **½ tsp. garlic powder**
- **½ tsp. grated lime zest**
- **¼ tsp. pepper**

1. Place corn in a large stockpot; add water to cover. Bring to a boil. Cook, covered, until crisp-tender, 6-8 minutes; drain. Cool slightly. Cut corn from cobs and place in a large bowl. Stir in red pepper, tomatoes, onion and basil.
2. In a small bowl, whisk dressing ingredients until blended. Pour over corn mixture; toss to coat. Refrigerate, covered, at least 1 hour.
¾ cup: 192 cal., 12g fat (1g sat. fat), 0 chol., 407mg sod., 21g carb. (9g sugars, 3g fiber), 3g pro. **Diabetic exchanges:** 2 fat, 1 starch, 1 vegetable.

CHUNKY KETCHUP

I made this chunky homemade ketchup to jazz up chopped steak sandwiches and hot sausage sandwiches. I gave some to our friends, too, and they enjoyed it on burgers and stuffed peppers. It's fresh-tasting and delicious.
—Susan Stahr, Driftwood, PA

Prep: 20 min. • **Cook:** 1½ hours
Makes: 3½ cups

- **4 cups chopped seeded peeled tomatoes**
- **1 medium onion, chopped**
- **1 medium green pepper, chopped**
- **1 cup sugar**
- **1 can (6 oz.) tomato paste**
- **1 Tbsp. salt**
- **¼ cup white vinegar**

1. In a large saucepan, combine tomatoes, onion, green pepper, sugar, tomato paste and salt; bring to a boil. Reduce heat; simmer, uncovered, until slightly thickened, about 1½ hours.
2. Stir in the vinegar; heat through. Cool to room temperature; store up to 2 weeks in the refrigerator.
2 Tbsp.: 40 cal., 0 fat (0 sat. fat), 0 chol., 258mg sod., 10g carb

OVERNIGHT SLAW

Think of slaw as a side for all seasons—but especially summer—no matter what you're serving. Fix this one ahead and don't forget to use your food processor for even easier prep.
—Nancy Brown, Janesville, WI

Prep: 15 min. + chilling • **Makes:** 8 servings

- **1 medium head cabbage, shredded**
- **4 mild white onions, thinly sliced**
- **2 large carrots, shredded**
- **½ cup vinegar**
- **½ cup sugar**
- **1 tsp. ground mustard**
- **1 tsp. celery seed**
- **1 tsp. salt**
- **⅛ tsp. pepper**
- **½ cup vegetable oil**

In a large bowl, combine cabbage, onions and carrots; set aside. In a saucepan, combine the vinegar, sugar, mustard, celery seed, salt and pepper; bring to a boil, stirring until sugar is dissolved. Remove from the heat and stir in oil. Pour over cabbage mixture. Cool to room temperature. Cover and refrigerate overnight; stir several times.
¾ cup: 238 cal., 14g fat (2g sat. fat), 0 chol., 325mg sod., 28g carb. (21g sugars, 5g fiber), 3g pro. (9g sugars, 1g fiber), 0 pro.

DOUBLE HOT HORSERADISH MUSTARD

My family enjoys spicy food and hot mustard is a favorite. We crave this in sandwiches.
—Madeline Cole, Willow, AK

Takes: 10 min. • **Makes:** ½ cup

- **¼ cup cider vinegar**
- **¼ cup ground mustard**
- **3 Tbsp. white wine vinegar**
- **2 Tbsp. mustard seed**
- **1 Tbsp. prepared horseradish**
- **1½ tsp. honey**

In a blender, combine all ingredients. Cover and process until smooth. Transfer to a small jar and cover tightly. Store in the refrigerator.
2 Tbsp.: 74 cal., 4g fat (0 sat. fat), 0 chol., 18mg sod., 6g carb. (3g sugars, 2g fiber), 3g pro.

SOUTHERN POTATO SALAD

SOUTHERN POTATO SALAD

This potato salad with a southern twist is perfect for a church supper or potluck. The pickles add an extra sweetness.
—Gene Pitts, Wilsonville, AL

Prep: 30 min. + chilling • **Makes:** 8 servings

- **5 medium potatoes, peeled and cubed**
- **6 hard-boiled large eggs, chopped**
- **½ cup thinly sliced green onions**
- **¼ cup chopped sweet pickles**
- **1 tsp. prepared mustard**
- **1 tsp. celery seed**
- **1 cup mayonnaise**
- **Salt and pepper to taste**

Place potatoes in a large saucepan; add water to cover. Bring to a boil. Reduce heat; cook, uncovered, until tender, 10-15 minutes. Drain; refrigerate until cold. Add eggs, onions and pickles; toss well. Stir in mustard, celery seed and mayonnaise. Season with salt and pepper and mix well. Refrigerate until serving.
¾ cup: 377 cal., 26g fat (4g sat. fat), 169mg chol., 275mg sod., 28g carb. (5g sugars, 2g fiber), 8g pro.

GRILLED LEMON CHICKEN

(PICTURED ON PAGE 207)

My grilled chicken gets its subtle bit of pucker from lemonade concentrate. It's so simple and so sweet!
—Linda Nilsen, Anoka, MN

Prep: 5 min. • **Grill:** 40 min.
Makes: 12 servings

- **¾ cup thawed lemonade concentrate**
- **⅓ cup soy sauce**
- **1 garlic clove, minced**
- **1 tsp. seasoned salt**
- **½ tsp. celery salt**
- **⅛ tsp. garlic powder**
- **2 broiler/fryer chickens (3 to 3½ lbs. each), cut up**

1. In a bowl, whisk the first 6 ingredients until combined. Pour half into a shallow glass dish. Cover and refrigerate remaining lemonade mixture. Dip chicken into lemonade mixture, turning to coat; discard lemonade mixture. Grill chicken, covered, over medium heat for 30 minutes, turning occasionally. Brush with the reserved lemonade mixture. Grill 10-20 minutes longer, brushing frequently, until a thermometer reads 165°.
5 oz. cooked chicken: 320 cal., 17g fat (5g sat. fat), 104mg chol., 504mg sod., 6g carb. (5g sugars, 0 fiber), 34g pro.

ROASTED STRAWBERRY SHEET CAKE

ROASTED STRAWBERRY SHEET CAKE

My Grandma Gigi loved summer berry cakes. Almost any time I'd call her during the warmer months, she'd invite me over to taste her latest masterpiece. This cake is an ode to her.
—Kristin Bowers, Rancho Palos Verdes, CA

Prep: 1 hour • **Bake:** 30 min. + cooling
Makes: 24 servings

- **4 lbs. halved fresh strawberries**
- **½ cup sugar**

CAKE

- **1 cup butter, softened**
- **1½ cups sugar**
- **2 large eggs, room temperature**
- **2 tsp. almond extract**
- **3 cups all-purpose flour**
- **3 tsp. baking powder**
- **2 tsp. salt**
- **1 cup 2% milk**
- **¼ cup turbinado (washed raw) sugar**

1. Preheat oven to 350°. Place strawberries on a parchment-lined rimmed baking sheet. Sprinkle with sugar and toss to coat. Bake until just tender, 35-40 minutes. Cool slightly.
2. Meanwhile, grease a 15x10x1-in. baking pan. In a large bowl, cream butter and sugar until light and fluffy. Add 1 egg at a time, beating well after each addition. Beat in extract. In another bowl, whisk flour, baking powder and salt; add to creamed mixture alternately with milk, beating well after each addition (batter may appear curdled).
3. Transfer to prepared pan. Top with 3 cups roasted strawberries; sprinkle with turbinado sugar. Reserve remaining strawberries for serving. Bake until a toothpick inserted in center comes out clean, 30-35 minutes. Cool completely in pan on a wire rack. Serve with reserved roasted strawberries.
1 piece: 235 cal., 9g fat (5g sat. fat), 37mg chol., 329mg sod., 37g carb. (23g sugars, 2g fiber), 3g pro.

DID YOU KNOW?

Fresh strawberries spoil within a few days. Roasting them is an excellent way to salvage a surplus on the brink of becoming moldy or shriveled. As the berries roast, their juice thickens into a sweet sauce. Bake the berries into this sheet cake for delicious dessert or use them to top pancakes, crepes, waffles, biscuits or toast. Or scoop them over ice cream or vanilla yogurt.

PULLED BBQ PORK

PULLED BBQ PORK

After years of vacationing on the North Carolina coast, I became hooked on their pork barbecue. The version I developed is a favorite at potluck dinners.
—Joseph Sarnoski, West Chester, PA

Prep: 15 min. • **Cook:** 10 hours
Makes: 8 servings

- **2 medium onions, finely chopped**
- **1 Tbsp. canola oil**
- **6 garlic cloves, minced**
- **1 tsp. crushed red pepper flakes**
- **1 tsp. pepper**
- **1 can (14½ oz.) diced tomatoes, undrained**
- **¼ cup packed brown sugar**
- **¼ cup cider vinegar**
- **2 Tbsp. hot pepper sauce**
- **1 Tbsp. Worcestershire sauce**
- **1 tsp. ground cumin**
- **1 boneless pork shoulder butt roast (3 to 4 lbs.)**
- **8 kaiser rolls, split**

1. In a large skillet, saute onions in oil until tender. Add the garlic, pepper flakes and pepper; cook 1 minute longer. Stir in the tomatoes, brown sugar, vinegar, hot pepper sauce, Worcestershire and cumin. Cook over medium heat until heated through and sugar is dissolved.
2. Cut roast in half. Place in a 5-qt. slow cooker; pour sauce over the top. Cover and cook on low for 10-12 hours or until meat is tender. Remove roast; cool slightly. Skim fat from cooking juices. Shred meat with 2 forks and return to the slow cooker. Heat through. With a slotted spoon, place ¾ cup meat mixture on each roll.
1 sandwich: 518 cal., 21g fat (7g sat. fat), 101mg chol., 528mg sod., 44g carb. (12g sugars, 3g fiber), 36g pro.

Summer in the City

Give your hot dog hometown flair with these fun frank flavors from across America.

PHILADELPHIA
- Cheez Whiz
- Sauteed peppers, onions and mushrooms
- Served on a hoagie roll

DETROIT
- Beanless chili
- Mustard
- Raw diced onion
- Shredded cheddar
- On a poppy seed bun

NASHVILLE
- Chicken hot dog
- Hot sauce
- Cayenne
- Mayo
- Sliced pickles
- Tucked into a plain bun

TUCSON
- Wrapped in bacon
- Pinto beans
- Chopped tomatoes
- Diced raw onion
- Avocado
- Mayo
- Jalapenos
- Piled on a bolillo roll

KANSAS CITY
- Melted Swiss cheese
- Sauerkraut
- Thousand Island dressing
- Served on a sesame seed bun

GOLDEN PEACH PIE

Years ago, I entered this pie in the Park County Fair in Livingston. It won a first-place blue ribbon plus a purple ribbon for Best All Around. Family and friends agree with the judges—it's a perfectly peachy pie!
—Shirley Olson, Polson, MT

Prep: 20 min. • **Bake:** 50 min. + cooling
Makes: 8 servings

2 sheets refrigerated pie crust
5 cups sliced peeled fresh peaches (about 5 medium)
2 tsp. lemon juice
½ tsp. grated orange zest
⅛ tsp. almond extract
1 cup sugar
¼ cup cornstarch
¼ tsp. ground nutmeg
⅛ tsp. salt
2 Tbsp. butter

1. Line a 9-in. pie plate with 1 crust; trim, leaving a 1-in. overhang around edge. Set aside. In a large bowl, combine the peaches, lemon juice, orange zest and almond extract. Combine the sugar, cornstarch, nutmeg and salt. Add to peach mixture; toss gently to coat. Pour into crust; dot with butter.
2. Roll out remaining crust to a ⅛-in.-thick circle; cut into strips. Arrange over filling in a lattice pattern. Trim and seal strips to bottom crust; fold overhang over. Lightly press or flute edge. Cover the edges loosely with foil.
3. Bake at 400° for 40 minutes. Remove foil; bake until crust is golden brown and filling is bubbly, 10-15 minutes longer. Cool on a wire rack. Store in the refrigerator.
1 piece: 425 cal., 17g fat (8g sat. fat), 18mg chol., 267mg sod., 67g carb. (36g sugars, 2g fiber), 3g pro.

RAINBOW FRUIT SALAD

RAINBOW FRUIT SALAD

When my children were young, I would often dress up fresh fruit in this easy-to-fix salad. Decades later, my grandchildren and great-grandchildren still love digging into the fruity layers. The salad goes well with barbecued meats or cold sandwiches.
—Jonnie Adams Sisler, Stevensville, MT

Prep: 20 min. + chilling • **Makes:** 20 servings

- **2 large firm bananas, sliced**
- **2 Tbsp. lemon juice**
- **2 cups seeded cubed watermelon**
- **2 cups fresh or canned pineapple chunks**
- **1 pint fresh blueberries**
- **3 kiwifruit, peeled and sliced**
- **1 pint fresh strawberries, halved**
- **6 oz. cream cheese, softened**
- **⅓ cup confectioners' sugar**
- **2 Tbsp. fresh lime juice**
- **½ tsp. grated lime zest**
- **1 cup heavy whipping cream, whipped**

1. Toss bananas and lemon juice; place in a 4-qt. glass serving bowl. Add remaining fruit in layers.
2. In a bowl, beat cream cheese until smooth. Gradually add sugar, lime juice and zest. Stir in a small amount of whipped cream; mix well. Fold in remaining whipped cream. Spread over fruit. Chill until serving.
¾ cup: 123 cal., 7g fat (5g sat. fat), 22mg chol., 31mg sod., 14g carb. (10g sugars, 2g fiber), 1g pro.

To add an extra punch of flavor to this fruit salad, consider adding fresh herbs. Mint pairs well with citrus fruits and melon. Basil is a great accompaniment to fresh strawberries and blueberries.

SUNDAE FUNDAY

Host a good old-fashioned ice cream social right in your kitchen with homemade recipes that will take you back to the simple pleasures of childhood. Whether you're partial to sundaes, parfaits, shakes, pops or other novelties, this icy recipe collection will keep you chill when the weather's hot.

Chocolate Chip Strawberry Ice Cream (p. 221)

HOT FUDGE
REAL
Ice Cream

BROWNIE WAFFLE ICE CREAM SUNDAES

I adore getting my four girls in the kitchen. They bake brownies from scratch on a weekly basis. This summer, we experimented and put our famous brownie batter in the waffle iron and served them with ice cream!
—Juliana Evans, Wesley Chapel, FL

Prep: 15 min. • **Cook:** 5 min./batch
Makes: 8 servings

- **½ cup unsalted butter**
- **1 cup sugar**
- **⅓ cup baking cocoa**
- **1 tsp. vanilla extract**
- **2 large eggs, room temperature**
- **½ cup all-purpose flour**
- **½ tsp. salt**
- **4 cups vanilla ice cream**
- **Chocolate or hot fudge ice cream topping and sprinkles, optional**

1. Preheat a round Belgian waffle maker. In a microwave, melt butter on high, stirring every 30 seconds. Stir in sugar, cocoa and vanilla. Add eggs, 1 at a time, whisking after each addition. Add flour and salt; stir just until combined.
2. Bake brownie waffles according to manufacturer's directions until cooked through, 4-5 minutes. Let stand on open waffle maker for 30-60 seconds to crisp before carefully removing. Cut the waffles into fourths. Top each wedge with a scoop of ice cream. If desired, top with ice cream topping and sprinkles.
¼ waffle with ½ cup ice cream: 394 cal., 20g fat (12g sat. fat), 106mg chol., 220mg sod., 49g carb. (39g sugars, 1g fiber), 5g pro.

BUTTERY PINEAPPLE & COCONUT FROZEN CUSTARD

This frozen custard is truly a decadent warm-weather dessert, thanks to toasted coconut and pineapple sauce. It has just the right tropical flavor to keep you coming back for more.
—Colleen Delawder, Herndon, VA

Prep: 1 hour + chilling
Process: 20 min. + freezing
Makes: 1¼ qt.

- **6 large egg yolks**
- **½ cup sugar**
- **¼ tsp. kosher salt**
- **2 cups heavy whipping cream, divided**
- **1 cup whole milk**
- **1 Tbsp. vanilla extract**

PINEAPPLE SAUCE
- **1 cup cubed fresh pineapple**
- **¼ cup sugar**
- **¼ tsp. kosher salt**
- **1 Tbsp. butter**

TOASTED COCONUT
- **1 Tbsp. butter**
- **1 cup unsweetened shredded coconut**

1. In a small heavy saucepan, whisk the egg yolks, sugar and salt until blended; stir in 1 cup cream and whole milk. Cook over medium-low heat until a thermometer reads at least 160°, stirring constantly. Do not allow to boil. Remove from heat.
2. Strain into a bowl; whisk in remaining 1 cup cream and vanilla. Place bowl in a pan of ice water. Stir gently and occasionally for 2 minutes. Press plastic wrap onto surface of custard. Refrigerate overnight.
3. For pineapple sauce, place the pineapple, sugar and salt in a food processor; process until pureed. Transfer to a small saucepan; add butter. Cook and stir over medium-high heat until sugar is dissolved, 2-3 minutes. Cover and refrigerate until chilled.
4. For toasted coconut, melt butter in a large skillet over low heat. Add coconut; cook and stir until golden brown, 5-10 minutes, stirring occasionally. Spread coconut on foil to cool completely. Store in an airtight container.
5. Pour custard into cylinder of ice cream freezer; freeze according to manufacturer's directions, adding toasted coconut during the last 5 minutes of processing.
6. Transfer custard to freezer containers, allowing headspace for expansion; drop pineapple sauce by tablespoonfuls over custard. Cut through custard with a knife to swirl. Freeze until firm, 8 hours or overnight.
½ cup: 177 cal., 14g fat (9g sat. fat), 87mg chol., 73mg sod., 11g carb. (10g sugars, 1g fiber), 2g pro.

TEST KITCHEN TIP

Straining the warm custard mixture ensures that you won't have any cooked egg bits in your frozen custard. That's also why you slowly add a little bit of warm cream mixture to the whisked eggs before adding them back into the saucepan.

BROWNIE WAFFLE
ICE CREAM SUNDAES

Scoop Dreams

Vanilla ice cream makes the coolest canvas for these tricked-out topping ideas we're all screaming for.

RITZ CRACKERS & CHOCOLATE SAUCE
Hershey's chocolate sauce and Ritz crackers!
—Brooklyn Reynolds, Anderson, IN

BACON & MAPLE SYRUP
I top mine with maple syrup and crispy thick-cut bacon.
—Carol Feldmann, Sheboygan Falls, WI

CORNFLAKES & CINNAMON
From my sister's brain: cornflakes and cinnamon. It tastes like apple pie. You don't even need the apples!
—Sabrina Eileen Stebbins Brown, Saratoga Springs, UT

JAM & CHOCOLATE
I load mine up with strawberry jam, mini chocolate chips and chopped pecans.
—Donna Paprocki, Des Plaines, IL

COOLED ESPRESSO
Pour on some cooled Cuban coffee or espresso. It's just plain awesome.
—Cathy Killinger Lopez, Charlotte, NC

FRENCH FRIES & FUDGE
Fresh-baked french fries and hot fudge sauce. So good.
—Tracy Strickland, Shipshewana, IN

NERDS CANDY
I like to top mine with rainbow Nerds candy. I love the fun color and crunch!
—Rachel Bernhard Seis, Taste of Home *Senior Editor*

MELTED PEANUT BUTTER
I drizzle mine with melted peanut butter.
—Rd Stendel-Freels, Albuquerque, NM

CRUSHED POTATO CHIPS
The flavor combo gives you both sweet and salty. Yum!
—Pam Slack, Freeburg, IL

MALT POWDER
This is best sprinkled on chocolate syrup. Or scoop the ice cream into a glass and pour in a little Baileys for a more adult serving.
—Amy Rabideau Silvers, Taste of Home *Copy Editor*

CHOCOLATE CHIP
STRAWBERRY ICE CREAM

CHOCOLATE CHIP STRAWBERRY ICE CREAM

My husband and I have a favorite DQ Blizzard that we enjoy as a special treat. I decided to come up with my own homemade version. Make sure the ice cream mixture is cooled for several hours or overnight before filling the ice cream maker.

—Sandy Martin, Elizabethtown, PA

Prep: 25 min. • **Process:** 15 min. + freezing
Makes: 1½ qt.

- 1⅔ **cups sugar**
- 5 **Tbsp. cornstarch, divided**
- 4 **cups 2% milk**
- 2 **large egg yolks**
- 1⅓ **cups heavy whipping cream**
- ⅔ **cup half-and-half cream**
- 3 **tsp. vanilla extract**
- ¼ **cup light corn syrup**
- 3 **cups fresh strawberries, hulled**
- 1 **dark chocolate candy bar (8 oz.), finely chopped**
- **Whipped cream and maraschino cherries, optional**

1. In a large heavy saucepan, whisk sugar and 4 Tbsp. cornstarch until blended; whisk in milk until smooth. Bring mixture to a boil, stirring constantly; cook and stir 1-2 minutes or until thickened. Reduce heat to low. In a small bowl, whisk a small amount of hot mixture into egg yolks; return all to pan, whisking constantly. Cook for 2-3 minutes over low heat or until mixture thickens and a thermometer reads 160°, stirring constantly. Remove from heat immediately.

2. Quickly transfer mixture to a large bowl; place the bowl in a pan of ice water. Stir gently and occasionally for 2 minutes. Stir in cream, half-and-half and vanilla. Press plastic wrap onto surface of custard. Refrigerate several hours or overnight.

3. Fill cylinder of ice cream freezer two-thirds full; freeze according to the manufacturer's directions.

4. Meanwhile, place the remaining 1 Tbsp. cornstarch in a large skillet. Whisk in corn syrup until smooth; add the strawberries. Bring to a boil over medium heat; cook and stir berry mixture until thickened, 2 minutes. Mash strawberries; cool.

5. During last 5 minutes of processing, add strawberry mixture and chopped chocolate. Transfer ice cream to freezer containers, allowing headspace for expansion. Freeze at least 4 hours or until firm. If desired, serve with whipped cream and cherries.

½ cup: 397 cal., 19g fat (12g sat. fat), 76mg chol., 59mg sod., 56g carb. (50g sugars, 2g fiber), 6g pro.

BLUEBERRY CREAM POPS

BLUEBERRY CREAM POPS

Blueberry and cream pops are such a fun afternoon snack. And they're simple to make!

—Cindy Reams, Philipsburg, PA

Prep: 15 min. + freezing • **Makes:** 8 pops

- ⅔ **cup sugar**
- ⅔ **cup water**
- 2 **cups fresh or frozen blueberries, thawed**
- ¼ **cup heavy whipping cream**
- 8 **freezer pop molds or 8 paper cups (3 oz. each) and wooden pop sticks**

1. For sugar syrup, in a small saucepan, combine sugar and water; bring to a boil, stirring to dissolve sugar. Cool completely.

2. Meanwhile, in a bowl, coarsely mash blueberries; stir in cream and sugar syrup. Spoon into molds or paper cups. Top molds with holders. If using cups, top with foil and insert sticks through foil. Freeze until firm. To serve, let pops stand at room temperature 10 minutes before unmolding.

1 pop: 112 cal., 3g fat (2g sat. fat), 10mg chol., 3mg sod., 22g carb. (21g sugars, 1g fiber), 0 pro.

RUM BANANA SAUCE

Plain vanilla ice cream becomes amazing thanks to this delectable recipe.

—Katherine Desrosiers, Trail, BC

Takes: 15 min. • **Makes:** 4 servings

- ¾ **cup packed brown sugar**
- ¼ **cup butter, cubed**
- ¼ **cup heavy whipping cream**
- 2 **Tbsp. maple syrup**
- 2 **large bananas, cut into ½-in. slices**
- ½ **tsp. rum extract**
- **Vanilla ice cream**

In a small saucepan, combine brown sugar, butter, cream and maple syrup. Cook and stir over medium heat until sauce is smooth, 4-5 minutes. Stir in bananas; heat through. Remove from the heat; stir in extract. Serve with ice cream.

½ cup: 397 cal., 17g fat (11g sat. fat), 50mg chol., 104mg sod., 63g carb. (54g sugars, 2g fiber), 1g pro.

PEACHY BUTTERMILK SHAKES

My husband and grandkids enjoy the tang of buttermilk blended with sweet peaches in these delightful shakes.
—Anna Mayer, Fort Branch, IN

Takes: 10 min. • **Makes:** 3 servings

- **1 cup buttermilk**
- **3 cups fresh or frozen unsweetened sliced peaches, thawed**
- **1 cup vanilla ice cream, softened**
- **¼ cup sugar**
- **¾ tsp. ground cinnamon**
- **Optional: Whipped cream and additional sliced peaches**

Place all ingredients in a blender; cover and process until smooth. Pour the mixture into chilled glasses; serve immediately. If desired, top shakes with whipped cream and additional sliced peaches.

1 cup: 250 cal., 6g fat (3g sat. fat), 23mg chol., 191mg sod., 46g carb. (42g sugars, 3g fiber), 6g pro.

BUTTER PECAN SAUCE

Buttery, smooth and full of pecans, this sauce is sensational over ice cream. It's hard to beat its homemade goodness.
—Kim Gilliland, Simi Valley, CA

Takes: 15 min. • **Makes:** 1½ cups

- **½ cup plus 2 Tbsp. packed brown sugar**
- **2 Tbsp. sugar**
- **4 tsp. cornstarch**
- **¾ cup heavy whipping cream**
- **1 Tbsp. butter**
- **½ cup chopped pecans, toasted**
- **Vanilla ice cream or flavor of your choice**

1. In a heavy saucepan, combine sugars and cornstarch. Gradually stir in cream until smooth. Bring to a boil over medium heat, stirring constantly; cook and stir until slightly thickened, 2-3 minutes.

2. Remove from the heat; stir in butter until melted. Add the pecans. Serve warm over ice cream.

2 Tbsp.: 148 cal., 10g fat (4g sat. fat), 23mg chol., 20mg sod., 15g carb. (14g sugars, 0 fiber), 1g pro.

PEACHY BUTTERMILK SHAKES

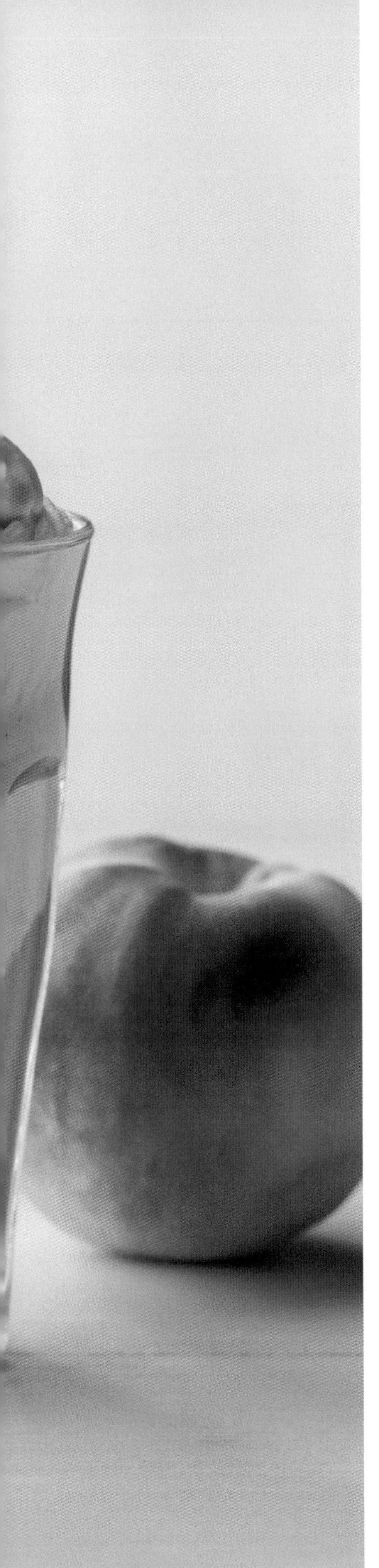

EASY RHUBARB SAUCE

Celebrate summer with the sweet-tart taste of rhubarb in this simple sauce. I enjoy it on toast, English muffins and pancakes, but it's just as good drizzled on pound cake or ice cream.
—Jackie Hutshing, Sonoma, CA

Takes: 20 min. • **Makes:** 1¼ cups

- **⅓ cup sugar**
- **¼ cup water**
- **2¼ cups sliced fresh or frozen rhubarb**
- **1 tsp. grated lemon zest**
- **⅛ tsp. ground nutmeg**
- **Pound cake or vanilla ice cream**

1. In a small saucepan, bring the sugar and water to a boil. Add rhubarb; cook and stir 5-10 minutes or until rhubarb is tender and mixture is slightly thickened. Remove from the heat; stir in lemon zest and nutmeg.
2. Serve warm or chilled over pound cake or ice cream. Refrigerate leftovers.
¼ cup: 64 cal., 0 fat (0 sat. fat), 0 chol., 2mg sod., 16g carb. (14g sugars, 1g fiber), 1g pro.
Diabetic exchanges: 1 starch.

CHOCOLATE FRAMBOISE PARFAITS

Expecting company? Have these quick delicious parfaits ready to pull out of the freezer for a welcoming treat.
—Charlene Chambers, Ormond Beach, FL

Prep: 15 min. + freezing • **Makes:** 6 servings

- **6 Tbsp. raspberry liqueur**
- **1½ pints vanilla ice cream**
- **1½ pints fresh raspberries**
- **2¼ cups chocolate wafer crumbs**
- **Sweetened whipped cream**

Layer each of 6 parfait glasses with 1 tsp. raspberry liqueur, 2½ Tbsp. ice cream, 4 or 5 raspberries and 2 Tbsp. chocolate wafer crumbs. Repeat layers twice. Freeze. To serve, top with sweetened whipped cream and the remaining raspberries.
1 parfait: 402 cal., 14g fat (6g sat. fat), 30mg chol., 297mg sod., 59g carb. (38g sugars, 6g fiber), 6g pro.

LADYFINGER LEMON TORTE

Golden ladyfingers frame the luscious custard filling of this lovely frozen dessert. Everyone loves the yummy combination of sweetness and lemony zest.
—J.H. Carroll, Ottawa, ON

Prep: 30 min. + freezing • **Makes:** 12 servings

- **5 large egg yolks, lightly beaten**
- **1½ cups sugar, divided**
- **¾ cup lemon juice**
- **2 large egg whites**
- **1 Tbsp. grated lemon zest**
- **2 cups heavy whipping cream**
- **2 pkg. (3 oz. each) ladyfingers, split**
- **Lemon slices and fresh mint leaves**

1. In a heavy saucepan, combine egg yolks, 1¼ cups sugar, lemon juice and egg whites. Bring to a boil over medium heat; cook and stir for 8-10 minutes or until mixture reaches 160° or is thick enough to coat a metal spoon. Remove from heat. Cool quickly by placing pan in a bowl of ice water; stir for 2 minutes. Stir in lemon zest. Transfer to a bowl, press plastic wrap onto surface of custard. Chill for 2-3 hours or until partially set.
2. In a large bowl, beat cream on medium speed until soft peaks form. Gradually beat in remaining sugar, 1 Tbsp. at a time, on high until stiff peaks form. Gradually fold whipped cream into the cooled lemon mixture.
3. Arrange 24 ladyfingers around the edge of an ungreased 9-in. springform pan. Arrange 16 ladyfingers on bottom of pan. Spread with half the lemon mixture. Layer with the remaining ladyfingers; top with remaining lemon mixture.
4. Cover and freeze overnight. Remove from the freezer 5 minutes before cutting. Remove sides of the pan. Garnish with lemon slices and fresh mint.
1 slice: 291 cal., 17g fat (10g sat. fat), 169mg chol., 38mg sod., 32g carb. (29g sugars, 0 fiber), 3g pro.

CHOCOLATE DESSERT DELIGHT

Some of my friends refer to this unbelievably rich ice cream dessert as Death by Chocolate. Then they ask for seconds! It's a scrumptious make-ahead treat perfect for parties.
—Lee Ann Stidman, Spirit Lake, ID

Prep: 25 min. + freezing • **Makes:** 20 servings

- **2 cups chocolate graham cracker crumbs (about 32 squares)**
- **½ cup butter, melted**
- **½ cup chopped walnuts**
- **1 Tbsp. sugar**

FILLING

- **½ gallon chocolate ice cream, softened**
- **1 jar (12¼ oz.) caramel ice cream topping**
- **1 jar (11¾ oz.) hot fudge ice cream topping**
- **½ cup miniature semisweet chocolate chips**
- **½ cup chopped walnuts**

TOPPING

- **2 cups heavy whipping cream**
- **3 Tbsp. sugar**
- **1 Tbsp. baking cocoa**
- **1 tsp. vanilla extract**
- **½ tsp. instant coffee granules**
- **Additional miniature chocolate chips and chopped walnuts**

1. For crust, combine crumbs, butter, walnuts and sugar; press into an ungreased 13x9-in. baking pan. Bake at 350° for 10 minutes; cool completely.
2. Spread half of the ice cream over crust; spoon caramel and hot fudge toppings over ice cream. Sprinkle with chocolate chips and walnuts; freeze until firm. Spread with the remaining ice cream over the top. Cover with plastic wrap. Freeze for at least 2 hours.
3. In a large bowl, beat cream until stiff peaks form. Fold in sugar, cocoa, vanilla and coffee granules. Pipe or spoon onto dessert. Sprinkle with additional chocolate chips and walnuts. Return to freezer. Remove from the freezer 10 minutes before serving.
1 piece: 443 cal., 26g fat (13g sat. fat), 63mg chol., 230mg sod., 50g carb. (39g sugars, 2g fiber), 6g pro.

WATERMELON BOMBE DESSERT

This sherbet dessert looks like watermelon slices—complete with seeds—when cut. It's fun to eat and refreshing, too.
—Renae Moncur, Burley, ID

Prep: 20 min. + freezing • **Makes:** 8 servings

- **About 1 pint lime sherbet**
- **About 1 pint pineapple sherbet**
- **About 1½ pints raspberry sherbet**
- **¼ cup miniature semisweet chocolate chips**

Line a 1½-qt. bowl with plastic wrap. Press slightly softened lime sherbet against the bottom and sides of bowl. Freeze, uncovered, until firm. Spread pineapple sherbet evenly over lime sherbet layer. Freeze, uncovered, until firm. (Lime and pineapple sherbet layers should be thin.) Pack raspberry sherbet in center of sherbet-lined bowl. Smooth the top to resemble a cut watermelon. Cover and freeze until firm, about 8 hours. Just before serving, uncover bowl of molded sherbet. Place a serving plate on the bowl and invert. Remove bowl and peel off plastic wrap. Cut the bombe into wedges; press a few chocolate chips into the raspberry section of each wedge to resemble watermelon seeds.
1 piece: 205 cal., 4g fat (2g sat. fat), 8mg chol., 60mg sod., 43g carb. (35g sugars, 0 fiber), 2g pro.

DID YOU KNOW?

Sherbet originated in the Middle East as a popular drink made by adding sweetened fruit juice to water. The version we know now gets its creamy texture from milk, egg whites and/or gelatin.

WATERMELON BOMBE DESSERT

BEACH PARTY

Grab your beach towel, flip-flops and shades—it's time for a beach bash! Whether you live on the water or just want to bring a seaside vibe to your summer gathering, turn to these easy-to-eat recipes that are portable, refreshing, cooler-friendly and delicious.

Mojito-Style Yellow Tomato Salsa (p. 229) **Garden Pesto Pasta Salad** (p. 233) **Chipotle Guacamole** (p. 231) **Italian Hero Braid** (p. 235)

MOJITO-STYLE YELLOW TOMATO SALSA

MOJITO-STYLE YELLOW TOMATO SALSA

With grilled tomatoes, crunchy peppers and a sprinkle of mint, this fresh salsa is good on just about everything. Try it in fish tacos, on tortilla chips or by the spoonful!
—Patterson Watkins, Philadelphia, PA

Prep: 20 min. • **Grill:** 10 min. + chilling
Makes: 4 cups

- **2 lbs. large yellow tomatoes, halved**
- **1 Tbsp. olive oil**
- **2 garlic cloves, minced**
- **1 tsp. chopped shallot**
- **¾ tsp. salt, divided**
- **3 medium limes**
- **2 tsp. coarse sugar**
- **12 fresh mint leaves**
- **¼ cup chopped Cubanelle or banana peppers**

1. Grill tomatoes, uncovered, on an oiled rack over high heat (or broil 3-4 in. from the heat) until the skin is slightly charred, 3-4 minutes on each side. Cool to room temperature. Meanwhile, combine oil, garlic, shallot and ¼ tsp. salt. When tomatoes are cool enough to handle, finely chop; stir in garlic mixture until well combined.
2. Finely grate zest of each lime; set aside. Peel and discard white membranes; section the limes. In a food processor, pulse lime sections, sugar, mint and remaining salt until finely chopped. Combine with tomatoes; add peppers and lime zest. Mix well.
3. Refrigerate at least 1 hour. Serve with chips or grilled meats.
¼ cup: 23 cal., 1g fat (0 sat. fat), 0 chol., 161mg sod., 4g carb. (1g sugars, 1g fiber), 1g pro. **Diabetic exchanges:** 1 vegetable.

FRESH CUCUMBER SALAD

Crisp, garden-fresh cukes are always in season when we hold our family reunion, and they really shine in this simple cucumber salad. The recipe can easily be expanded to make large quantities, too.
—Betsy Carlson, Rockford, IL

Prep: 10 min. + chilling
Makes: 10 servings

- **3 medium cucumbers, sliced**
- **1 cup sugar**
- **¾ cup water**
- **½ cup white vinegar**
- **3 Tbsp. minced fresh dill or parsley**

Place cucumbers in a 1½- to 2-qt. glass container. In a jar with a tight-fitting lid, shake remaining ingredients until combined. Pour over cucumbers. Cover and refrigerate overnight. Serve with a slotted spoon.
½ cup: 87 cal., 0 fat (0 sat. fat), 0 chol., 0 sod., 22g carb. (21g sugars, 1g fiber), 1g pro.

TEXAS TEA

Make a pitcher full of this tea for a get-together on a hot summer day. It's a potent drink, so enjoy responsibly!
—Taste of Home *Test Kitchen*

Takes: 10 min. • **Makes:** 8 servings

- **1 cup cola**
- **1 cup sour mix**
- **½ cup vodka**
- **½ cup gin**
- **½ cup Triple Sec**
- **½ cup golden or light rum**
- **½ cup tequila**
- **Lemon or lime slices**

In a pitcher, mix the first 7 ingredients; serve over ice. Garnish servings with lemon.
¾ cup: 246 cal., 0 fat (0 sat. fat), 0 chol., 2mg sod., 24g carb. (22g sugars, 0 fiber), 0 pro.

Pack Like a Pro

Transport food with confidence with these easy hacks.

BUILD A DIY MULTI-LEVEL TOTE
If you have more dishes than hands, reach for a cooling rack with folding legs. Fold out the legs and use the rack to create sturdy, stable levels inside a carrying tote without crushing what's below. You can also build layers by propping up a sheet pan with ring molds or cans.

ENSURE A NO-SLIP TRIP
Place grippy drawer liners or silicone baking mats in the car before loading your food. The lining will keep dishes from sliding and contain any errant spills. A yoga mat works, too.

KEEP A LID ON IT
Use a bungee cord, painter's tape or thick ribbon to keep the lid for your slow cooker, Dutch oven or other serving vessel in place. Secure the cord around the handles and over the top. Now you're ready to transport without risk of a mess.

BRING A SALAD
Yes, you can serve a crisp, freshly tossed salad when you're far from home. Just bring the fixings in a serving bowl, along with the utensils. Toss the salad at your destination. Voila!

GRILL SKILLS
If you're bringing a portable grill, place the grill on a solid surface, away from any activities so no one bumps into it. Don't set the grill near shrubs, grass, overhangs or fences.

TAILGATE KIT
Store all your tailgate needs (such as linens, serveware, utensils, napkins, trash bags, games and sunblock) in a plastic bin inside a cooler. You'll be ready to go at a moment's notice.

PINEAPPLE & MINT INFUSED WATER

This pineapple and mint water is like a tropical cocktail but without the sticky-sweet taste.
—James Schend, Pleasant Prairie, WI

Prep: 5 min. + chilling
Makes: 2 qts.

- **2 qt. water**
- **¼ fresh pineapple, sliced**
- **3 fresh mint sprigs**

Combine all ingredients in a large glass carafe or pitcher. Cover and refrigerate 12-24 hours. Strain before serving.
1 cup: 0 cal., 0 fat (0 sat. fat), 0 chol., 0 sod., 0 carb. (0 sugars, 0 fiber), 0 pro.

TEST KITCHEN TIP

Gently crush fresh herbs, toast dry spices or lightly muddle fresh fruit to get the most flavor in the water.

BLT TORTILLAS

I first sampled these BLT wraps at a bridal luncheon years ago. Now I make them for our weekly neighborhood dinners.
—Darla Wester, Meriden, IA

Takes: 15 min. • **Makes:** 8 servings

- **½ cup mayonnaise**
- **½ cup sour cream**
- **2 Tbsp. ranch salad dressing mix**
- **¼ tsp. crushed red pepper flakes**
- **8 flour tortillas (8 in.), room temperature**
- **16 cooked bacon strips**
- **2 to 3 cups shredded lettuce**
- **2 cups chopped seeded tomato**
- **Green and sweet red pepper strips, optional**

Mix the first 4 ingredients; spread onto the tortillas. Top with remaining ingredients and roll up.
1 wrap: 402 cal., 25g fat (7g sat. fat), 27mg chol., 890mg sod., 32g carb. (2g sugars, 2g fiber), 13g pro.

CHIPOTLE GUACAMOLE

My guacamole is so good because it has just a hint of smoke from the chipotle peppers. Stir them in or put a dollop in the center of the dip so people who aren't fans of peppers can easily scoop around them.
—Gayle Sullivan, Salem, MA

Prep: 15 min. + chilling • **Makes:** 3 cups

- 4 **medium ripe avocados, peeled and pitted**
- 1 **small tomato, seeded and chopped**
- ⅓ **cup finely chopped red onion**
- 3 **garlic cloves, minced**
- 2 **Tbsp. lemon juice**
- 2 **Tbsp. olive oil**
- ¼ **tsp. salt**
- 1 **to 2 Tbsp. minced fresh cilantro, optional**
- 1 **finely chopped chipotle pepper in adobo sauce plus 1 tsp. adobo sauce**
- **Tortilla chips**

Mash avocados. Stir in next 6 ingredients and, if desired, cilantro. Dollop chipotle pepper and adobo sauce over center of guacamole. Refrigerate 1 hour. Serve with tortilla chips.
¼ cup: 103 cal., 9g fat (1g sat. fat), 0 chol., 70mg sod., 5g carb. (1g sugars, 3g fiber), 1g pro.

PEACH
CRUMB BARS

PEACH CRUMB BARS

I had the most beautiful peaches and wanted to put them to good use in a tasty baked treat. I started with my blueberry crumb bar recipe, and after a little trial-and-error, came up with these delicious peach bars.
—Amy Burns, Newman, IL

Prep: 30 min. • **Bake:** 40 min. + cooling
Makes: 2 dozen

- **3 cups all-purpose flour**
- **1½ cups sugar, divided**
- **1 tsp. baking powder**
- **½ tsp. salt**
- **Dash ground cinnamon**
- **1 cup shortening**
- **1 large egg**
- **1 tsp. vanilla extract**
- **9 medium peaches, peeled and chopped**
- **1 tsp. almond extract**
- **4 tsp. cornstarch**

1. Preheat oven to 375°. Whisk flour, 1 cup sugar, baking powder, salt and cinnamon; cut in shortening until crumbly. In another bowl, whisk egg and vanilla until blended; add to flour mixture, stirring with a fork until crumbly.
2. Reserve 2½ cups crumb mixture for topping. Press remaining mixture onto bottom of a greased 13x9-in. baking pan.
3. Toss peaches with almond extract. In another bowl, mix cornstarch and remaining sugar; add to the peaches and toss to coat. Spread over crust and sprinkle with the reserved topping.
4. Bake until lightly browned and filling is bubbly, 40-45 minutes. Cool completely in pan on a wire rack. Cut into bars.
1 bar: 207 cal., 9g fat (2g sat. fat), 8mg chol., 73mg sod., 30g carb. (17g sugars, 1g fiber), 2g pro.

TEST KITCHEN TIP

If you're craving a bit of summer in the off-season, you can make these bars with canned peaches. Just substitute 5½ cups canned peaches (drained well before measuring) for the fresh fruit. Want a bold and fresh flavor combination? Sprinkle minced fresh basil over these right before serving. The anise-y bite pairs surprisingly well with the juicy fruit flavor.

GARDEN PESTO PASTA SALAD

GARDEN PESTO PASTA SALAD

My family and I live on a homestead in the Missouri Ozarks and produce much of our own food. In the summer, when the garden is bursting with fresh vegetables and it's too hot to cook, I use the seasonal veggies for pasta salads and other cool meals.
—Sarah Mathews, Ava, MO

Prep: 15 min. + chilling • **Makes:** 10 servings

- **3 cups uncooked spiral pasta (about 9 oz.)**
- **½ cup prepared pesto**
- **3 Tbsp. white wine vinegar**
- **1 Tbsp. lemon juice**
- **½ tsp. salt**
- **¼ tsp. pepper**
- **¼ cup olive oil**
- **1 medium zucchini, halved and sliced**
- **1 medium sweet red pepper, chopped**
- **1 medium tomato, seeded and chopped**
- **1 small red onion, halved and thinly sliced**
- **½ cup grated Parmesan cheese**

1. Cook spiral pasta according to package directions; drain. Rinse with cold water and drain well.
2. Meanwhile, whisk together pesto, vinegar, lemon juice and seasonings. Gradually whisk in oil until blended.
3. Combine the vegetables and pasta. Drizzle with pesto dressing; toss to coat. Refrigerate, covered, until cold, about 1 hour. Serve with Parmesan cheese.
¾ cup: 217 cal., 11g fat (2g sat. fat), 3mg chol., 339mg sod., 23g carb. (3g sugars, 2g fiber), 6g pro. **Diabetic exchanges:** 2 fat, 1½ starch.

WATERMELON SLICE COOKIES

Once when I made these butter cookies for a party, a neighbor thought they were so cute that she took one home and froze it to show her friends. They're easy to make, too!
—Sue Ann Benham, Valparaiso, IN

Prep: 25 min. + chilling • **Bake:** 10 min./batch
Makes: about 3 dozen

- **¾ cup butter, softened**
- **¾ cup sugar**
- **1 large egg, room temperature**
- **½ tsp. almond extract**
- **2 cups all-purpose flour**
- **¼ tsp. baking powder**
- **⅛ tsp. salt**
- **Red and green gel food coloring**
- **⅓ cup miniature semisweet chocolate chips or raisins, chopped**
- **1 tsp. sesame seeds, optional**

1. In a large bowl, cream butter and sugar until light and fluffy. Beat in egg and extract. In another bowl, whisk flour, baking powder and salt; gradually beat into creamed mixture. Reserve 1 cup dough.
2. Tint remaining dough red; shape into a 3½-in.-long roll and wrap. Tint ⅓ cup of reserved dough green; wrap. Wrap remaining plain dough. Refrigerate dough for 2 hours or until firm.
3. On a lightly floured surface, roll plain dough into an 8½x3½-in. rectangle. Unwrap red dough and place on a short end of the plain dough; roll up.
4. Roll the green dough into a 10x3½-in. rectangle. Place red and plain roll on a short end of the green dough; roll up. Wrap and refrigerate overnight.
5. Preheat oven to 350°. Unwrap and cut dough into 3/16-in. slices (just less than ¼ in.). Place 2 in. apart on ungreased baking sheets. Lightly press chocolate chips and, if desired, sesame seeds into red dough to resemble watermelon seeds.
6. Bake cookies for 9-11 minutes or until firm. Immediately cut each cookie in half. Remove to wire racks to cool.
1 cookie: 82 cal., 4g fat (2g sat. fat), 16mg chol., 52mg sod., 11g carb. (5g sugars, 0 fiber), 1g pro.

PICNIC FRUIT BOWL

Mint gives melon a delicious zip. Mixed with fruit juices and served over melon, here's a medley that's both sweet and refreshing.
—Dorothy Pritchett, Wills Point, TX

Prep: 15 min. + chilling • **Makes:** 8 servings

- **2 cups watermelon balls**
- **2 cups honeydew balls**
- **2 cups cantaloupe balls**
- **½ cup orange juice**
- **¼ cup lime juice**
- **2 Tbsp. sugar**
- **1 Tbsp. snipped fresh mint**
- **1 Tbsp. grated orange zest**
- **1 cup lemon-lime soda**

1. Combine melon balls in a glass bowl. In a small bowl, whisk together juices, sugar, mint and orange zest; pour over melon and toss gently.
2. Cover and refrigerate for 2 hours. Just before serving, add soda and toss gently.
¾ cup: 77 cal., 0 fat (0 sat. fat), 0 chol., 13mg sod., 19g carb. (18g sugars, 1g fiber), 1g pro.
Diabetic Exchanges: 1 fruit, ½ starch.

GREEK DELI KABOBS

For an easy Mediterranean-style appetizer, marinate broccoli and mozzarella, then skewer with sweet red peppers and salami. Who doesn't love food on a stick?
—Vikki Spengler, Ocala, FL

Prep: 30 min. + marinating • **Makes:** 2 dozen

- **1 lb. part-skim mozzarella cheese, cut into 48 cubes**
- **24 fresh broccoli florets (about 10 oz.)**
- **½ cup Greek vinaigrette**
- **24 slices hard salami**
- **2 jars (7½ oz. each) roasted sweet red peppers, drained and cut into 24 strips**

1. In a shallow dish, combine the cheese, broccoli and vinaigrette. Turn to coat; cover and refrigerate for 4 hours or overnight.
2. Drain cheese and broccoli, reserving the vinaigrette. On 24 appetizer skewers, alternately thread cheese, salami, broccoli and peppers. Brush with reserved vinaigrette.
1 kabob: 109 cal., 7g fat (4g sat. fat), 19mg chol., 374mg sod., 2g carb. (1g sugars, 0 fiber), 8g pro.

ITALIAN HERO BRAID

ITALIAN HERO BRAID

My mother-in-law used to make these pastry pockets for my husband when he was growing up. After we got married, I changed her recipe a little to fit our family's tastes.
—*Amanda Kohler, Redmond, WA*

Prep: 20 min. • **Bake:** 25 min.
Makes: 8 servings

- **½ lb. bulk Italian sausage**
- **1 pkg. (¼ oz.) active dry yeast**
- **1 cup warm water (110° to 115°)**
- **2¾ to 3¼ cups all-purpose flour**
- **1 Tbsp. butter, melted**
- **⅓ lb. sliced provolone cheese**
- **⅓ lb. thinly sliced Genoa salami**
- **1 cup shredded cheddar cheese**
- **1 large egg white**

1. Preheat oven to 400°. In a large skillet over medium heat, cook and crumble Italian sausage until no longer pink, 4-6 minutes; drain.
2. Meanwhile, dissolve yeast in warm water. In another bowl, combine 1½ cups flour and butter; add yeast mixture. Beat on medium speed until smooth. Stir in enough remaining flour to form a soft dough.
3. Turn onto a lightly floured surface; roll into a 13x10-in. rectangle. Transfer to a parchment-lined baking sheet. Layer cheese and salami slices down center of rectangle; top with crumbled sausage and shredded cheddar. On each long side, cut 1-in.-wide strips about 2 in. into the center. Starting at 1 end, fold alternating strips at an angle across filling. Pinch both ends to seal.
4. Whisk egg white; brush over pastry. Bake until golden brown, 25-30 minutes.
1 piece: 436 cal., 23g fat (11g sat. fat), 64mg chol., 823mg sod., 35g carb. (0 sugars, 1g fiber), 21g pro.

BOOK CLUB PARTY

Celebrate the joys of reading and good food by hosting a book club party for your foodie friends. It's easy to create a warm setting that invites fellow bibliophiles to linger and relax over a glass of wine and a spread of amazing offerings. So crack open your favorite book—whether it's a timeless classic or a juicy novel—and serve this modern menu to feed the conversation.

Jam-Topped Mini Cheesecakes (p. 239) **Rustic Chocolate Raspberry Tart** (p. 240)

JAM-TOPPED
MINI CHEESECAKES

JAM-TOPPED MINI CHEESECAKES

Presto! We turned cheesecake into irresistible bite-sized snacks with these cute little treats. Feel free to swap in your favorite flavor jam.
—Taste of Home *Test Kitchen*

Prep: 20 min. • **Bake:** 15 min. + chilling
Makes: 9 servings

- **⅔ cup graham cracker crumbs**
- **2 Tbsp. butter, melted**
- **1 pkg. (8 oz.) cream cheese, softened**
- **⅓ cup sugar**
- **1 tsp. vanilla extract**
- **1 large egg, room temperature**
- **3 Tbsp. assorted jams, warmed**

1. In a small bowl, combine the graham cracker crumbs and butter. Press gently onto the bottom of 9 paper-lined muffin cups. In another small bowl, beat the cream cheese, sugar and vanilla until smooth. Add egg; beat on low speed just until combined. Spoon over crusts.
2. Bake at 350° for 15-16 minutes or until centers are set. Cool for 10 minutes before removing from pan to a wire rack to cool completely. Refrigerate for at least 1 hour.
3. Remove paper liners; top each cheesecake with 1 tsp. jam.
1 mini cheesecake: 198 cal., 13g fat (7g sat. fat), 53mg chol., 141mg sod., 19g carb. (14g sugars, 0 fiber), 3g pro.

FRENCH DIP SANDWICH WITH ONIONS

When I want to impress company, these satisfying sandwiches are my first pick for the menu. I serve them au jus, dishing up the cooking juices in individual bowls for dipping.
—Florence Robinson, Lenox, IA

Prep: 30 min. • **Cook:** 7 hours + standing
Makes: 14 servings

- **2 large onions, cut into ¼-in. slices**
- **¼ cup butter, cubed**
- **1 beef rump roast or bottom round roast (3 to 4 lbs.)**
- **5 cups water**
- **½ cup soy sauce**
- **1 envelope onion soup mix**
- **1½ tsp. browning sauce, optional**
- **1 garlic clove, minced**
- **14 French rolls, split**
- **2 cup shredded Swiss cheese**

1. In a large skillet, saute onions in butter until tender. Transfer to a 5-qt. slow cooker. Cut roast in half; place over onions.
2. In a large bowl, combine the water, soy sauce, soup mix, browning sauce if desired and garlic; pour over roast. Cover and cook on low until meat is tender, 7-9 hours.
3. Remove roast with a slotted spoon and let stand for 15 minutes. Thinly slice meat across the grain. Place on roll bottoms; sprinkle with Swiss cheese. Place open-faced sandwiches on an ungreased baking sheet.
4. Broil 3-4 in. from the heat until cheese is melted, about 1 minute. Replace bun tops. Skim fat from cooking juices; strain and serve as a dipping sauce if desired.
1 sandwich: 399 cal., 15g fat (7g sat. fat), 81mg chol., 1099mg sod., 34g carb. (2g sugars, 2g fiber), 30g pro.

SAVORY CRACKER SNACK MIX

I love everything bagel seasoning, so I decided to put those flavors into a snack mix. Now it's a deliciously addictive snack!
—Cyndy Gerken, Naples, FL

Prep: 15 min. • **Bake:** 15 min. + cooling
Makes: 4½ cups

- **1½ cups potato sticks**
- **1½ cups cheddar-flavored snack crackers**
- **1½ cups sourdough pretzel nuggets**
- **3 Tbsp. butter**
- **¼ cup grated Parmesan cheese**
- **3 Tbsp. olive oil**
- **1½ tsp. sesame seeds**
- **1½ tsp. dried minced garlic**
- **1½ tsp. dried minced onion**
- **1½ tsp. poppy seeds**
- **¼ tsp. kosher salt**

1. Preheat oven to 350°. In a large bowl, combine the potato sticks, crackers and pretzels. In a small saucepan, melt butter; stir in remaining ingredients. Drizzle over pretzel mixture; toss to coat.
2. Spread in a greased 15x10x1-in. baking pan. Bake until crisp and lightly browned, 12-15 minutes, stirring every 4 minutes. Cool completely in pan on a wire rack. Store in an airtight container.
¾ cup: 306 cal., 20g fat (7g sat. fat), 20mg chol., 468mg sod., 26g carb. (1g sugars, 1g fiber), 5g pro.

How to Plan a Book Club Party

Be it Reese Witherspoon's latest pick, a spicy new thriller or a celeb memoir bound to spur an invigorating debate, book clubs have long been a fun excuse to get friends together for good food, fun drinks and enlightening discussion.

If it's your turn to host, turn to these creative ideas that will make your book club party a real page-turner.

LITERARY-INSPIRED EATS
Draw menu inspiration from the day's book selection, basing your picks around the food or wine of the region where the plot is set or making the main character's favorite dish. For example, choose grape preserves to embellish the Jam-Topped Mini Cheesecakes, as an ode to *The Grapes of Wrath*. Or give a nod to *Like Water for Chocolate* with Rustic Chocolate Raspberry Tarts and Chocolate Caramel Rum Coffee.

BOOKISH INVITATIONS
Remember the library check-out cards that used to be in a pocket inside every library book you checked out as a kid? Use those as inspiration for your book club party invitations.

A COZY SETTING
Just like the book itself, the setting of your book club party should be rich with detail and interest. The easiest way to do this is by using what you already have—books. Assemble books in stacks of two or three down a dining table or in the center of a coffee table. Top each stack with a vase of flowers or a candle safely tucked inside a jar.

Also make sure your setting for deep literary discussion is warm and cozy—if a fireplace is available, you might want to utilize this. Give guests a selection of blankets to snuggle underneath while they share their favorite parts of the romance/political thriller/celebrity memoir you're discussing.

A HAPPY ENDING
Surprise guests with a parting gift such as a handmade bookmark or treat bags constructed from old book pages.

To choose the book club's next book, wrap four to five options in brown craft paper and have one guest choose at random. Oh, the suspense!

RUSTIC CHOCOLATE RASPBERRY TART

Here's a delectable dessert that's simple but feels upscale. With its fresh raspberries and Nutella-covered homemade pastry crust, you and your guests won't be able to get enough.
—*Christina Seremetis, Rockland, MA*

Prep: 20 min. + chilling
Bake: 45 min. + cooling
Makes: 8 servings

- **5 oz. cream cheese, softened**
- **6 Tbsp. butter, softened**
- **1½ cups all-purpose flour**

FILLING

- **2 cups fresh raspberries**
- **2 Tbsp. sugar**
- **1 tsp. cornstarch**
- **⅓ cup Nutella**

1. Process cream cheese and butter in a food processor until blended. Add flour; process just until a dough forms. Shape into a disk; wrap and refrigerate 1 hour or overnight.
2. Preheat oven to 350°. In a small bowl, toss raspberries, sugar and cornstarch with a fork, mashing some of the berries slightly.
3. On a lightly floured surface, roll dough into a 14x8-in. rectangle. Transfer the crust to a parchment-lined baking sheet. Spread with Nutella to within 1 in. of edges. Top with the raspberry mixture. Fold edge of pastry toward center of tart, pleating and pinching as needed.
4. Bake until crust is golden brown, 45-50 minutes. Transfer tart to a wire rack to cool.
1 piece: 315 cal., 19g fat (10g sat. fat), 41mg chol., 130mg sod., 34g carb. (12g sugars, 3g fiber), 5g pro.

RUSTIC CHOCOLATE RASPBERRY TART

ALMOND BISCOTTI

I've learned to bake a double batch of these crisp dunking cookies, because one batch goes too fast!
—H. Michaelsen, St. Charles, IL

Prep: 15 min. • **Bake:** 35 min. + cooling
Makes: 3 dozen

- **½ cup butter, softened**
- **1¼ cups sugar, divided**
- **3 large eggs, room temperature**
- **1 tsp. anise extract**
- **2 cups all-purpose flour**
- **2 tsp. baking powder**
- **Dash salt**
- **½ cup chopped almonds**
- **2 tsp. 2% milk**

1. In a large bowl, cream butter and 1 cup sugar until light and fluffy, 5-7 minutes. Add eggs, 1 at a time, beating well after each addition. Beat in anise extract. Combine the dry ingredients; gradually add to creamed mixture and mix well. Stir in almonds.
2. Line a baking sheet with foil and grease the foil. Divide dough in half; on the foil, shape each portion into a 12x3-in. rectangle. Brush with milk; sprinkle with remaining sugar.
3. Bake at 375° until golden brown and firm to the touch, 15-20 minutes. Lift foil with rectangles onto a wire rack and let cool for 15 minutes. Reduce heat to 300°.
4. Transfer the rectangles to a cutting board; cut diagonally with a serrated knife into ½-in. slices. Place cut side down on ungreased baking sheets.
5. Bake for 10 minutes. Turn and bake until firm, 10 minutes longer. Remove to wire racks to cool. Store in an airtight container.
1 cookie: 207 cal., 9g fat (4g sat. fat), 50mg chol., 129mg sod., 29g carb. (16g sugars, 1g fiber), 4g pro.

CLASSIC COBB SALAD

Making this salad is a lot like putting in a garden. I plant everything in nice, neat sections, just as I do with seedlings. It's easy to double for a larger group.
—Patricia Kile, Elizabethtown, PA

Takes: 20 min. • **Makes:** 4 servings

- **6 cups torn iceberg lettuce**
- **2 medium tomatoes, chopped**
- **1 medium ripe avocado, peeled and chopped**
- **¾ cup diced fully cooked ham**
- **2 hard-boiled large eggs, chopped**
- **¾ cup diced cooked turkey**
- **1¼ cups sliced fresh mushrooms**
- **½ cup crumbled blue cheese**
- **Salad dressing of choice**
- **Optional: Sliced ripe olives and lemon wedges**

Place lettuce on a platter or in a large serving bowl. Arrange remaining ingredients in rows or sections as desired. Serve with dressing of choice; if desired, serve with sliced ripe olives and lemon wedges.
1 serving: 260 cal., 15g fat (5g sat. fat), 148mg chol., 586mg sod., 10g carb. (5g sugars, 4g fiber), 23g pro.

DIY Page-Turner Table Runner

Using a craft knife, carefully cut pages out of a discarded book. Use double-sided tape to randomly attach the pages to each other to the desired length and width.

CHOCOLATE-CARAMEL RUM COFFEE

This decadent coffee drink can stand alone as a final course or as a delightful complement to any chocolate or caramel dessert. Our family loves it after a special dinner or just for sipping in front of the fireplace.
—Joyce Conway, Westerville, OH

Takes: 25 min. • **Makes:** 8 servings

- **2 cans (12 oz. each) evaporated milk**
- **¾ cup rum**
- **½ cup chocolate syrup**
- **½ cup caramel sundae syrup**
- **¼ cup packed brown sugar**
- **4 cups hot brewed coffee**
- **2 Tbsp. coffee liqueur**

COFFEE WHIPPED CREAM

- **1 cup heavy whipping cream**
- **6 Tbsp. confectioners' sugar**
- **2 Tbsp. coffee liqueur**
- **Instant espresso powder, optional**

1. In a large saucepan, combine the milk, rum, syrups and brown sugar. Cook over medium heat until hot (do not boil). Stir in coffee and liqueur.
2. Meanwhile, in a small bowl, beat cream until it begins to thicken. Add confectioners' sugar; beat until stiff peaks form. Fold in liqueur until combined.
3. Pour coffee mixture into mugs. Garnish with a dollop of coffee whipped cream and, if desired, espresso powder.

1 cup coffee with ¼ cup coffee whipped cream: 437 cal., 16g fat (11g sat. fat), 68mg chol., 166mg sod., 50g carb. (43g sugars, 0 fiber), 7g pro.

LOADED TWICE-BAKED POTATO CASSEROLE

My husband loves potatoes in any incarnation, so I try new combinations for variety. In this party-pleasing dish, twice-baked potatoes and potato skins make a scrumptious casserole.
—Cyndy Gerken, Naples, FL

Prep: 1½ hours • **Bake:** 30 min.
Makes: 8 servings

- **4 large baking potatoes (about 3¼ lbs.)**
- **1 Tbsp. olive oil**
- **¾ tsp. salt, divided**
- **¾ tsp. pepper, divided**
- **¼ cup butter, cubed**
- **⅔ cup heavy whipping cream**
- **¼ cup sour cream**
- **2 cups shredded cheddar cheese, divided**
- **6 bacon strips, cooked and crumbled, divided**
- **2 green onions, sliced, divided**
- **Additional sour cream, optional**

1. Preheat oven to 375°. Scrub potatoes; pierce several times with a fork. Brush with oil; sprinkle with ½ tsp. salt and ¼ tsp. pepper. Place in a foil-lined 15x10x1-in. baking pan; bake for 1-1¼ hours or until potatoes are tender. Cool slightly.
2. In a small saucepan, melt the butter over medium heat. Whisk in whipping cream and ¼ cup sour cream. Add 1½ cups cheese; stir until melted. Remove from the heat; cover to keep warm.
3. When potatoes are cool enough to handle, cut each potato lengthwise in half. Scoop out pulp and place in a large bowl. Cut 2 potato skin shells into 1-in. pieces; save the remaining skins for another use.
4. Mash pulp with the remaining salt and pepper. Stir in the cheese mixture, half the bacon and 2 Tbsp. green onion. Transfer to a greased 1½-qt. baking dish. Top with the cut-up potato skins. Sprinkle with remaining cheese and bacon.
5. Bake until heated through and lightly browned, 30-35 minutes. Sprinkle with the remaining green onion. If desired, serve with additional sour cream.

½ cup: 367 cal., 27g fat (16g sat. fat), 84mg chol., 458mg sod., 20g carb. (2g sugars, 2g fiber), 12g pro.

CHAI CUPCAKES

You'll get a double dose of the spicy blend that's frequently used to flavor tea in these tender single-size cakes. Both the cupcake and frosting use the sweet blend of spices.
—Taste of Home *Test Kitchen*

Prep: 25 min. • **Bake:** 25 min. + cooling
Makes: 1 dozen

- **½ tsp. each ground ginger, cinnamon, cardamom and cloves**
- **⅛ tsp. pepper**
- **½ cup butter, softened**
- **1 cup sugar**
- **1 large egg, room temperature**
- **½ tsp. vanilla extract**
- **1½ cups cake flour**
- **1½ tsp. baking powder**
- **¼ tsp. salt**
- **⅔ cup 2% milk**

FROSTING

- **6 Tbsp. butter, softened**
- **3 cups confectioners' sugar**
- **¾ tsp. vanilla extract**
- **3 to 4 Tbsp. 2% milk**

1. In a small bowl, combine ginger, cinnamon, cardamom, cloves and pepper; set aside.
2. In a large bowl, cream butter and sugar until light and fluffy. Beat in egg and vanilla. Combine the flour, baking powder, salt and 1½ tsp. spice mixture. Gradually add to creamed mixture alternately with milk, beating well after each addition.
3. Fill 12 paper-lined muffin cups two-thirds full. Bake at 350° for 24-28 minutes or until a toothpick inserted in the center comes out clean. Cool for 10 minutes before removing from pans to wire racks to cool completely.
4. In a large bowl, beat butter until fluffy; beat in the confectioners' sugar, vanilla and the remaining spice mixture until smooth. Add enough milk to reach desired consistency. Pipe frosting over cupcakes.

1 cupcake: 377 cal., 14g fat (9g sat. fat), 54mg chol., 209mg sod., 61g carb. (46g sugars, 0 fiber), 3g pro.

CHAI CUPCAKES

HAUNTING HALLOWEEN MOVIE NIGHT

Dim the lights, grab some cozy blankets and stock up on snacks. Then invite your bravest movie buffs over for a fearsome film fest! Rely on these terrifyingly delicious recipes and ideas to get mouths watering and hearts racing. Everyone will eat, drink and scream the night away!

Vampire Killer Martini (p. 253) **Garlic Pizza Wedges** (p. 248)

MONSTER COOKIES

This recipe combines several flavors—peanut butter, butterscotch and chocolate—in one colossal cookie. Before baking, press a few extra M&M's on top for added color.
—Patricia Schroedl, Jefferson, WI

Prep: 15 min. + standing • **Bake:** 15 min./batch
Makes: about 2½ dozen

- **1 cup peanut butter**
- **½ cup butter, softened**
- **1¼ cups packed brown sugar**
- **1 cup sugar**
- **3 large eggs, room temperature**
- **2 tsp. baking soda**
- **1 tsp. vanilla extract**
- **4 cups quick-cooking oats**
- **1 cup M&M's**
- **1 cup butterscotch chips**
- **1 cup salted peanuts**
- **2 cups all-purpose flour**

1. In a large bowl, cream peanut butter, butter and sugars. Add 1 egg at a time, beating well after each addition. Add baking soda and vanilla. Add oats, M&M's, butterscotch chips and peanuts; let stand for 10 minutes. Stir in flour (the dough will be crumbly).
2. Shape by ¼ cupfuls into balls. Place on greased baking sheets, about 9 cookies on each sheet. Gently flatten cookies. Bake at 325° for 15-18 minutes or until edges are lightly browned. Remove to wire racks.
1 cookie: 318 cal., 15g fat (6g sat. fat), 28mg chol., 180mg sod., 41g carb. (25g sugars, 2g fiber), 7g pro.

TEST KITCHEN TIP

If your cookies crumble when removed from a baking sheet, let them cool for 1-2 minutes first. But if they cool too long, they can become hard and can break when removed. If this happens, return the baking sheet to the oven to warm the cookies slightly so they'll release more easily.

NACHO CHEESE DIP

Our family is always on the go with jobs, school and sport activities, so we relish our evenings when things slow down. This zippy dip is a favorite to munch on while we spend time together or watch one of our favorite movies. It's perfect for parties, too.
—Dawn Taylor, Milton, KY

Takes: 10 min. • **Makes:** 3 cups

- **¼ lb. bulk spicy pork or Mexican-style sausage**
- **2 Tbsp. chopped green pepper**
- **2 Tbsp. chopped onion**
- **1 lb. American cheese, cubed**
- **¾ cup salsa**
- **Tortilla chips or raw vegetables**

In a 1½-qt. microwave-safe container, cook sausage, green pepper and onion on high for 1-2 minutes or until sausage is fully cooked; drain. Add the cheese and salsa. Cover and microwave on high for 1-2 minutes, stirring frequently until cheese is melted and mixture is smooth. Serve dip with tortilla chips or vegetables.
2 Tbsp.: 75 cal., 6g fat (3g sat. fat), 14mg chol., 279mg sod., 2g carb. (2g sugars, 0 fiber), 4g pro.

MONSTER COOKIES

GARLIC PIZZA WEDGES

Our pastor made this for a get-together, and my husband and I just couldn't stay away from the hors d'oeuvres table. The cheesy slices are usually served warm, but they're still wonderful when they've cooled slightly.
—Krysten Johnson, Simi Valley, CA

Takes: 25 min. • **Makes:** 2 dozen

- **1 prebaked 12-in. pizza crust**
- **1 cup grated Parmesan cheese**
- **1 cup mayonnaise**
- **1 small red onion, chopped**
- **3½ tsp. minced garlic**
- **1 Tbsp. dried oregano**
- **Alfredo sauce, optional**

Place crust on an ungreased 14-in. pizza pan. In a small bowl, combine Parmesan cheese, mayonnaise, onion, garlic and oregano; spread over crust. Bake at 450° until edges are lightly browned, 8-10 minutes. Cut into wedges. If desired, serve with Alfredo sauce.

1 piece: 119 cal., 8g fat (2g sat. fat), 4mg chol., 193mg sod., 8g carb. (0 sugars, 0 fiber), 3g pro.

SCARY SCREENERS

From monsters and ghosts to haunted hotels, here are some of the best scary movies to watch during your Halloween party.

FOR THE HORRORHEADS:

- *Bram Stoker's Dracula*
- *Friday the 13th*
- *Halloween*
- *Nightmare on Elm Street*
- *Poltergeist*
- *The Ring*
- *The Shining*

FRIENDLY FOR THE FAMILY:

- *Beetlejuice*
- *Casper*
- *Coraline*
- *Ghostbusters*
- *Hocus Pocus*
- *Hotel Transylvania*
- *Monster House*

GARLIC PIZZA WEDGES

CARAMEL SNICKERDOODLE BARS

What did I do when I couldn't decide between two of my favorite desserts? I combined them! This snickerdoodle-blondie hybrid proved even better with caramel, always a favorite ingredient.
—Niki Plourde, Gardner, MA

Prep: 30 min. • **Bake:** 25 min. + chilling
Makes: 4 dozen

- **1 cup butter, softened**
- **2 cups packed brown sugar**
- **2 large eggs, room temperature**
- **2 tsp. vanilla extract**
- **2½ cups all-purpose flour**
- **2 tsp. baking powder**
- **1 tsp. salt**
- **¼ cup sugar**
- **3 tsp. ground cinnamon**
- **2 cans (13.4 oz. each) dulce de leche**
- **12 oz. white baking chocolate, chopped**
- **⅓ cup heavy whipping cream**
- **1 Tbsp. light corn syrup**

1. Preheat oven to 350°. Line a 13x9-in. baking pan with parchment, letting ends extend over sides by 1 in.
2. In a large bowl, cream butter and brown sugar until light and fluffy, 5-7 minutes. Beat in eggs and vanilla. In another bowl, whisk flour, baking powder and salt; gradually beat into creamed mixture. Spread onto bottom of prepared pan.
3. In a small bowl, mix sugar and cinnamon; sprinkle 2 Tbsp. mixture over batter. Bake until edges are light brown, 25-30 minutes. Cool completely in pan on a wire rack.
4. Spread dulce de leche over crust. In a small saucepan, combine white baking chocolate, cream and corn syrup; cook and stir over low heat until smooth. Cool slightly. Spread over dulce de leche. Sprinkle with the remaining cinnamon sugar. Refrigerate, covered, at least 1 hour.
5. Lifting with parchment, remove from pan. Cut into bars. Refrigerate leftovers.
1 bar: 197 cal., 8g fat (5g sat. fat), 27mg chol., 137mg sod., 28g carb. (23g sugars, 0 fiber), 2g pro.

To help the dulce de leche layer set up a bit, pop it in the fridge for 30 minutes before adding the white chocolate layer. If you're a dark chocolate fan, substitute dark baking chocolate for the white.

SPICED CHOCOLATE TRUFFLES

I make truffles for gift-giving and family events. Someone once asked me to add pumpkin spice—now my recipe is legendary.
—Gerry Cofta, Milwaukee, WI

Prep: 45 min. + chilling • **Cook:** 5 min,
Makes: about 2 dozen

- **12 oz. milk chocolate baking bars, divided**
- **½ cup heavy whipping cream**
- **2 Tbsp. canned pumpkin**
- **¼ tsp. ground cinnamon**
- **¼ tsp. ground ginger**
- **¼ tsp. ground nutmeg**
- **Dash ground cloves**
- **Baking cocoa**
- **Candy eyeballs, optional**

1. Finely chop 10 oz. chocolate; place in a bowl. In a small heavy saucepan, combine cream, pumpkin and spices; heat just to a boil. Pour over the chocolate; let stand 5 minutes.
2. Stir with a whisk until smooth. Cool to room temperature. Refrigerate, covered, at least 4 hours.
3. Finely grate remaining chocolate; place in a small microwave-safe bowl. With hands dusted lightly with baking cocoa, shape the chocolate mixture into 1-in. balls; roll in grated chocolate. (Mixture will be soft and truffles may flatten slightly upon standing.)
4. If desired, melt unused grated chocolate in a microwave and use to attach eyeballs. Store in an airtight container in the refrigerator.
1 truffle: 89 cal., 6g fat (4g sat. fat), 10mg chol., 7mg sod., 9g carb. (8g sugars, 0 fiber), 1g pro.
Note: This recipe was tested with Ghirardelli Milk Chocolate Baking Bars; results may vary when using a different product.

CHEESY MEATBALL SLIDERS

CHEESY MEATBALL SLIDERS

These sliders are a fun way to serve meatballs without using a slow cooker. Made on mini Hawaiian rolls, they have a hint of sweetness to balance out all the great Italian seasonings.
—Taste of Home *Test Kitchen*

Prep: 1 hour • **Bake:** 30 min.
Makes: 12 servings

- **2 lbs. lean ground beef (90% lean)**
- **1 cup Italian-style bread crumbs**
- **3 Tbsp. prepared pesto**
- **1 large egg, lightly beaten**
- **1 jar (24 oz.) pasta sauce**
- **1 pkg. (18 oz.) Hawaiian sweet rolls**
- **12 slices part-skim mozzarella cheese**
- **½ tsp. dried oregano**
- **¼ cup melted butter**
- **1 Tbsp. olive oil**
- **3 garlic cloves, minced**
- **1 tsp. Italian seasoning**
- **½ tsp. crushed red pepper flakes**
- **2 Tbsp. grated Parmesan cheese**
- **1 cup shredded part-skim mozzarella or shredded Italian cheese blend**
- **Minced fresh basil**

1. Preheat oven to 350°. Combine ground beef, bread crumbs, pesto and egg; mix lightly. Shape into 12 meatballs; place on a greased rack in a 15x10x1-in. baking pan. Bake until browned and a thermometer reads 160°, about 35 minutes. Toss meatballs with sauce; set aside.
2. Meanwhile, without separating rolls, cut horizontally in half; arrange bottom halves in a greased 13x9-in. baking dish. Place half of cheese slices over roll bottoms; sprinkle with oregano. Add meatballs and sauce. Top with remaining cheese slices and bun tops.
3. Combine the butter, olive oil, garlic, Italian seasoning and red pepper flakes; brush over buns. Bake, covered 20 minutes. Uncover, sprinkle with Parmesan and shredded mozzarella.
4. Bake uncovered until cheese is melted, 10-15 minutes longer. Sprinkle with basil before serving.
1 slider: 514 cal., 25g fat (12g sat. fat), 120mg chol., 856mg sod., 39g carb. (15g sugars, 3g fiber), 33g pro.

Scary Movie Survival Kit
After shrieking the night away, guests will appreciate calm-down comforts. Wrap mini flashlights, packets of chamomile tea and small roller bottles of soothing lavender oil in black tulle.

SWEET POTATO & CHORIZO CROQUETTES

Chorizo and paprika add smokiness to these mashed potato balls fried inside a crispy shell. You can prepare the balls in advance and fry them right before the party.
—*Nick Iverson, Denver, CO*

Prep: 55 min. + chilling • **Cook:** 5 min./batch
Makes: 3 dozen

- **2 large sweet potatoes (about 12 oz. each), cut into 1-in. pieces**
- **1 Tbsp. canola oil**
- **14 oz. fresh chorizo or bulk spicy pork sausage**
- **2 cups (8 oz.) queso fresco or shredded Mexican cheese blend**
- **1 large egg**
- **½ tsp. smoked paprika**
- **¼ tsp. salt**
- **¼ tsp. pepper**
- **¾ cup panko bread crumbs**
- **Oil for deep-fat frying**
- **Pretzel sticks and fresh cilantro leaves**

1. Preheat oven to 400° Place sweet potatoes on a 15x10x1-in. baking pan. Drizzle with oil; toss to coat. Roast potatoes 30-40 minutes or until tender. Meanwhile, in a large skillet, cook chorizo over medium heat 6-8 minutes or until no longer pink. Drain and transfer to a large bowl.
2. Mash sweet potatoes; add to chorizo. Stir in the cheese, egg, paprika, salt and pepper. Refrigerate until cold, about 1 hour.
3. Shape into 1¼-in. balls. Place bread crumbs in a shallow bowl. Roll balls in crumbs to coat. In an electric skillet or a deep fryer, heat oil to 375°. Fry balls in batches 4-6 minutes or until golden brown, turning occasionally. Drain on paper towels.
4. Decorate with pretzel sticks and cilantro.
1 croquette: 110 cal., 8g fat (2g sat. fat), 19mg chol., 174mg sod., 6g carb. (2g sugars, 1g fiber), 5g pro.

SUN-DRIED TOMATO HUMMUS

A jar of sun-dried tomatoes adds rich color and flavor to this smooth hummus that can be whipped up in minutes. Garlic and red pepper flakes nicely spice it up, too.
—Todd Schmeling, Gurnee, IL

Takes: 20 min. • **Makes:** 3½ cups

- **2 cans (15 oz. each) garbanzo beans or chickpeas, rinsed and drained**
- **1 jar (7 oz.) oil-packed sun-dried tomatoes, undrained**
- **⅔ cup water**
- **3 Tbsp. olive oil**
- **2 garlic cloves, halved**
- **1 tsp. crushed red pepper flakes**
- **½ tsp. salt**
- **¼ tsp. pepper**
- **Chopped fresh basil, optional**
- **Baked pita chips and/or assorted fresh vegetables**

In a food processor, combine the garbanzo beans, tomatoes, water, oil, garlic, pepper flakes, salt and pepper; cover and process until blended. Place in a serving bowl; sprinkle with basil if desired. Serve with pita chips and/or vegetables.

¼ cup: 113 cal., 6g fat (1g sat. fat), 0 chol., 201mg sod., 13g carb. (1g sugars, 3g fiber), 3g pro.

BUFFALO CHICKEN CRESCENT ROLLS

My husband loves Buffalo wings, but they are so messy! These Buffalo chicken rolls are mess-free and always go fast at parties—and they're much tastier than regular Buffalo wings, if you ask me.
—Tiffinie Cichon, Gulfport, MS

Prep: 20 min. • **Bake:** 15 min.
Makes: 16 servings

- **1 cup shredded cooked chicken**
- **4 oz. cream cheese, cubed**
- **½ cup shredded cheddar cheese**
- **2 Tbsp. prepared ranch salad dressing**
- **2 Tbsp. Buffalo wing sauce**
- **2 tubes (8 oz. each) refrigerated crescent rolls**
- **⅓ cup crumbled blue cheese**

1. Preheat oven to 375°. In a small saucepan, combine chicken, cream cheese, cheddar cheese, ranch dressing and wing sauce. Cook and stir over low heat until the cheeses are melted, about 5 minutes. Remove from heat.
2. Unroll each tube of crescent dough; separate into 16 triangles. Place 1 Tbsp. chicken mixture in the center of each triangle; sprinkle with 1 tsp. blue cheese. Bring corners of dough over filling and twist; pinch seams to seal (filling will not be completely enclosed). Place on ungreased baking sheets.
3. Bake until golden brown, 15-20 minutes. Serve warm.

1 appetizer: 175 cal., 11g fat (3g sat. fat), 21mg chol., 372mg sod., 13g carb. (3g sugars, 0 fiber), 6g pro.

VAMPIRE KILLER MARTINI

VAMPIRE KILLER MARTINI

If you're going to hang with vampires, you're going to need a strong drink. A little garlic helps, too! Be aware this drink needs a full week to steep so the flavors infuse.
—Taste of Home *Test Kitchen*

Prep: 5 min. + standing • **Makes:** 8 servings

- **1 serrano pepper, seeded and quartered**
- **2 garlic cloves, crushed**
- **1 lemon zest strip (2 in.)**
- **1½ cups vodka**
- **Ice**

GARNISH

- **Pickled baby beets**

1. Place the pepper, garlic, lemon zest strip and vodka in a large glass or plastic container. Cover and let stand at room temperature for 1 week.

2. For each serving, fill a shaker three-fourths full with ice. Add 1½ oz. infused vodka to shaker; cover and shake until condensation forms on outside of shaker, 10-15 seconds. Strain into a chilled martini glass. Garnish with a beet.

1½ oz.: 96 cal., 0 fat (0 sat. fat), 0 chol., 0 sod., 0 carb. (0 sugars, 0 fiber), 0 pro.

Tricked-Out Treats

Add chocolate-covered raisins or candies like Swedish Fish, Hot Tamales and M&M's to individual popcorn containers for a festive flare. If you want to amp up the flavor, mix together 2 Tbsp. grated Parmesan, ¼ tsp. salt, ¼ tsp. dried oregano and ⅛ tsp. garlic salt and sprinkle over popcorn. Or simply add black salt for a spooky twist.

RECIPE INDEX

TIMELINES, PARTY PLANNING TIPS & MORE

SHARE YOUR MOST-LOVED RECIPES

Do you have a cherished recipe or a special tradition that has become part of your family's holiday? Are homemade gifts and crafts included in your celebrations? We want to hear from you. Visit ***tasteofhome.com/submit*** to submit a recipe, craft or other idea for editorial consideration.